Values, Virtues and Violence: Education and the Public Understanding of Morality

Other books in this series:

Values, Virtues and Violence: Education and the Public Understanding of Morality

GRAHAM HAYDON

ISBN 0-631-21532-8

First published in 1999

Blackwell Publishers
108 Cowley Road, Oxford OX4 1JF, UK

350 Main Street, Malden, MA 02148, USA

British Library Cataloguing in Publication Data
Cataloguing in Publication data applied for

Library of Congress Cataloging-in-Publication Data
Haydon, Graham.
    Values, virtues, and violence: education and the public understanding of morality/Graham Haydon.
        p. cm.
    Special issue of The journal of philosophy of education.
    Includes bibliographical references (p. 175) and index.
    ISBN 0-631-21532-8
    1. Moral education. 2. Values–Study and teaching. I. Journal of philosophy of education. Special issue. II. Title.
LC268.H294 1999   99-33932
370.11′4–dc21   CIP

Printed in Great Britain by MPG Books, Bodmin, Cornwall
This book is printed on acid-free paper

Contents

Foreword

From time to time we remember that the world can be a nasty place in which people are capable of inflicting great harm on each other in the most casual ways. Outrages from Northern Ireland to Rwanda show us what can happen when the ties of shared humanity snap. We discover too that children themselves are entirely capable of murdering schoolfellows or teachers. At such times we may wonder whether education which concentrates relentlessly on levering up standards of literacy and numeracy might be in danger of leaving something out.

Recent burgeoning of interest, in many countries, in moral education and citizenship education forms part of the background to Graham Haydon's monograph. The title takes us a long way from some of the older approaches to moral education which saw children's moral universe rather in terms of overdue library books or inconsiderate treatment of siblings. Acknowledging public perceptions of our moral condition, he asks: *if* this is how things are with our young people, what kind of moral education ought we to give them?

Another part of the background to this book is the philosophical one. Many recent writers on morality have been impressed by the Aristotelian account and re-emphasised the place of the virtues in the moral life. This does seem to put back something which had long been neglected. But it threatens to obscure the place in moral education of rules and principles, and it is a major part of Haydon's purpose here to explain in what sense rules and principles are properly at the heart of morality and moral education and in what sense they are not.

In thus addressing both public concerns about education and recent philosophical thinking Graham Haydon has done important work in philosophy of education. His monograph stands as a major contribution to the literature on moral education and should significantly inform public debate on the topic.

Richard Smith

Preface

'This book is a response to renewed and widespread public interest in moral education.'

That, the opening sentence of *Teaching Right and Wrong: Moral Education in the Balance*, edited by Richard Smith and Paul Standish (1997), could equally apply to the present book. Is there room for another book in response to that same public interest? In certain moods, I might think we can never have too many books on moral education (in other moods, I might think there are far too many to keep up with already). But more specifically, I think there is room for a further response to that public interest just because its nature as a *public* interest has not yet been sufficiently addressed. I shall try only briefly to explain that point here, since the bulk of this book will be about the requirements for a public educational response to that public interest.

As is well known to readers of the philosophical literature on moral education, and of moral philosophy generally, there has been a swing in recent years away from a morality of rules and principles and towards an ethics of virtue. Much of the current literature is concerned with developing the virtues theme and arguing its superiority over a rules and principles approach. (This is, of course, a simplification of a more complex picture.)

Meanwhile, the public concern has been rather different. As the editors of *Teaching Right and Wrong* point out, renewed public interest in moral education has to an important extent been a response to certain specific events, especially the murders of James Bulger and Philip Lawrence. It is widely thought that if people, and young people in particular, can do things like this, then something must have gone wrong in schools. More and better moral education seems, to many people, to be the answer.

What, in the public mind, might this moral education consist in? The public does not generally seem to be calling for the cultivation of virtues; it may be calling for something more like the stamping in of certain hard-and-fast rules of conduct. I think that philosophers of education should take such public concerns seriously. That is not to say that philosophers must adopt the language in which those concerns are sometimes expressed. But it is to say that there is an important question about the kind of language in which such concerns can best be addressed within public discourse.

While the public concerns are by no means only about violence, I take violence here as my dominant example. It is an example that brings out well the uncertainties we have about the kind of language in which it is appropriate to treat matters of public moral concern. I am well aware that in treating violence in this way I shall not have done justice to many of the questions that can be raised both about the nature of violence and about the judgements we make on it. I hope to take these issues further on another occasion. I do here express some opinions about particular issues concerning violence, but I do not claim to demonstrate the truth of these opinions; their status is more that of illustrations.

Briefly, my overall argument here is that if schools are to be able to address such concerns adequately there needs to be, not only a considerable measure of agreement on at least some moral 'standards' (for want of a better word at this point), but also a measure of agreement on the nature of morality itself. And this agreement needs to be on a conception of morality which teachers can be comfortable with and can articulate. It is doubtful how far we have this kind of agreement, and this kind of understanding, at present, but there is (I shall argue) a viable conception of morality which might, through education, come to be widely shared. In working out such a conception I shall suggest that the language of rules and principles is indispensable; to that extent I hope to redress the balance in a literature which is becoming more interested in different ways of talking.

The writer of a recent popular book on moral education suggests that we have to 'make virtue sexy' (Houghton, 1998, p. 181) among teenagers — a hard task. But the hard task in addressing philosophers in the present climate is to make rules and principles sexy; so I did not include 'rules and principles' in my own title. My actual title encapsulates notions which are important, but which we must not get obsessed with. We need to talk of the broad field of values education, but within that we still need the notion of morality; we do and will continue to talk about virtues, but we should not think that talking about virtues is a panacea for the ills that moral education needs to address; and we are right to be concerned about violence, but we should not expect moral education to be concerned with that to the exclusion of all else.

It will be clear that in part I am addressing my fellow philosophers of education; there are questions I want to air with them about the responsiveness of our discipline to public concerns. But there are not, after all, very many of us, and there would be little point in my saying to my colleagues that we should be addressing these public concerns if I were not myself trying to do so. So this book is addressed at the same time to a wider readership.

This may mean on occasions that the general reader has to be patient with reflections on philosophy of education which seem to have little direct bearing on the public concerns themselves. But the reader will not, I think, find any obtrusive philosophical technicalities (unless they are so ingrained in me that I fail to notice them); more likely, he or she may feel that, with typical philosophical detachment, I have still failed to get to grips sufficiently with the practical issues that teachers, and others engaged in education, face. But I still share the faith of philosophers, or at any rate of a certain kind of philosopher, that trying to think clearly about the practical issues — even though this often means attending to words and ideas rather than 'things' — is an essential part of tackling the issues.

SOURCES AND ACKNOWLEDGEMENTS

This book is a substantially rewritten version of my London University doctoral thesis (1999). The thesis says much less about violence, but goes into more detail on some other parts of my argument, particularly the idea of the public understanding of morality. Some of the ideas in this book are anticipated in various chapters and articles, and particularly in my *Teaching about Values: A New Approach* (Haydon, 1997), but I have tried to avoid very much direct overlap.

Much of the writing of this book (and of my doctoral thesis) was done during a period of study leave granted by the Institute of Education, University of London. I am grateful to the Director and Council for giving me this opportunity.

In this book I frequently refer to the Smith and Standish volume. It is a timely and very valuable collection, which in several ways I take to be representative of current thinking about moral education within, especially, the British philosophy of education community. My own aims in contributing to the debate will have been well realised if people read this book alongside and in comparison with that.

I would like to thank Richard Smith in particular for encouragement at just the right time, and John White for his comments on the thesis which have helped me, I hope, to make my position clearer in this book. The extent to which, in this book, I react against certain points abstracted from their writings is an odd way of repaying a debt. It is, of course, all part of an ongoing discussion, and I hold no one else responsible for my contribution.

I would like to thank too the students with whom I have talked about some of the concerns of this book, including Wilmette Brown and Helen Young. They have both raised with me points about violence in an educational context which I know I have not yet responded to adequately.

This book is, I hope, relatively free of postmodern irony, except for many of the head-of-chapter quotations, which are taken from Tom Stoppard's *Jumpers*, a play about conceptions of morality both in academia and in public discourse; page references are to Stoppard (1972). George, Professor of Moral Philosophy, who wants to defend an objectivist, realist position (but can't find good arguments for it), is preparing a paper in response to McFee, Professor of Logic, whose view of morality, it has to be said, is closer to the one I defend here. Meanwhile McFee has been shot dead in confusing circumstances, which Bones, the detective inspector, is investigating. Among other characters are the Vice-Chancellor, Archie, whose position could be described as pragmatist, but not in the philosophical sense; Dotty, wife of George, former philosophy student and musical-comedy star; and Crouch, the janitor. Outside the University public attention has been drawn to questions of morality and conduct by a live television broadcast from the Moon, where there are two astronauts, Scott and Oates, but their damaged rocket can only bring one back to earth . . .

Chapter 1 Violence and the Demand for Moral Education

TV VOICE: 'Millions of viewers saw the two astronauts struggling at the foot of the ladder until Oates was knocked to the ground by his commanding officer . . . Captain Scott has maintained radio silence since pulling up the ladder and closing the hatch with the remark, "I am going up now. I may be gone for some time." ' (*Jumpers*, p. 23)[1]

THE POPULAR EQUATION

Next time some more-than-usually striking act of violence hits the headlines, consider the opinions expressed in the media. Will you find a reference to education? Quite possibly, if the violence has not involved schools or young people, you will not. But if children or young people who have only recently left school are involved as perpetrators, it will be surprising if you do not encounter the view that there must be something amiss in education; that if young people were getting a proper moral education, events like these would never happen. This kind of view was expressed, for instance, after the murder of two-year old James Bulger by two ten-year old boys, after the murder of the headteacher Philip Lawrence, and after the shooting of children in a school in Jonesboro, Arkansas, by two classmates.

Such a view is often expressed in a rather unsophisticated way; thus it will be appropriate to refer to it here initially in a deliberately simplistic form, in the formula: 'more morality in schools = less violence in society'.

This is not intended strictly as an equation. Rather the suggestion is of a causal relationship: more morality in schools will lead to less violence in society. I use the form of words 'more morality in schools' as an indication, not just of a demand for more moral education, but of a demand for moral education according to a certain conception of what it is. My impression has been that the view that schools should do something about the 'moral crisis' in society often goes with an understanding of morality as a matter of conformity to certain basic rules, and of moral education as essentially a matter of inculcating this conformity. Whether this is an appropriate way of seeing morality and moral education will be one of my central topics.

On the other side of the equation I have written 'violence in society'. Yet if the event in the news is, say, terrorist bombings, or 'ordinary' violent crime by 'mature' adults, the question 'What has gone wrong with these people's education?' is not usually prominent. It is when the violence is committed by young people that one is most likely to hear the popular formula. Perhaps the thought is that while children are actually attending school, or for young people who have only recently left school, the influence of their education must be especially strong.

Yet it does not seem entirely rational that education should be expected to make a difference especially for these categories. Is it that the influence of education is expected gradually to wear off with time, so that it would be unreasonable to expect the moral education that someone received as a child to have any influence at all on whether that person behaves violently at the age of fifty? This would fit oddly with the very common idea that education is a preparation for adult life.

In any case, even if the thought expressed in my slogan does tend to appear in the media especially after violence committed by children, there may be a thought of more general applicability behind it. Many people see our society, our culture, as being violent, or as putting insufficient constraints on violence; and they do think that schools should have some effect on the nature of the culture. So it is right, I think, to express the right-hand side of the equation as 'less violence in society', not just as something like 'less violence in and around schools'. It is also necessary, of course, to ask whether schools can reasonably be expected to have an effect on the whole culture.

That there is an argument *for* the slogan is fairly easy to show. The argument could go like this:

1. Violence is morally wrong.
   Therefore
2. People who behave morally will not be violent (*by definition*).
3. People who are morally educated will behave morally.
   Therefore (putting 2 and 3 together)
4. People who are morally educated will not be violent.
   Conclusion
5. Moral education will reduce violence.

Perhaps the connection with the nature of the wider culture could be initially indicated in some further steps:

6. Everybody in society, when they are young, receives some education.
   Therefore

7. If children, from now on, begin to receive an adequate moral education, there will come a time when everyone within the society has received an adequate moral education.
   Therefore
8. The effects of an adequate moral education will not just be on this individual or that; they will be on everybody in the society.
   Conclusion
9. This will constitute a change in the culture.

The argument appears simple. It is so simple that almost any element of it, and the transitions from one element to the next, can be challenged. Nevertheless, it does seem to constitute a *prima facie* case for the popular equation. Perhaps we can add yet one more stage to the argument:

10. If moral education can do something about violence, it ought to.
    Therefore
11. If an approach to moral education contains no adequate response to violence, that is a deficiency in the approach.

I am suggesting, then, that it is not unreasonable to see the issue of violence as a kind of test case for approaches to moral education. If a proposed programme for moral education, or more broadly a way of talking and thinking about moral education, seems to have nothing adequate to say to public concerns about violence, or seems likely in no way to affect the incidence of violence, this might be seen as a major weakness. If moral education can not make a difference in this way, it might be said, what good is it?

THE CASE AGAINST

There is, of course, something to be said on the other side. If there is a widespread sense that moral education could, and should, be addressing violence more effectively than it now does, there is also the frequent thought that thinking or talking about morality is *not* the way to address whatever problems society has about violence. Perhaps this thought is found more frequently among academics and social commentators than among the general public; it too has a claim on philosophical attention.

The following example comes from the Report of The Commission on Children and Violence convened by the Gulbenkian Foundation (which is hardly a hotbed of radicalism or moral scepticism):

> In considering violence and how to reduce it, a concentration on moral judgements is unlikely to be helpful, acting as a distraction from issues amenable to change. (Gulbenkian Commission, 1995, p. 32).

Two things are not untypical here (though they are not necessarily to be attributed to the individual members of the Gulbenkian Commission): a certain suspicion about the making of moral judgements at all, and a conviction that it is the causes of behaviour that need most to be addressed.

Look again at the argument set out above. To accept the first step of the argument is to endorse a moral judgement: 'violence is morally wrong'. Many people are uncomfortable about taking such a definite moral stance. There may be various reasons for such discomfort (some of which will emerge later),[2] but the result is that some people would prefer to avoid moral talk altogether. That may be one reason why some people see moral talk as a distraction from the real job of tackling violence.

There is also the idea that to reduce violence it is necessary to identify the causes or contributory conditions of violence and do something about them. This is not a matter of moral discourse, but of other kinds of discourse, for example sociological or economic. The approach through such kinds of discourse can appear rational and empirically based where moral talk can appear woolly and subjective.

A possible argument, in outline, runs like this. When someone is violent, there will be in principle a causal explanation of that behaviour. Various factors may come into that explanation: the person's family background, social circumstances, ongoing frustrations and immediate provocation. Morality, or the absence of it, simply does not figure in the explanation. Perhaps certain observers may use moral language in talking about what has happened, but the explanation of what happens will often be presented as, in a strict sense, amoral. Morality in this kind of picture is not a causal force in the world at all;[3] or if it is, it is too weak to make much difference.

You may wonder how morality is the sort of thing that could be a causal force. I mean that moral ideas, people's moral thinking, people's use of moral language, might be among the factors which result in their acting in one way or another. It might be, for instance, that sometimes a person refrains from doing something because she thinks to herself 'this would be wrong'. Then the fact that she thinks in that way would be part of the explanation of why she does not do it. The view in which morality drops out of the explanation seems to be denying that this kind of thing can happen. (Some philosophers would invoke here a distinction between reasons and causes, saying that if a person's reason for not doing something is that she thinks it would be wrong, this cannot at the same time be a cause of her refraining. But even if that view is taken, the upbringing or education which the person received, which enabled such a consideration to be a reason for her, can be counted among the causal factors which contributed to her eventual decision.)

The extensive literature on bullying in schools illustrates the point. References to morality, and the use of any distinctively moral language,[4] are largely conspicuous in this literature by their absence. There will often be some moral evaluation made by the authors early on in identifying why bullying is a problem (e.g. people have a right not to be victimised).[5] But when the text goes on to make practical suggestions about how schools should respond to bullying and try to prevent it, the idea that pupils' behaviour might be influenced by any moral talk is as likely to be condemned as 'moralising' as to be advocated.

If morality is seen in this way as impotent, then so is moral education. Whether the level of violence in our society in the years to come increases or decreases may have nothing to do with anything that moral educators do or fail to do.

The view that morality is impotent in changing the behaviour of those people who are, or who may become, violent, may be complemented by the view that for other people, morality and moral education are irrelevant because unnecessary (so far as any likelihood of violence is concerned). Most people most of the time are not violent; perhaps many people are unlikely to behave violently anyway. For such people, their non-violence may have nothing to do with their moral education or lack of it. As John White says about not killing people (in a passage I shall quote at greater length in the next chapter): 'with few or no exceptions children don't need moral education programmes in order to learn not to do it.'

So, if the concern is to reduce violence, it can easily seem that moral education must be either irrelevant, because most people are not going to be violent anyway, or impotent, because moral education lacks the capacity to prevent violence. Then the popular equation will be simply wrong. And if morality and moral education are either impotent or irrelevant, in relation to something like violence, which can be such a negative factor in the quality of human life, then what, one could say, is the point of morality? Why do we bother with it? Why not forget all about it?

In the face of such a challenge, I would like to defend the popular equation. At the same time I have to recognise that the popular equation, as it stands, is simplistic, and that it may often be associated with views I do not share. Defenders of the equation may often have over-simple views both about violence and about morality and the nature of moral education. If I am to defend the popular equation, I cannot take the popular understanding of its vocabulary for granted.

You might think that this is the point at which I need to define my terms. What is 'violence'? What is 'morality'?

ON NOT DEFINING ONE'S TERMS AT THE BEGINNING

Students writing essays often think they should start by defining their terms. So, sometimes, do writers of reports. This is not necessarily a good idea. For instance, the Gulbenkian Commission report already referred to prints at the beginning of its 'Definition of Violence':

> Violence is defined as behaviour by people against people liable to cause physical or psychological harm (p. 4).

Unfortunately, there is no particular reason to think that all the mentions of violence throughout the 300 or so pages of the report actually conform to this definition. The Gulbenkian Commission drew heavily on other reports from other bodies, and on many research studies. It would hardly have been doing its job if it had tried rigorously to exclude any work which was not written with an eye to just the same definition. In particular, the Gulbenkian Commission no doubt had good reason for including in its definition behaviour liable to cause psychological harm, even in the absence of any physical harm. But most of the other work on which the Commission drew was probably working, explicitly or implicitly, with a narrower notion of violence, closer to everyday usage, in which physical force is an essential element. The discussion throughout the report also reads generally as if this narrower notion is the focus.

Definitions at the beginning, then, can too easily be left idle, like pivots on which nothing in the argument actually turns (the same phenomenon which can often be observed in student essays). Where philosophical writing is concerned, much of the argument may be about the understanding of terms; there is no point in trying to pre-empt the necessary discussion by stipulating the answer at the beginning. So far as this book is concerned, both 'morality' and 'violence' are contested concepts (as is 'education', but so much has been written on that notion within philosophy of education that it — the concept, not the reality — will be a lesser focus here).

Apart from the general reasons for not stipulating the meaning of one's terms at the beginning, there is the particular reason that understandings of violence and morality can interact. First, few uses of the word 'violence' are morally neutral. It may look as if it is possible to define the term in such a way that we can tell whether violence is taking place purely by observing what goes on. We see one person hitting another: that appears to be a central case of violence, which we can describe as such before and independently of any moral judgement of its rightness or wrongness. But even in the apparently simplest cases we make assumptions about the intentions of the persons involved. We need to know, or assume, for instance, that we are not watching two people pretending, perhaps in a piece of street theatre (most violence on stage and in screen fiction is, after all, not actually violence: it is a representation of violence, in which people are pretending to be violent).

When we make a moral evaluation of some action (to put explicitly what may take place implicitly) we are often evaluating an intention. Was one person hitting the other for reasons which we regard as justifying the action? If so, will we still describe the action as violence? Often, too, we cannot grasp what the intention was without knowing the moral evaluations *of the agent*. Perhaps the person hitting was an adult and the person hit was a child. What was the adult's intention? To hurt? To frighten? Or perhaps the action as the adult saw it was a 'smack' as an act of moral education: 'you were naughty (evaluation) and I know better than you (evaluation) and I have a right (evaluation) to teach you a lesson'.

Many people are less likely to call an action violent if they believe that it is justified; many will not describe an action as violent at all without at the same time and by the same token seeing it as wrong. This means that how we conceive of violence is not independent of how we conceive of moral evaluation. If moral evaluation is indeed primarily a matter of seeing whether an action conforms to certain rules or principles, then counting an action, of hitting, say, as unjustified and therefore as violent will be a matter of seeing it as a violation of norms. And indeed academic discussions of violence have often written into their definitions that an action which is violent is — besides other conditions — one that violates norms or is illegitimate (i.e. violating laws or quasi-legal norms) (e.g. Garver, 1981, Honderich, 1980, Wolff, 1969).

For the virtue ethics of which so much has been heard recently (more on this below: see pp. 41 ff.), moral (or ethical) evaluation is not primarily a matter of reference to norms. Evaluation is primarily of persons, or of the quality of character of persons. So we might expect that a virtue theorist would be more interested in the grounds on which we might describe someone as a violent (or non-violent) person. This does not mean that a virtue theorist cannot focus on individual actions, but when she does it will be the motivation of the action which will be central, rather than whether it conforms to norms. If she sees the motivation of the adult smacking the child as good — if she sees this as the kind of action one would expect from a caring responsible parent, or the kind of action which could flow from a loving disposition — she might not describe the action as violence. If she sees the action as manifesting a malicious or sadistic character, she will be much more ready to describe it as violence.

Is this all a matter of verbal quibbles, of no relevance to the practical business of education? Not at all. This is partly for the reason — which is of application far beyond the present context — that we cannot respond to practical situations without conceptualising them in some way. How teachers respond to violence in schools has a lot to do with what they recognise as violence and with the moral evaluations they make. But they are not only using these notions in their own thinking: they are also inevitably, even if unconsciously, engaged in teaching them. No child's use of language is complete by the time the child starts school. The child's encounters with the concepts of violence and of morality within school themselves constitute part of the child's education. Whether teachers use these notions in a clear or a confused way, then, does make a difference to the education of the children passing through our schools. It is because of this that the idea that schools could change the culture does have some purchase.

Is that not an argument for laying down a usage of the terms, so as to impose some clarity and coherence? It is not, because we are dealing with ideas which are of common currency in our language, not the technical terms of a specialised discipline. A recommendation to use a term in a particular way, even if it is backed up by an argued case, may have no effect, or a very gradual one, on entrenched linguistic habits.

Consider a teacher who is taking a part-time Masters course in the sociology of education. Perhaps she has become acquainted with the notion of 'systemic violence', which 'has been defined as any institutional practice or procedure that adversely impacts on individuals or groups by burdening them psychologically, mentally, culturally, spiritually, economically or physically' (Epp and Watkinson, 1996, p. i). Talking to colleagues in the staff room, worrying about the incidence of violence in the school, she could, by this definition, be uneasy about the school's collective worship marginalising Muslims, or about a particular teacher's tendency to use sarcasm towards pupils; but she is far more likely to be concerned about fighting between pupils or physical attacks by pupils on teachers.

It is the physical kind of violence which is likely to come to mind first in most contexts in which the term is used (except where its use seems clearly to be metaphorical; someone might think, for instance, that the notion of systemic violence does violence to the ordinary understanding of the word).[6] Up to this point it is likely that most readers have tacitly been taking the term this way, though some may indeed have been questioning my usage. It is physical violence of person against person which I shall take as the central case. There are arguments for extending this usage, but these arguments will almost invariably be appealing to moral evaluations. It will be said, for instance, that certain ways in which people can be humiliated, perhaps by calling them names, are morally equivalent to physically hurting people; that is, they are morally as bad, and for similar sorts of reason (consider the different ways in which one person can treat another which may be counted as bullying). Thus the notion of psychological violence comes into use (and is perhaps now gaining a wider currency).

If we extend our notion of violence by treating one kind of behaviour as morally equivalent to another, which we already count as violence, then what we count as violence is going, as before, to depend importantly on what kind of moral evaluations we give priority to. Do we count one kind of treatment as equivalent to another because it has consequences which are bad in the same sort of way? Then we open the way to notions such as that of systemic violence, where it is 'adverse impact' that counts, not the motivation of any person responsible for the adverse impact, or even whether there is any identifiable person who is responsible at all. Or do we count one kind of treatment as equivalent to another because it stems from a similar motivation, or similar state of character? Then we might count as morally equivalent both physical and psychological violence which is seen as stemming from maliciousness, but not 'systemic violence' which may be an unintended by-product of arrangements made for quite other purposes.

HOW TO PROCEED

I have not so far tried to lay down a way of conceiving either of violence or of morality; I have only shown that the questions are complex, not least because of the interactions between them. In particular I have mentioned some of the variety of conceptions of violence, but I have also touched on some different ways of conceiving of morality. Do I then, need to review all possible conceptions of morality and relate them to all possible conceptions of violence, or is there some less exhaustive, and exhausting, way to proceed?

Here, I suggest, it will be helpful to go back again to the popular equation. If this equation is to have any plausibility, it must be drawing on an understanding of morality which has certain features. It must be possible to see morality as having a point, as being good *for* something (as opposed to just good in itself), because the popular equation in effect wants to *use* morality as a means to an end. And it must be possible to see morality as being at least in some respects shared and public. There must be sufficient agreement in the language people use for them not to be merely talking at cross purposes; and there must be some actual agreement on the judgements people make within their common language (a broadly Wittgensteinian point which will recur in the next chapter). The outline argument, as an argument within public discourse, assumes agreement on its premises: the rest of the argument would not go through if the first premise were merely '*some people think* that violence is morally wrong'.

One question we have to consider, then (and would have to consider even if we were not taking violence as our central example), is: 'Do we have, or is there available to us, a conception of morality which can fulfil the public role that popular demands for moral education presuppose?' This is the question I wish to pursue. I have already suggested that the popular view tends to think in terms of basic rules or constraints which are not to be overstepped. How far that way of thinking will survive within a more reflective consideration of morality remains to be seen. Initially I want to ask how philosophical writing on education, and on moral education in particular, has responded to public concerns about violence. Later I shall go on to recommend — for certain public and educational purposes — a particular way of conceiving of morality. I shall not, in this book, recommend a way of conceiving of violence. Rather, I shall say that, given a certain understanding of morality, the question of how we conceive of violence is itself a question to be addressed publicly within that understanding of morality. This book will not, then, be telling teachers, or anyone else, what to do about violence. Like much philosophy, it will be a set of prolegomena — which is simply Greek for 'things which need to be said in advance'.

NOTES

1. See sources and acknowledgements in the Introduction.
2. See also Chapter 6, 'What's wrong with morality?' in *Teaching about Values*.
3. In philosophical jargon, it is an epiphenomenon.
4. I shall say more later about what kind of language counts as moral.
5. For example Tattum and Lane (1988), p. 1.
6. The distinction between the literal and the metaphorical may not be clear-cut. I am inclined to count the notions of 'systemic violence', 'structural violence' (Galtung, 1969) and 'the Marxist concept of violence' (Harris, 1980) as extensions of the literal meaning of the term (it being a further question whether there is good reason for the extensions). On the other hand, the notion of 'symbolic violence' (Bourdieu and Passeron, 1994) seems to me metaphorical. But perhaps nothing substantial hangs on the literal/metaphorical distinction.

Chapter 2 Right, Wrong and Murder

BONES (about McFee): He thinks there's nothing *wrong* with killing people?
GEORGE: Well, put like that, of course . . . But *philosophically*, he doesn't think it's actually, inherently wrong in itself, no.
BONES: What sort of philosophy is that?
GEORGE: Mainstream, I'd call it. Orthodox mainstream. (*Jumpers*, pp. 48–49)

PHILOSOPHY OF EDUCATION AND VIOLENCE

Whatever may be the case for philosophy in general, philosophy of education has had rather little to say about violence. The *Journal of Philosophy of Education*, for instance, from its conception in the 1960s under the title of *Proceedings of the Philosophy of Education Society of Great Britain*, has contained very little discussion of violence. There have been occasional papers in which violence is referred to, from discussions of the justification of punishment in schools, which include corporal punishment within their remit, to discussions of peace education. But the idea of violence itself has hardly been a focus at all.

Part of the explanation for this, perhaps, is that philosophy of education has an inbuilt bias towards 'sweet reason'. We (I am one of this community) are still to a large degree part of the tradition epitomised by the title of the collection edited by Dearden, Hirst and Peters in the early 1970s: *Education and the Development of Reason*. That, to many of us, is still what it is about. Of course, other perspectives, within postmodernism and feminism especially, have made the link between education and reason, and the nature of reason itself, more problematic than it once appeared. But even if we are not quite so sure that rationality is what it is about, it is still reasoning (especially in philosophy, where empirical investigation is not the driving force) that we have to try to use to understand what it is about. There may, then, be an inbuilt reluctance to do much thinking about anything that seems quite so much 'brute fact' — contingent, empirical and messy (in more than one sense of the word) — as violence. As one of my colleagues remarked 'it's not a nice subject' (and I have myself sometimes found it a difficult one to pursue, for just that reason).

A lot of philosophy of education, though, has been pursuing explicitly ethical concerns, so that one might expect some consideration of the ethical status of violence. In fact, this has been largely absent, not only in writing by professional philosophers of education, but also in philosophical writing about moral education by 'mainstream' philosophers. Part of the reason for this, I suspect, is that philosophers like to have intellectually interesting problems to deal with. The ethical status of violence, when compared with problematic issues such as whether telling the truth is always required, or whether it can sometimes be right to break a promise — may seem simply too clear-cut to be interesting. But actually this thought applies, if anywhere, only to personal violence — assault, mugging and the like — and even there it may turn out to be too simple. There are considerable ethical problems about violence in what might be called 'public' contexts — including political protest, and much police and military action. In some way a public moral education surely has to address issues such as these.

It would, however, be a diversion from the public concerns I have in mind if philosophers of education were to limit their interest in violence to such ethically and politically controversial matters. The public call, as I understand it, is not primarily for the kind of education (which we might call an aspect of political education or citizenship education) which would equip the public for its participatory democratic role in debates over the justifiability of, say, capital punishment, gun control, the arming of the police, or military intervention for alleged self-defence or peace-keeping (though for my part I certainly think education should at least lay the groundwork for such debates). The public perception[1] seems to be more that there is a form of education, labelled moral education, which would be a means of reducing the level of violence in society, as manifested in, for instance, bullying, assault on teachers, football riots and mugging.[2]

If this is a widespread public perception, is this sufficient reason for philosophy of education to take the idea seriously? I think it is, if philosophy of education is to have a public role. While it is good that individual philosophers of education should pursue the matters that interest them, because for one thing they are likely to do better work that way, it is also reasonable to expect them, as a group, to respond to public concerns about education. If philosophy of education is to be a species of applied philosophy — and if that is to mean, not just that it says things which could be applied, but that it actually gets some application — then it cannot afford to ignore popular conceptions.[3]

At the least, philosophy of education surely should be able to offer some guidance to teachers who are faced with popular demands for their engagement in moral education, whether or not those demands are well founded. In doing this it needs to recognise that if there are differences between popular understandings and philosophers' understandings, the untutored understandings of teachers for the most part (especially if there is no philosophical content in teacher education) are going to be closer to the popular ones than to the philosophers' ones. So philosophy of education needs to engage with the popular conceptions — to understand their motivation, and to see whether, perhaps in some aspects if not in all, there is point in retaining those conceptions.

TEACHING RIGHT AND WRONG

Of the recent philosophical literature on moral education, Smith and Standish's *Teaching Right and Wrong* (1997) is probably the book which contains the clearest acknowledgements that public demands for attention to moral education in schools have been fuelled by reaction to violence. The murders of James Bulger and Philip Lawrence are mentioned by Smith and Standish on the first page, and several further times by other contributors.[4] There are also occasional references in various places to the horrors of murder, mugging and rape. But within the overall argument, not only of Smith and Standish themselves, but of other contributors too, these are almost references in passing. How to get people not to be violent is far from being the main topic of the book.

There are good reasons why this should be so. If Smith and Standish had made that the main topic of their book they would have given a different impression of moral education from that which they, and their contributors generally, wanted to convey. They would have risked giving the impression that moral education is a matter of 'us' and 'them' in which 'we', who know what is what (and would never, of course, be violent) put across the elements to 'them', who do not (and might well be). Smith and Standish and their contributors quite rightly acknowledge that morality is not something that only impinges on life from time to time, that we only have to take account of in special circumstances: it is all-pervasive (e.g. Smith, *Teaching Right and Wrong* p. 116). We are all involved in morality and we all have problems with it. 'Literature on moral education often conveys a curious sense of looking on from the sidelines, as if values were only problematic in terms of how they are to be got across to children and teenagers' (Smith and Standish, 1997, p. viii).

But although it is not a criticism of *Teaching Right and Wrong*, or of any other single book on moral education, that it does not say a lot about violence, the overall impression from much recent philosophical writing on moral education is that it is 'looking on from the sidelines' in a different sense from that which Smith and Standish intended: that it seems, not so much to argue against popular perceptions of what moral education should be, as to ignore these conceptions. The reasons for that, I think, do not have to do only with reluctance to discuss violence. They also have to do with the view taken of the place of rules in morality.

My first example from *Teaching Right and Wrong* is not from a philosopher, but from a sociologist also well versed in psycho-analysis, Michael Rustin:

> In the sphere of education, there is the demand that moral standards should be taught in schools. . . . The implicit idea seems to be that morality consists of a self-evident set of rules and precepts. (p. 76)

Rustin himself takes quite a negative view of this demand:

> The demand for prescriptive teaching of moral principles has recently functioned mainly as a mechanism of denial of the damage that is being done by the weakening of many social institutions, including the family. . . . Whilst there have been many demands that more attention be given to moral issues, this prescriptive climate has been largely inimical to rather than supportive of moral thinking. (p. 90)

Several things are worth noting here. First, Rustin makes no distinction (in these passages, or as far as I can see elsewhere in the chapter) between 'rules' and 'principles' (and indeed 'precepts'). In terms of the distinction I shall make later, he is talking about rules. Second, the idea of teaching rules or principles, and recognition of social and institutional factors, are seen as if they were opposed. Rustin may well be right that one can function as a distraction from the other. On the other hand, there need be no inconsistency between the two lines of thought. There is a possibility to be considered that the teaching of rules or principles could actually strengthen social institutions, including the family. Third, the teaching of rules or principles is seen as inimical to moral thinking. The possibility that the two could be mutually supportive needs more attention (I shall come back to it in later chapters).

Carole Cox in the same volume writes in similar vein, but apparently going further:

> . . . when we express our concerns about the moral education of the young, we can find ourselves wanting children to know what the rules are and how to apply those rules. Unfortunately, there is no set of tablets of stone on which these rules are inscribed. Instead, moral situations are specific and particular, concrete and local. They require us to respond to these particulars, rather than obey a rule or maxim. (p. 68)

Cox appears here to be rejecting the role of rules altogether, though she does not expand on her reasons. She appears in this passage to be adopting the position which Dancy has labelled particularism, though Cox herself is perhaps more likely to be following feminist arguments than those of Dancy.[5] Straight after this passage Cox turns to virtue ethics, thus incidentally illustrating how easy it is in current writing about moral education within philosophy of education almost to take for granted a rejection of anything that smacks of Kantianism or universalism, without even running through the arguments.

In the same volume, Richard Smith takes a view that is in several ways similar to Cox's, emphasising the inescapable role of judgement and the value of literature in developing judgement; but whereas Cox apparently denies that there are any moral rules, Smith uses his opening examples from *Huckleberry Finn* to remind us that '*as well as moral principles or rules*' [my italics] there are many other elements of the moral life (p. 106). Smith, then, does explicitly recognise that rules and principles have a role, but he does not say very much about what that role is. And this would be true of many philosophical writers on moral education, at least subsequent to Richard Peters.[6]

As in moral philosophy generally, so in philosophy of education we can distinguish in principle two quite different positions regarding rules, which in pure forms would be incompatible with each other, though both mean that little space is given to rules.

One position is essentially negative about the role of rules. It may actually give some space to discussing them, but only in order to reject or minimise their role. Some writing on an ethic of care is like this, as is some virtue ethics, and as is much of the writing critical of what I shall later call morality in the narrow sense (these categories overlap). A good deal of recent philosophical writing about moral education adopts this kind of position, while sometimes, as in Cox's case, assuming rather than explicitly using the arguments that have been made elsewhere in philosophy. (I am sure that it must be legitimate for philosophy of education sometimes to assume arguments that have been made elsewhere; otherwise it would constantly be going over ground already covered. On the other hand, the arguments do need to be brought out and examined from time to time, if an unchallenged orthodoxy is not to take hold.)

A second position is much more positive about rules: it allows that there is a significant, perhaps important, even perhaps a basic role for rules in morality; but it holds (sometimes only implicitly) that because this is fairly obvious and a well-worn point, we do not actually need to say much about it.

A particularly explicit example of this position, outside of philosophy of education, occurs in a writer who has been heavily influenced by postmodernist thought but who has retained the analytical penchant for clear distinctions: the philosopher of religion Don Cupitt. In a work on ethics, in which he distinguishes between morality and ethics in much the way that Bernard Williams does (see Chapter 4 below), Cupitt writes:

> Morality, for the most part, can be left to look after itself. Where in any particular sphere of life rules of practice are needed, people can be relied upon to evolve them. So long as the rules are working well people can be relied upon to maintain them, and when they have become redundant or archaic, nothing can revive them and people will let them drop.
>
> ...the renegotiation of the rules of morality looks like a straightforwardly political task. Through public debate one tries to obtain and establish an agreed code of practice, backed where necessary by sanctions. And philosophy nowadays does not need to say very much more about moral codes than that. (Cupitt, 1995, pp. 11–12, paragraphs transposed.)

Cupitt's view of morality here seems to be similar to the one I shall be developing later in this book. Where I differ from Cupitt is in thinking that philosophy, and philosophy of education in particular, does need to say rather more about moral rules: it cannot afford to take their existence and maintenance for granted.

In the rest of this chapter I shall try to illustrate this point by further reference to some of the contributors to *Teaching Right and Wrong*: Richard Smith and Paul Standish themselves, and more especially John White. All three have something to say about the wrongness of murder. Whether all murder counts as violence is itself a moot point when we think about what makes an act one of violence; even those, for instance, who describe euthanasia as murder would not necessarily class it as violence. And, of course, there is much violence that does not kill. But for the rest of this chapter I shall concentrate on killing.

Standish asks 'Do you teach children that murder is wrong?' and replies 'The wrongness is built into our world and the young child absorbs this as part of the background' (p. 51). Similarly in their joint conclusion Smith and Standish say: 'No-one normally *teaches* their children that murder is wrong' (p. 146).

These remarks could be read as an interpretation of what it is for the rule against killing another human being to be *basic*, though Smith and Standish do not themselves put it that way. On this interpretation the rule against killing would be basic in the sense of being part of the background (though more would at least have to be said about what it is in the background that allows some killing not to be counted as murder). The point is perhaps a broadly Wittgensteinian one: for language to function, some agreement is needed, not just in the use of words, but in *judgements*, that is, in the application of at least some terms to at least some cases. If people do not recognise that *murder* is wrong, then the word 'wrong' is idle; moral language cannot function. (This sort of point was made by the Swansea school of philosophers influenced by Wittgenstein: cf. Phillips and Mounce, 1969).

It would perhaps be a further loosely Wittgensteinian point that it is only philosophers who need or are inclined to focus their attention on the wrongness of murder; outside the philosopher's study, this can be taken for granted, precisely because it is part of the background. And in the same loosely Wittgensteinian vein one could suggest, as perhaps Smith and Standish mean to, that formal education has no need to focus on the wrongness of murder. If the child has not absorbed the wrongness of murder, says Standish, 'it is not that she doesn't know the rules: something has gone wrong with her world' (p. 51). And this sort of existential or cosmic wrongness is not the sort of thing, presumably, that we expect teachers to address.

It seems to me that there is a certain danger in the idea that the wrongness of murder can be taken for granted so far as formal education is concerned. I do not know whether Smith and Standish would quite say this, or whether John White would, though he certainly uses the phrase 'take for granted' about the prohibition on killing. It is by unpacking some of White's remarks that I shall pursue my argument here.

THINKING ABOUT THE 'UNTHINKABLE'

John White has been consistent over the years in recognising that there are basic rules that play a part in morality (e.g. White, 1982, p. 78; 1990, p. 37), and also in wanting to put more emphasis on other aspects of ethics. In his chapter in *Teaching Right and Wrong* one of his points is that we should have confidence in insisting on the basic rules such as the prohibitions on killing and injuring, while we should also have confidence in building up certain virtues. (I shall come back to the concern about virtues later.) That we should have confidence, and are justified in having confidence, is part of White's answer to the worries that people like Nick Tate (Chief Executive of the Qualifications and Curriculum Authority and formerly of the School Curriculum and Assessment Authority) have about the prevalence of 'relativism' in our society.

There is a sense in which it is not clear how confident we can be about rules against violence in general, or even against killing in general, because of the uncertainties over the nature of violence and over which acts of killing might be justified — a matter to which I shall eventually return in Chapter 14. White recognises some of the standard problem cases, such as self-defence and voluntary euthanasia, where it is at least arguable that killing is not wrong. In fact, though he uses the word 'killing', it seems to be murder that White is talking about.

'Murder' is, of course, a term in our language that allows for the existence of problem cases about killing, since murder by definition is wrongful killing. Given that, White can hardly be wrong in saying that we should have confidence in the rule against it. But he also says of this rule that it 'is *so* fundamental as to be utterly taken for granted' (I shall quote this remark in context below). It seems to me rather important to distinguish 'having confidence in' from 'taking for granted'.

The rule we are talking about now — the prohibition of murder — is the one which Smith and Standish say is not taught. In some sense, however, it clearly has to be learned: human beings are not born innately programmed with knowledge of this rule; they have, after all, to learn the language in which it is expressed. Smith and Standish say the rule is absorbed. But this surely is just what we should not take for granted.

Why are many people worried about the level of portrayed violence in films and on television? No doubt for several reasons, among them the possibility, which may have been reality in just a few cases, that people committing violent crimes are consciously copying what they have seen in some film. But there is, I think, a more general worry, which is that the prevalence of images of violence and killing may counteract the 'absorption' to which Smith and Standish refer.

The question of the attitude which society should take towards images of violence is a complicated one, for reasons which are not unique to this issue. There are factual questions mixed up with evaluative ones, and there is a lack of indisputable evidence on the factual questions. Even if we did know for certain that images of violence lead to real violence, there would still be arguments against legal restrictions on the grounds of freedom of expression and consumer choice. In fact, we do not know; again, as in so many public policy issues, any evidence is going to be challenged. It may be that challenges come because of vested interests, but in any case they are there.

As citizens, and especially as educators, we need a way of proceeding which does not have to wait for unchallenged evidence, but which nevertheless is reasonable. If there is a possibility that the wrongness of murder is not being as thoroughly or universally absorbed as perhaps it used to be, then we should not take its absorption for granted. We should, then, pay explicit attention to the matter in schools. In a sense, this does mean, odd though it may sound, that it is a responsibility of schools to *teach* the rule that murder is wrong. (It would not, perhaps, have sounded so odd to earlier generations.)

If we say this, though, we should remember that 'teaching' can take many forms. In most areas of the curriculum we do not suppose, because a teacher is teaching, that he or she is didactically handing something down. We tend now to assume that there are ways of teaching which involve the student in the learning, and have the student coming to see the reasons behind what is learned, rather than simply being told the reasons. Can the 'teaching' of basic moral rules be non-didactic and participatory? I think this is not only possible but essential if morality is not to appear as some sort of alienating force; but the possibility depends on a conception of morality which can be widely shared. It is such a conception that I shall be unpacking further in later chapters.

If we do have a responsibility as educators to *teach* the prohibition on murder (in some meaningful sense of the word 'teach') then we also need to do some thinking of our own about this prohibition: we cannot take it for granted in the sense of thinking that nothing further needs to be said in its support.

Consider this passage from White's discussion:

> In fact, when you think about it, if you take the rule against killing, there's not much to do here in the way of inducting children into it. By this, I don't mean that the prohibition against killing is not important. Quite the opposite. It is *so* fundamental as to be utterly taken for granted. Killing a human being belongs to the realm of the unthinkable. With few or no exceptions children don't need moral education programmes in order to learn not to do it . . .
>
> Some ethical considerations, like the one just mentioned, should be seen as embedded in the very framework of a civilised life. Reject them and you reject civilisation. You outlaw yourself from your community. Not killing is one example, so is not injuring, so is not stealing. (*Teaching Right and Wrong*, pp. 21–2)

In some ways it is unfair to focus on this passage. White would not have expected his contribution to *Teaching Right and Wrong* to be evaluated on the basis of remarks which are made almost in passing. And indeed I am not intending here any evaluation of the whole chapter. What I want to bring out is that if academic thinking about moral education takes prohibitions on killing and injuring for granted, then it leaves too many questions unaddressed. White here is doing what much philosophy of education does: addressing 'us'. ('This gives *us* a useful way of thinking about values education.') But does it give something useful to 'our' pupils? Or do we need to do rather better than this?

Consider: does killing a human being really belong to the realm of the unthinkable? Is that so in some sense which would mean that philosophers writing on moral education need give little attention to the point?

It is not clear what White means by 'the realm of the unthinkable', but it is pretty clear that on some interpretations of that phrase killing a human being is far from unthinkable. Some people do kill others. In cases where we might say that the action is done unthinkingly (in the heat of the moment, in reaction to immediate and great provocation, and so on), then in a sense we could say that such an act of killing is not an exception to the idea that killing is unthinkable. But, first, not all cases of killing are ones in which the action is taken unthinkingly. And second, even in the cases where the act on the part of an individual is unthinking, it is still the case that killing is within the possible repertoire of behaviour for the individual concerned. And because it is not, in fact, utterly exceptional, it *is* within the realm of possibilities in our culture. (Whether or not it would be within the realm of possibilities in all actual or conceivable human cultures does not affect this point.)

So there is at least an important sense in which killing is not unthinkable (if it were, it would be neither possible nor necessary for educationalists to think about killing at all; but if killing is in some sense thinkable, it can hardly come outside the purview of education). What of White's further points, that if you reject the prohibition on killing you reject civilisation, and outlaw yourself from your community? These are points, I suggest, about how we would like people to perceive the situation, or how they need to perceive it if morality is to work, not truths about the facts of the case.

That by killing you reject civilisation may be true in a literal sense of a minority of killers who see their own killing as a protest against civilisation. This seems to have been true, for instance, of the so-called Unabomber in the United States in the mid-1990s. Against such killers it may be possible to argue, in a loosely Kantian way, that one who takes such a stance is inconsistent, for he or she necessarily relies on some features of civilisation while ostensibly rejecting it (the Unabomber relied on the mass media; his bombing-as-protest would have made no sense if his message had not been heard). But it would only be in a minority of cases that such arguments would have bite. There is no reason to think that most killers either see themselves as rejecting civilisation, or actually are in any substantial sense rejecting it; there may be many aspects of civilisation that one who has killed continues to value (including, to anticipate a point, a civilised society's procedures of justice).

As a claim of fact, that you outlaw yourself from your community by killing does not fare any better. First, it is not difficult to think of examples of communities, from Homeric Greece onwards, in which people (usually men) who kill, far from being rejected, are highly regarded. It will probably be said that this is missing White's point. Certainly many communities have been in varying degrees militaristic, seeing themselves (whether reasonably or not) as threatened by enemies, and positively valuing those who kill the community's enemies. But presumably White's point is that the same community which accepts or may positively value the killing of outsiders, will outlaw the one who kills within his (or her) own community.

What sort of claim is this? It is not straightforwardly a matter of fact, since so much turns on what is to count as a person's community. The anthropologist von Furer-Haimendorf (1967) reports on the head-hunting culture of the Naga in Northern India, which survived well into this century. It was not acceptable to kill a member of one's own village, but merit could be acquired by bringing back the head of an innocent person from a neighbouring village — a village which culturally could hardly have been considered totally alien. Something similar may apply to the sort of 'subculture of violence' identified by some sociologists within Western urban contexts (Wolfgang, 1977, pp. 37–38, and see Chapter 6 below). In such a subculture (if the sociological accounts can be trusted) a person will not outlaw himself by using violence: rather he will be doing what is expected. If there is a community from which a person will outlaw himself by using violence within it, that community may be as small as a particular street gang. There may be loyalty among gang members, but hostility towards rival gangs — who again are recognisably of the same culture, sharing many of the same expectations.

Yet another example may be found among terrorist groups. In the summer of 1998 the group calling itself the Real IRA claimed responsibility for the car-bombing in Omagh in Northern Ireland. It was widely perceived that the rest of the Irish community, both North and South, Protestant and Catholic, turned their back on this remnant of 'the armed struggle'. These terrorists were, in other words, seen as outlawing themselves from their community. Yet presumably there remained a community of a kind — the community of the Real IRA itself — from which the people who planted the bombs were not outlawing themselves.

Putting weight on the idea that killing has the effect of outlawing one from one's community is likely, then, to lead towards a relativistic morality in which the nature and strength of the prohibitions against killing depend on which community one has in mind. And this is not, I think, the kind of morality White had in mind. Though he is (rightly) suspicious of the term 'absolute', he clearly has in mind elements of morality which are to be part of any moral framework. He wants us to see the killer as isolating himself (if I may continue to use the masculine pronoun in this context) from civilisation and community *as such*.[7] And this claim, I have argued, cannot be interpreted as a straightforwardly factual one.

There is also a sense in which the claim is itself morally suspect. Many would argue that it is the mark of a civilised society that it does not totally reject the killer, that it still acts toward him or her in a civilised fashion, and allows a possibility over time of rehabilitation. (In Northern Ireland, it is possible that the people who have recently been influential in moves towards peaceful coexistence include among their number some individuals who have themselves killed or been responsible for killings in the past. Perhaps there is good reason for the community, or communities, of Northern Ireland to be grateful that such individuals were not irrevocably outlawed.)

Despite these queries about how we should take the idea that to kill is to reject civilisation and to outlaw yourself from your community, I do take these claims to be pointing in the right direction. There is something certainly right in the understanding of morality behind them; it is that kind of understanding that I shall try to unpack in more detail in the chapters which follow.

To come finally to a point which I anticipated in the first chapter. White claims: 'with few or no exceptions children don't need moral education programmes in order to learn not to do it [i.e. killing]'. If this is on the right lines at all, it may seem that little hangs on whether 'few' or 'no' is correct. But from the point of view of the popular view I am examining, a great deal will hang on it.

Suppose first that there are no exceptions. That is, *no* children need a moral education programme in order to learn not to kill;[8] there is nothing children need to learn about not killing that they cannot and will not learn perfectly well without a moral education programme. That really would make moral education programmes irrelevant to any social goal of reducing the number of killings (it would be a further question whether this applies to the broader goal of reducing violence in general).

But suppose instead that there are some exceptions: that is, there are *some* children who *do* need a moral education programme to learn not to kill. What follows? If the children who do need a moral education programme for this could be identified in advance, then (in trying to reduce the number of killings) society would need to provide moral education just for those children. But suppose there is no way of identifying such children in advance. Then even if there are only a few children who will be liable to kill if they do not get a moral education programme, society might decide (if it is sufficiently concerned about killing) that everybody ought to get such a programme, including all those who do not actually need it.

Some would think that given the importance of the aim — which is, literally, a matter of life and death — it would be reasonable to try to use the opportunities which schooling provides to reinforce a condemnation of murder, even if for the great majority of pupils the message is unnecessary. Even if only one or two murders in a generation were prevented by a moral education programme in schools, it would be worthwhile. (It would take some time and resources away from all the other things we want schools to do; but are we sure that the other things are more important?)[9]

This does seem to me reasonable, provided the effort is not counterproductive. There is a danger — as Rustin, for instance, sees — that heavy moralising in schools will alienate people from their community and so contribute to the very thing it is trying to avoid. But this is very much a matter of what kind of conception of morality schools are putting across. And that is why it is important to articulate a non-alienating conception of morality. This is what I shall try to do in the chapters which follow. The conception I am working towards is one that may indeed be already implicit in White's remarks about basic rules; but I am arguing that it should not be taken for granted and does therefore need to be spelt out.

NOTES

1. I do not have any well-grounded evidence about the extent of this public perception. I am relying largely on media comment, which no doubt reflects strands of public opinion, but also has a role in forming it.
2. Domestic violence is less often mentioned in the same breath. Feminists have rightly pointed out the problematic nature of the public/private distinction which has sometimes been used to exclude domestic violence from public concern.
3. For a certain scepticism about philosophy of education as applied philosophy, see Cooper (1998). For my purposes here it is enough that at least some philosophy of education is properly seen as applied philosophy.
4. See *Teaching Right and Wrong* p. 2 (Talbot and Tate), p. 16 (White), p. 67 (Cox), p. 121 (Blake). Perhaps philosophers of education — together with many other academics and commentators — should make some acknowledgement to the relatives of James Bulger and Philip Lawrence, who to us have so often provided merely convenient examples. I hope we do not entirely take their names in vain.
5. Dancy (1993) defends particularism. In an earlier piece of writing (Dancy 1992) he explicitly aligns particularism with feminist arguments for an ethic of care. Particularism will come up again below.
6. Richard Peters, as White points out (1990, p. 41), did give an important role to rules and a good deal of space to them.
7. Surprising as it may seem to readers who know White's work, and the extent to which he has been influenced by MacIntyre and by Williams, I suspect that if we are to make sense of his claims that killing is 'unthinkable' and that it entails outlawing from civilisation and community, we have to interpret these claims in a quite Kantian way. The thought of killing another will involve some sort of deep contradiction in the agent's thinking (this does not make such thinking impossible as a matter of fact: people are contradicting themselves all the time). And the community from which one outlaws oneself will be Kant's ideal community of rational moral agents, the 'kingdom of ends'.
8. It is not quite clear what is meant by 'learn not to kill'. Does it mean 'learn that killing is wrong' (Smith and Standish's absorption), or something like 'grow up in such a way that killing is, for oneself, unthinkable'?
9. cf. *Teaching about Values*, Chapter 2.

Chapter 3 From Values to Morality

DOTTY: . . . actions . . . can be *disapproved of*, or comical, unexpected, saddening or good television, depending on who frowns, laughs, jumps, weeps or wouldn't have missed it for the world. (*Jumpers*, p. 41)
GEORGE: Not all value judgements, however, are the proper study of the moral philosopher. (p. 62)

DOUBTS ABOUT MORALITY

I have suggested that popular demands for moral education, and beliefs that it can be effective, for instance in reducing violence, presuppose some appropriate and shared conception of morality and moral education. But the existence, and even the possibility, of such a shared conception is often now called into question. The focus is very often on diversity within a plural society. And I have myself argued before that not only do we have differences of opinion over whether certain sorts of conduct are morally right or wrong, we also have different conceptions of what it means to call something morally right or wrong, and even disagreement over whether such terminology has any useful role at all. (cf. Haydon, 1995; 1999c; 1997 Chapter 6; White, 1990, Chapter 3; Williams, 1985, Chapter 10.)

Certainly many people are uncomfortable with the *word* 'morality'. Standish, for instance, puts it like this: 'For many the very word "morality" has become tainted, suggesting the stiff correctness of Victorian behaviour, sexual repression (if not hang-ups), timid subjection to conformity, and a certain starchiness of tone. . . . People *do* avoid speaking of morality — as if something were amiss with it, as with an outmoded ceremony' (*Teaching Right and Wrong*, p. 50).

That many people avoid talking about morality is one of our problems; another is that when they do talk about it they may have different ideas in mind about what morality is. Is it a set of commandments issued by a divinity? Is it an ideological device which functions to uphold the interests of the ruling classes? Is it a matter of what seems important to each individual, and hence a subjective matter in no way open to argument? Is it a set of prescriptions for conduct which can be explained — and even justified — by an evolutionary account of human nature? Is it a set of conventions which serve a social function in particular circumstances and can therefore be changed as circumstances change? It would be surprising if the reader has not encountered at least as much diversity as this in ideas about morality, not just in the pages of academic writing, but in everyday talk.

If many people — including teachers — are uncomfortable with talk about morality, and people who are comfortable with it do not agree about what morality is, it might seem better to use some different terminology. There are other terminologies which many people are more comfortable with. That of 'values' is one. Talk of values seems to fit readily with a recognition of diversity, that is, of variation both between cultures and between individuals. Smith and Standish suggest that 'talk of "values" . . . plays into the hands of instinctive subjectivists . . . since "values" have the air of something personal to the individual' (*Teaching Right and Wrong*, p. 141). In educational contexts, that has to some people no doubt been a positive feature of the terminology of values. People who are wary of talk of morality, partly because such talk suggests to them some form of imposition if not indoctrination, can comfortably talk of helping individuals to clarify and indeed to choose their own values.

On the other hand, the demand for moral education to do something about perceived problems such as violence clearly cannot be content with the idea of values as something personal and up for choice. At the very least, it needs values which are widely shared (it actually needs more than just that: what more will, I hope, be brought out below).

THE SCAA FORUM

It was in this confused terminological context that the School Curriculum and Assessment Authority (SCAA) in 1996 began to do some work bearing on, but not confined to or indeed labelled as, moral education. Other aspects of the context of that work were the popular reaction to events like the murder of Philip Lawrence; and the educational legislation of the late 1980s and early 1990s which required schools to attend to, and OFSTED (Office for Standards in Education) to inspect their provision for, the 'spiritual, moral, social and cultural' development of pupils.

After a conference in January 1996, shortly after the Lawrence murder,[1] SCAA set up its National Forum for Values in Education and the Community. This had a twofold remit: to see whether there were any values upon which there was agreement across society, and to see how schools could be supported in their task of promoting pupils' spiritual, moral, social and cultural development. A deliberate attempt was made to draw into the Forum representatives of a wide range of opinion (cf. Tate and Talbot in *Teaching Right and Wrong*).

Given the task of finding common agreement, there were probably good pragmatic reasons for using the language of values in the first part of the remit. To ask people to converge on a shared morality — *without further explanation* — would be to set a task which might be puzzling to some people, and perhaps even abhorrent to others. To ask them to see if there are values which they share at least holds open the possibility that they will find something that fits the bill, if only on the contingent grounds that there are limits to the extent to which everyone's values can be different.

I want to argue that, given the remit, and the background to that remit, the task set to the Forum always was, *in effect*, to agree on the elements of a common morality. But that task was partly obscured by the wording of the remit, and was not necessarily clear to the participants. (I write partly from experience, as one of the members of the Forum. Reference to moral and spiritual development was there from the beginning in the materials provided to members. My own feeling in the first meeting, though I did not articulate it until later, was that if there was to be agreement at all, within the terms of the remit, it would be on moral values. But this was not the view of all members. Some, in particular, at least at the beginning, thought that the important task was to find agreement on matters of spirituality. So far as I am aware, the Forum in its discussions never explicitly focused on the idea of morality.)

By arguing here that the task of the Forum was to find the elements of a common morality, I want to take the first steps towards establishing that there can be a publicly shared understanding of morality which could, for instance, underpin the popular equation about moral education and violence. I am not claiming that there is in fact, at present, such a conception shared across the whole society (and I do not think the results of the SCAA exercise establish that there is). The task of education may be to construct a shared understanding of morality, rather than to transmit a preexisting one; but it could not be constructed *de novo*, so it is important to show at least that some materials for such a construction exist.

What lay behind the setting up of the Forum in the first place — as behind much of the public concern with morality to which I have already referred — was a concern about people's behaviour. The underlying concern was not, for instance, 'too many people like the Spice Girls and too few people appreciate Bach: what can we do about people's aesthetic values?'; or 'too many of the people who say they believe in God lack sufficient respect for God; and of the others, too many people think it doesn't matter whether they believe in God or not' — which arguably could indicate a concern about religious values. It was much more 'It's terrible that someone like Philip Lawrence has been murdered by a youth outside his own school; what can we do about this sort of thing?'

The items in the list drawn up by the Forum (reprinted in *Teaching Right and Wrong*, pp. 10–14) are expressed (a) in terms of things to be done (there are possible exceptions, as in 'we should respect' or 'we should care for', but it is plausible that such terms are intended to be cashed out as actions rather than only as attitudes); (b) as things that people *should* do; i.e. it is not a matter of indifference whether people act in these ways or not — these ways of acting are prescribed; and (c) as things which *we* should do, where 'we' means all of us.

These, I suggest, are three common marks of morality; or at least, of what I shall refer to below, following Mackie and others, as 'morality in the narrow sense': that morality (a) concerns conduct rather than (or rather than merely) belief, attitude and the like;[2] (b) is prescriptive, telling us what we are to do (unlike, say, aesthetics which does not — unless it is already merging into morality — carry demands that we should do or refrain from doing anything in particular);[3] and (c) is seen as applying not just to one or the other of us but to everyone.

These marks of moral values so far leave room for the notion of an individual's moral values, perhaps even idiosyncratic ones: something may be a moral value which I hold if I think that it makes demands on people's action and that it does this for everyone, even if others do not in fact recognise this. But we also have the notion of morality as a system of values existing within society[4] and putting constraints on the actions of different persons within society, particularly as they affect each other: this is a fourth element of the notion of 'morality in the narrow sense' which I shall pursue further in the coming chapters.

Arguably the existence of morality as a social system is prior to our being able to conceive of such a thing as an individual morality. In any case, morality cannot serve a social function if it does not contain at least some considerable degree of agreement on values across a society. So we can take it as yet a further mark of moral values, in their social manifestation, that they are fairly widely shared. And this appears to be true of the values in the Forum's list: not only were they put forward as being values which the Forum members both agreed on and thought to be more widely agreed on, but SCAA also claimed empirical evidence (gleaned through a professional public-opinion survey) of a widespread consensus on them. (There is a further question, to which I shall return in Chapter 10, of how far agreement at verbal level may mask underlying disagreement.)

What was aimed at when the Forum was set up (given the background from which that move had come) was something which could influence how people across society would behave. If we are trying to draw up an itemised statement of what people should do, where the items in the statement are to apply to everyone, and there is to be wide agreement on the items across society, then moral values are what we are going to get, because this (on one plausible understanding of morality) is the sort of thing moral values are. (As regards the actual items in the Forum's list, this conclusion will require some qualification: see Chapter 13.)

DEVELOPMENT: MORAL AND SPIRITUAL CONTRASTED

We have begun, then, to see a way — one way at least, and one I shall take further — in which we can differentiate the sphere of morality within the wider sphere of values. The picture in the recent rhetoric of moral education is, however, far from clear-cut, and I have already suggested that it was by no means clear within the deliberations of the Forum. In particular, both within the Forum and in other related rhetoric, the 'moral' has often been linked with the 'spiritual'. They were explicitly coupled in a discussion paper first issued by the National Curriculum Council (1993), then again by Nick Tate, then Chief Executive of SCAA, at the 1996 conference. One way of helping to clarify the scope of the moral will be by trying to drive a wedge between these notions which so many people want to connect.[5]

In Nick Tate's speech and many of the position papers prepared for the January 1996 conference, out of which the Forum was born, there seems to be something like the following connection. There is a concern with people's conduct, as pointed out above. But it is acknowledged that the recognition of a common set of values, even where this takes the form of a moral code, does not by itself guarantee anything about how people will behave. This means that some attention has to be paid to people's motivation. And the idea of the spiritual seems to be introduced in order to provide a necessary motivational context. People's motivation to take moral values seriously is seen as an aspect of their spiritual condition.

One can see how this can make good sense within many religious traditions. But too close a coupling, in educational rhetoric, of the moral and the spiritual, risks making it more difficult to find or construct a shared understanding of morality across a society in which a variety of religious traditions coexists with secular outlooks. This is *not* because the idea of the spiritual has to be tied to religion. It is because, even if we recognise a secular sense of spirituality, we also have to recognise that spirituality can be an individual matter in ways in which morality is not, since in certain ways morality has to be shared where spirituality does not.

I can best illustrate this point, I think, by focusing on the notions of moral and spiritual *development*. How is the distinction to be drawn between these notions? In an individual case it may indeed be difficult. It will not do to say simply — though I have been tempted by this — that spirituality is an individual matter while morality is a social matter. For there is a sense in which both must be social. The beliefs and attitudes involved in either must draw on some culturally available stock of concepts and understandings (for both moral and spiritual development must in part be species of conceptual development). But in a modern plural society, with centuries behind it of the most diverse thought about the human condition and about the universe — theistic and atheistic, scientific and artistic — the stock of ideas on which spiritual development can draw is so vast that there is no reason in advance to expect that the spiritual development of different individuals will take similar forms — rather the reverse. By contrast, in the case of moral development the possibilities are limited by the public social reality and function of morality. We are constrained to look for common elements in moral development which we do not have to expect in spiritual development.

Consider a minimal but evaluatively positive notion of development, which only requires that it be a change for the better. To apply this notion, to say that someone has *developed*, requires *some* standpoint from which to judge whether a change is a change for the better. And if notions such as moral and spiritual development are to be useful *in public discourse*, there will have to be a standpoint which is at least fairly widely shared. While it is true for both moral and spiritual development that any standpoint which could be adopted will be drawing on a culturally available set of materials, it is also true that there is more likely to be agreement on a standpoint from which the notion of moral development can be applied than on any from which the notion of spiritual development can be applied.

Suppose we say, rather formally, that the moral development of an individual implies an improvement in the individual's moral condition (whatever that may be) and similarly that the spiritual development of an individual implies an improvement in the individual's spiritual condition (whatever that may be). Although in each case I have inserted 'whatever that may be' in order to indicate that there is room for differences of interpretation, the notion of an individual's moral condition lends itself to an interpretation in terms of adherence or otherwise to recognised values. That is (to put it in a schematic way which will admittedly appear crude) if values *a*, *b* and *c* are among the values which are central to the morality of a given society, one might say that a member of that society has progressed in his or her moral development just in so far as he or she has come to share the values *a*, *b* and *c*. Development here is being judged from the standpoint of values widely shared, which have (to quote the preamble to the SCAA Forum's Statement of Values) 'the authority of consensus'.

There is a sense in which this way of looking at moral development makes the judgement of development culture-relative. I think that if there is to be a common public policy for moral education and moral development, reference to at least some shared values is unavoidable. (It is true that in such terms one could speak of moral development from a Nazi perspective; but the objection to that is the objection to Nazi values, not an objection to a way of conceiving of moral development.) In fact most, if not all, accounts of moral development do turn out to have some substantive content built into the standpoint from which development is judged. Aristotle's certainly did; Kohlberg's scheme judges moral development to have progressed further to the extent that people adopt a morality of universal rights (which is the liberal morality of a certain kind of society); theorists of caring judge moral development to have progressed further to the extent that people have come to exercise care and responsibility.

On any such account of moral development, then, there can be a common policy for moral development just in so far as there are certain shared moral values, from the standpoint of which the degree of development can be assessed (these shared values may include the ideas that it is a good thing for people to be able to think for themselves and that it is a bad thing for people to be indoctrinated). Admittedly such a conception of moral development could be applied in rather crude behavioural terms, and I would not want to endorse it in that form. But it is in any case significant that a standpoint which judges moral development in terms of adherence to shared values is available and is usable in public discourse. Not only that, but such a standpoint does reflect some of the public concerns which lie behind calls for more effective moral education in schools.

In contrast there is no such publicly available and agreed standpoint for speaking of spiritual development. This is actually for two interlocking reasons: first, there is no shared sense of what constitutes a spiritually better condition; second, the notion of spiritual condition does not lend itself to interpretation in terms of observable behaviour. The first of these points depends on the pluralism of our society; there have been societies in which it would have been just as widely agreed that becoming an atheist is not an improvement in spiritual condition as that becoming a murderer is not an improvement in moral condition. But in modern plural societies there is so much room for disagreement in interpretations of an improvement in spiritual condition (as well as for disagreement over whether there is *anything* that counts as a spiritual condition) that the prospect of a publicly agreed standpoint for judging spiritual development is remote.

What I am suggesting, then, and indeed recommending, is that we can, and should, distinguish moral values — as values which are seen as prescriptive for everyone within a society — from other values which may be involved in certain patterns of spiritual — and indeed social or cultural — development but which will not be prescriptive for everyone. It would follow from this recommendation that we would be able to identify a certain common pattern of moral development, in terms of content, while we would not be able to identify a common pattern — common in the sense that everyone ought to be encouraged to follow it — for spiritual, cultural or social development. And we could then use the question, 'Do we think that everyone will be more developed to the extent that they come to hold this or that value?', as one way of distinguishing whether it is moral development or some other kind of development that we are talking about.

In this chapter I have tried to differentiate morality from the wider field of values, and from the field of spirituality in particular, by referring to a set of values which are shared, which are seen as prescriptive for conduct, and which are seen as applying to everyone. What this does not yet bring out is what the point of the whole phenomenon is. Why do we, or should we, care about morality, if this is the sort of thing we understand by that term? The question may or may not seem to have an obvious answer (if years of doing philosophy teaches one anything, it is that obviousness is in the eye of the beholder). At any rate, I shall try to give an answer in the next chapter.

NOTES

1. Marianne Talbot and Nick Tate, referring to these events in their contribution to *Teaching Right and Wrong*, say that the conference 'coincided' with Lawrence's murder (p. 2); it was actually about a month later. Nigel Blake is mistaken, though, or at least misleading, in saying in the same volume (p. 120) that 'the conference . . . was a conscious and explicit response to' the murder. Much that was said at the conference may have been an explicit response to that, but the conference had certainly been planned some time before.
2. This is, of course, controversial. I shall not leave it unquestioned in my discussion of what I shall call morality in the narrow sense, or morality(n); the chapter on motivation will be especially relevant.
3. It may appear that aesthetic reasons can underpin prescriptions for action. E.g. 'If doing a given dance-step in a given way is aesthetically better than doing it in some different way, isn't it reasonable to conclude that the first way is the way the step *should* be done . . .?' (Slote, 1996, p. 108, italics in original). The obvious answer to this is the Kantian one, that any imperative deriving from this aesthetic judgement is hypothetical; there is nothing to say anyone has to be doing this dance-step in the first place. The issue would bear more discussion, but is not particularly germane to my argument.
4. See for example (among many other sources) Cooper (1981) and Strawson (1974).
5. See also Nigel Blake's paper in *Teaching Right and Wrong*.

Chapter 4 Morality in the Narrow Sense

GEORGE (about McFee): Well, in simple terms he believes that on the whole people should tell the truth all right, and keep their promises, and so on — but on the sole grounds that if everybody went around telling lies and breaking their word as a matter of course, normal life would be impossible. (*Jumpers*, p. 48)

MORALITY AND LAW

I have suggested that in looking for shared values which were seen as having force for people's conduct, the SCAA Forum was in effect looking for a shared morality. This does not yet show that a shared understanding was achieved on what kind of thing morality is — no such agreement was explicitly aimed at — but it does point in the direction in which such an agreement might be found. The key is to be found, I think, in the idea that morality has a social function, and in a certain understanding of what that function is.

In pursuing that line of thought, it will be best to forestall certain objections at the beginning. I do not intend what I say about the function of morality to capture everything which the notion of morality means to many of the people to whom that notion is important. I shall have more to say about what the notion of morality which I am developing leaves out. For the moment, it is best to refer to the notion I am discussing in a terminology first used, to my knowledge, by John Mackie: 'morality in the narrow sense', which I shall henceforth usually abbreviate to morality (n).

Briefly, the suggestion is that morality has a similar function to that of law. Better put, there seems to be a function which morality and law offer different, though related, means of fulfilling. The plausibility of this can be shown by telling a story of the common origins of law and morality(n). Whether this story is anthropologically accurate is beyond my competence to judge; but if it sounds plausible, that fact by itself demonstrates the plausibility of an analysis of morality(n) which likens it to law.

We can, like Hart (1961, p. 89) in *The Concept of Law*, think of a community (perhaps of hunter–gatherers) in which there are common expectations about conduct but no systematic way, either in form or content, in which one class of expectations is differentiated from another.[1] Where there is divergence from a certain expectation there may be disapproval in some form — it might be in facial expression or body language — and this will be among the ways in which ways of doing things are learned and hence maintained from one generation to another.

Simply in talking of expectations, of a shared sense of what is done and what is not done, we are not yet talking of morality *as opposed* to law — or indeed to etiquette, say, or religious observance. But we are already referring to the roots of both morality and law as the social practices or institutions which, later, they would become; and since we are already talking of ways of doing things which are not instinctive, but have to be learned, we are talking of the roots of education too.

Though there is no single function which the expectations about conduct in such a community would have performed, some of them will in fact have tended to help the affairs of the community to run smoothly, by protecting its members against their vulnerability both to external dangers and to other members of the same society (Hart, 1961, Chapter 9). For example, once weapons are in use, there are likely to be norms about maintaining them in effective condition; and also since weapons which could be used in hunting will be potentially lethal to members of the group, there are likely to be norms about safe and non-malicious use too. In the conduct of the hunt, co-operation and co-ordination of the actions of members of the group will be vital (the consequences of lack of co-operation and co-ordination will not just be inconvenience, but at times could be starvation). So expectations about co-operation and co-ordination will develop and will need to be taken very seriously. Then again, there are likely to be norms about how an animal killed is to be used by the group, whether divided up or not, and so on. So a variety of expectations will tend either to protect members of the community or to protect the way of life of the community itself against things which can go wrong.[2]

We can make sense of the existence of such expectations independently of the distinction between law and morality. Perhaps in time it will happen that if someone takes a larger than usual share of the kill, there are mutterings of disapproval but nothing more; whereas if one member of the group turns their weapon on another, the first member is brought before a gathering which prescribes a penalty. Then with hindsight, we might say that fairness in division is a moral expectation but the prohibition on violence within the group is (also) legal. There still need not be any significant difference in the way that the expectations are initially learned by children; they will learn that certain things are done and certain things not done before they have any clear or differentiated sense of what happens, in the adult world, when one expectation or another is violated.[3]

Much in the picture sketched so far can be carried over, I suggest, to education in expected ways of behaving even in a modern complex society. Children today learn all kinds of ways in which things are done, and also learn that certain things are not to be done; and they are likely to acquire such vocabulary as 'ought not to' and 'wrong' — as part of the repertoire they recognise, even if they do not use it themselves — well before they acquire the terms 'morality' and 'law', or are able to differentiate between what is morally wrong and what is legally wrong.[4] Perhaps, too, for many adults the idea that children should be taught what is right and what is wrong — where this in turn is conceived in terms of adherence to norms — is used in a blanket way with little weight given to the morality/law distinction. When an event like the murder of Philip Lawrence leads to calls that schools must do more to stamp in and reinforce a sense of right and wrong, this popular reaction may see little need to distinguish between moral and legal right and wrong. Perhaps this is correct, in the sense that society's need for certain sorts of conduct to be ruled out is more basic than the division between morality and law. (It is significant in this respect that when MacIntyre (1981, p. 141) argues that any community needs, in addition to virtues, a recognition of certain offences as beyond the pale, he uses for the latter kind of 'evaluative practice' the phrase 'a morality of laws'.)

What we have so far, then, is the notion that any society needs a basic framework of expectations (and that these, of course, need to be sustained from generation to generation). The need for this framework is in a sense prior to the distinction between morality and law. (One of the clearest statements of this idea is in Hobbes, where 'the state of nature' is the name for the human condition prior to both morality and law. In Hobbes, moral rules by themselves would be of no avail if they were not backed up by political sovereignty and so, in effect, treated precisely *as* laws.) The notion of the basic framework is also in Hart, as mentioned above; and within philosophy of education it is recognised, as we have seen, by John White among others.

One matter on which theorists differ is just how the distinction between morality and law is to be made; granted it may seem obvious to us now, in a modern Western society, what is law and what is not, but even if it is obvious there is still a task for philosophy in explicating the rationale of the distinction; and once theorists try to give that explication, it can turn out, as in the writings of Ronald Dworkin, that the distinction is not so clear after all.

Here I shall not enter into discussion of what makes certain norms law, rather than (merely, as some might say) moral expectations. I shall assume that the distinction can be made in a sufficiently clear way for it to make sense (in modern societies, but not in the kind of community in the story above) to talk about an analogy between morality and law. If we claim such an analogy we are saying that law and morality are not (now) the same thing, but that there are important similarities between them. For instance, morality has often been seen, like law, as containing many prohibitions on certain kinds of act; and violations of the prohibitions have sometimes been seen in both cases as liable to call forth some sort of sanction (even though, in the case of morality, it may be only a sanction of public disapproval).

To refer to such similarities is not, in logic, to endorse any particular story of the origins of morality and of law, though some story of common origins may in fact explain the similarities. Even if a story of common roots is true, many distinctions will have developed over time, so that it is now normal in common practice and usage to distinguish law and morality. Whatever the analogies, then, there are certainly also going to be disanalogies. For instance, if both law and morality involve sanctions of a kind, the sanctions of morality may be unenforceable, and may indeed be internal (as in Mill's *Utilitarianism*, Chapter 3). There are certainly going to be points at which an analogy between law and morality cannot be sustained; this means that pointing out particular points of difference will not in itself be an argument against the analogy.

There is also an important ambiguity to be considered at this point. While it is clear that there has been much argument in recent moral philosophy against construing morality on a model of law, from writers as varied as Anscombe (1997, first published 1958) and Bauman (1993), and in philosophy of education John White (1990, pp. 41 ff.), many of the objections have been against the idea, not of morality as analogous to the positive law of states, but of morality as a system of law which is universal, and independent of and authoritative over the positive law of states. Construing morality in this latter way retains some points of analogy between morality and law but also sets up clear differences. It makes it evident, for instance, that morality applies much more widely than just to the citizens of a state; and it can set law and morality against each other, in that morality can be appealed to in criticism of the law.

In effect, then, there are two versions of the analogy between morality and law. Many of the criticisms of such an analogy in the literature — such as general criticisms of the role of rules in morality — will apply to both versions, but some will apply to one only. Criticisms of natural law and Kantian conceptions of morality will not necessarily have force against morality construed as much closer to positive law. Anscombe, for instance, puts weight on the point that (if we no longer have God as lawgiver in the picture) there can be nothing in the role of legislator for a universal moral law. If the Kantian conception of the autonomous self as lawgiver is also rejected (see K. Baier, 1973, pp. 101–14, as well as Anscombe), then there can be no moral law.

Here, however, I shall consciously be pursuing an analogy between morality and the positive law of states (one also remarked by Griffin, 1996). On this, objections of Anscombe's kind largely miss the mark. Law in the positive sense (which is surely, at least now, the standard sense, whether or not it was the original sense of the word) clearly does not lack a legislator (which need not, of course, be a single person), and, since it does exist, is clearly not impossible. What if anything stands in the role of legislator in the case of morality(n) will be taken up in Chapter 12.

MORALITY AND THE WIDER ETHICAL SPHERE

For all that has been said so far, once we look further away from matters of function and form, and bring into our sights matters of individual feelings, attitudes, perceptions, ideals (the list could go on), it becomes clear (and has been emphasised in much recent moral philosophy) that there are many aspects of morality that cannot be captured in the analogy with law. That is why we need something like the notion of morality *in the narrow sense*, which seems to correspond approximately to that area of morality which does share its function (though not necessarily, as we shall see in the next chapter, its *form*) with that of law.

This notion of morality in the narrow sense has come in for a certain amount of criticism from moral philosophers in recent years. However, most of the criticism has been of one of two kinds. (What I say in this paragraph and the next will be far from satisfying to philosophers of education who in recent years have been convinced by writers such as Charles Taylor and Bernard Williams that there is something seriously amiss with narrow notions of morality. I therefore add more at the end of this chapter.) Some criticism has been of particular ways of unpacking the form of morality(n); for instance, seeing it very much in terms of obligations. The question of the form that morality(n) should take is one I have still to address, so this kind of criticism will be addressed as the argument proceeds.

Other criticisms have been directed against the idea that morality(n) is all there is to morality — or to ethics, which is often now taken as the broader term. But this is not a criticism that applies to the position I am arguing here. I not only acknowledge, but I would myself stress, that the sphere of the moral or the ethical can and does extend well beyond morality(n). It can encompass individuals' deepest concerns about how they should live their lives and about what sort of persons they are to be: thus it can involve various sorts of evaluation: evaluations of actions, of attitudes, of personal qualities, of individual lifestyles, even of whole cultures. Roughly speaking, the further the sphere of morality or ethics is extended, and the more kinds of evaluation it takes in, the more room there is for differences and disagreements within the sphere. My aim here is to delineate a minimal conception which could, despite wider variations, be shared.

I want to try, then, to construe morality(n) in a positive light, and to see whether, in making sense of the notion, we are committed to interpretations which will not stand up to criticism. I also want to see morality(n) here as the morality which we can expect to be shared across a society of diversity (without wishing that formulation to be taken as a definition). In this respect morality(n) may be a core; it may be that on which it can reasonably be expected that there will be a consensus. This consensus may not go very deep; in Rawls's (1993) terms, it may be a matter of overlapping consensus in which very different comprehensive world-views are able to converge, from their different directions, on similar norms or values. The SCAA Forum (in the Preamble to its Statement of Values) was making a similar point in saying that members of society may agree on certain values but not on where they come from.

The idea of morality(n) also fits well with the idea, common in recent Anglo-American liberal theory, as well as in Habermas, that there is both more need for and more scope for agreement on the right than the good, and that in a certain sense an ethic of the right must have priority in a liberal society. Thus Habermas (1990, p. 178) distinguishes *moral* questions from what he calls *evaluative* or *ethical* questions 'which fall into the general category of issues of the *good life*'.

I have no quarrel with the widespread view that education should be concerned with enabling people to live, if possible, a good life; that a good life for one will not, in details, be the same as a good life for another; hence that, in modern plural societies especially, much of the purpose of education will be to enable individuals to find for themselves and to pursue a good life; and that (to put it rather crudely) individuals in doing this will have to integrate whatever allegiance they may have to shared moral values with other values which are important to them. But what I am concerned about here is whether we can still, recognising all this, keep open the possibility of a shared morality which actually helps to make the pursuit of a good life possible.

Notice that this position not only recognises that the field of values is wider than that of morality. It also in a sense makes certain values more fundamental than morality; these are the values which morality itself subserves. Philosophers such as Hobbes, and more recently

Mackie and Geoffrey Warnock, did see certain things clearly, even if their focus was a narrow one (some might say blinkered). They saw that human beings do value, and would be likely in almost all circumstances to value, freedom from pain and injury, from assault and danger of death, from hunger and isolation. They may have been wrong in supposing (if they did suppose) that in all conceivable circumstances morality(n) would be necessary if these values were to be realised; maybe, as more optimistic views of the human condition would have it, fellow-feeling and altruism could eliminate the need for morality(n) as we know it. But that does not alter the point that morality(n) can be seen as one way at least in which human communities may to a degree obtain something of what they value. To that extent the popular perception of morality as a way of protecting people from violence is fully in line with a long-standing philosophical conception of morality.[5]

CRITICISMS OF A NARROW NOTION OF MORALITY

(Readers not familiar with or particularly interested in the literature may want to skip this section.)

There have been influential critics in recent years of morality(n) — at least this is what I have often taken them to be criticising. I have in mind especially Bernard Williams and Charles Taylor. A number of writers in philosophy of education, including John White, have been influenced by Williams and Taylor. Williams, as is well known, criticised 'morality, the peculiar institution', in *Ethics and the Limits of Philosophy* (1985), and Taylor (1995) has expressed his broad agreement with Williams, having previously in his own right contributed to the critique of morality(n) in *Sources of the Self* (1989b).

Here I do not need to take up all of the many points raised by Williams and Taylor. I do need to say enough to show that there is still point in being concerned with morality(n) even after their criticisms. To do this, it is important to distinguish criticism of morality(n) itself — that is, of the institution or practice — from criticisms of philosophers' interpretations of morality. (Note that the last word of the previous sentence is *not* 'morality(n)'.) It is explicit in Mackie's (1977) account of morality(n), and is implicit in the label itself, that morality(n) is not the whole of morality, since there is also what Mackie calls 'morality in the broad sense'. So, at least on Mackie's interpretation, any philosopher who offers what is in effect an account of morality(n), as an account of morality *tout court*, is mistaken. Clearly, to take an over-narrow view of something that needs to be understood in all its breadth and richness, is to take a distorted view of the phenomenon; but to take a narrow view of what is in fact broad, is not the same as to take an accurate view of something which is in fact narrow. Once we make this distinction, between a narrow interpretation of morality, and an interpretation of morality-in-the-narrow-sense, we can see that a concern with morality(n) can quite properly survive much of Williams's and Taylor's critiques.

Writers such as Mackie are saying that within the whole field of what he calls morality in the broad sense we can distinguish a particular institution, or practice, or way of thinking, which can be described as morality(n). Writers such as Williams and Taylor are not disputing that. Indeed Williams explicitly distinguishes what he calls 'morality' from the broader area of concern which is roughly what Mackie calls 'morality in the broad sense' and which Williams labels 'the ethical'; and some years later Williams (1995) himself uses the phrase 'morality in the narrow sense' for what he called in 1985 'the peculiar institution'.[6] Williams and Taylor are not disputing the existence of morality(n). A large part of what they are doing is criticising the mistaken philosophical interpretation which sees morality(n) as being the whole of the relevant area of concern. But they are also criticising the way that morality(n) has itself been interpreted by philosophers (and in doing so they are, of course, acknowledging its existence).

Thus Williams, in *Ethics and the Limits of Philosophy* (1985), criticises the interpretation of morality(n) which gives a particular kind of centrality to obligation. Roughly, morality(n) on the interpretation Williams is criticising is a Kantian morality. He acknowledges that utilitarianism can share some of the same features (p. 178). I take this to imply that a less Kantian, much more utilitarian, interpretation of morality(n) is a possibility. At times, while acknowledging the existence of morality(n), Williams seems to be saying that we would be better off without it. In his 1995 collection, he seems to me to be taking a somewhat softer line. I find it significant, for instance, that in his essay in that volume on what would normally be called 'professional ethics', he uses the term 'professional morality'. This may well be because he realised that, having defined ethics as the very broad area of thought about how one should live one's life, he could hardly use the same term of something intended to apply within strict professional limits. In any case, the sense of the term 'morality' in the phrase 'professional morality' does seem to be that of 'morality(n)'.

In *Sources of the Self* (1989b, p. 3) Taylor complains that

> much contemporary moral philosophy...has given such a narrow focus to morality that some of the critical connections I want to draw here are incomprehensible in its terms....This philosophy has accredited a cramped

and truncated view of morality in a narrow sense, as well as of the whole range of issues involved in the attempt to live the best possible life...

Here Taylor appears to be acknowledging that there is such a thing as morality(n), in contradistinction to the broader field (however that is to be labelled), while also saying that philosophical interpretations even of morality(n) are *too* narrow.

Two more examples from recent moral philosophy. Griffin (1996, p. 79) explicitly treats ethics as the broader field which includes both morality and prudence, and it seems fair to interpret morality here as morality(n). This makes the whole situation appear clear-cut (even though Griffin has spoken earlier in the book of the interpenetration of prudence and morality). Perhaps, to Taylor and Williams, Griffin's treatment might seem rather shallow in its clear-cutness; no doubt this is partly a matter of style.[7] Slote (1992) is closer to Williams in treating ethics as a broad field of evaluation, wider than prudential, but not confined to morality in either its utilitarian, Kantian or common-sense forms. But there is no consistency of terminology across writers; nor, probably, is there likely to be.[8]

Taylor, in *Sources of the Self*, acknowledged that 'morality' can be and often is defined purely in terms of respect for and obligation towards others, and went on:

> If we adopt this definition, then we have to allow that there are other questions beyond the moral which are of central concern to us, and which bring strong evaluation into play.

These 'other questions beyond the moral' are the questions which Williams labels ethical, but which Taylor himself in *Sources of the Self* continues to refer to as moral (in other words, he does not himself adopt the possible narrow definition, but continues to use 'moral' in a broad sense). Later, Taylor (1995) appears to endorse Williams's terminology, but as Williams (1995) himself says, 'The suggestion that we might use the words in this way has hardly, as yet, swept all before it, and it no doubt has its own powers to mislead'. The editors of *Teaching Right and Wrong*, expressing a general suspicion of systematic theory in relation to moral education, say 'For similar reasons, and in line with ordinary usage, we have avoided systematic differentiation between "morality" and "ethics" in this book' (p. x). ('Avoided' suggests that, but for this deliberate intent, they might have slipped into this differentiation. But avoiding it is easy; it is maintaining the distinction that is difficult.)

Another complication which interacts with that of terminology is that the distinction between the phenomena and interpretations of the phenomena is not sharp. If there were no moral philosophers, then indeed there would be no technically *philosophical* interpretations of morality, narrow or broad. But interpretations are written into the phenomena. This is much of the burden of Williams's discussion of the peculiar institution in Chapter 10 of *Ethics and the Limits of Philosophy*, and when Taylor (1989b, p. 14) says 'morality can be, of course, and often is, defined purely in terms of respect for others. The category of the moral is thought to encompass just our obligations to other people' he is (as I read him) referring to the thought of many ordinary people in modern cultures, not just the philosophers.

This means that another kind of criticism is open to writers like Williams and Taylor. Besides criticising (a) the philosophers who treat morality(n) as if it were the whole of the relevant area of concern, and (b) the philosophers who misrepresent morality(n), they can also be criticising (c) morality(n) itself for inherently working with mistaken interpretations. This kind of criticism goes back at least to Marx.[9] As Lukes (1985) and many others have noted, Marx was highly critical of morality, if this was understood as the 'official' morality of his day (and earlier). This was what Lukes described as 'the morality of *Recht*', and Lukes explicitly treats this as similar to Mackie's morality(n) (*ibid.*, p. 31). Morality in this sense was to Marx inherently ideological: in other words, it incorporated — independently of philosophers coming onto the scene — understandings which were false but which, as a matter of false consciousness, could not be seen as false: had morality not been experienced as putting objective, universal constraints on people, it would not have been able to serve its actual social function, which was to protect the existing structure of social relations.

Williams, while dissociating himself from a vulgar Marxist interpretation (1985, pp. 195–196), also believes that 'morality, the peculiar institution' rests on an illusion — which is, at least in part, that morality is somehow insulated from luck (see also Williams, 1995, pp. 241–247). It is not clear, however, that morality(n) necessarily has to be subject to the interpretations that Marx or Williams, or any other particular theorist, read into it. In this sense, such writers are giving us a particular, still narrower, reading of morality(n). (Morality n^2, so to speak.)

It seems to me that morality(n) does not have to rest on an illusion. It should be possible for people to be fully conscious of the nature of morality(n), and still take it seriously. But to try to bring this about would be an educational task.

NOTES

1. Hart (*ibid.*) speaks of the norms of conduct, even prior to the differentiation of law and morality, as 'rules of obligation', but this may be already to have read back into the

description of the situation a conception from a later way of thinking. I shall be considering below whether morality(n) has to be articulated in terms of rules.

2. Contrary to the way some might interpret talk of morality(n), such an account does not commit one to a Hobbesian individualism or to anachronistically reading into the consciousness of the members of the community any specifically modern conception of 'the individual'.

3. Notice that once the morality/law distinction is made, it need not be a distinction in content. It is to be expected that moral and legal norms will overlap considerably in what they prescribe or proscribe (deliberate killing of another member of the group is one obvious example; cf. Hart, 1961, Chapter 9, for some others). How far the similarity between law and morality extends will turn to a large extent on matters of form rather than content.

4. It is possible, though I shall not pursue the point, that the psychological emergence of certain distinctions in individual consciousness parallels their historical emergence in human societies; cf. Habermas's (1979) way of applying the developmental theories of Piaget and Kohlberg to the evolution of society.

5. There is certainly a question as to why it should be particularly *human* interests which morality protects or promotes; I shall come back to this in Chapter 14.

6. There is, however, at least one important difference between Mackie's 'morality in the broad sense' and Williams's 'ethics' or 'the ethical'; that is, that Mackie considers morality, even in the broad sense, to be 'a body of principles'.

7. In some respects Griffin is still an Oxford philosopher of the old school, a point recognised in the review of his *Value Judgement* by A. W. Price (*Philosophical Books* 39.1, 1998), quoted on the back cover of the paperback.

8. Bauman (1993, p. 21), for instance, uses the terms differently.

9. I used Marx in my exposition of criticisms of morality in *Teaching about Values*, p. 66.

Chapter 5 The Language(s) of Virtues

BONES (to George): But you're wasted on her, mate. What on earth made *her* marry *you*, I'll never know, when there are so many better men — decent, strong, protective, understanding, sensitive — . (*Jumpers*, p. 59)

CAN MORALITY(n) USE A LANGUAGE OF VIRTUES?

If there is to be a convergence in public understanding on a minimal conception of morality, morality(n), there has to be a way of talking about the content of that morality which can be both readily understood and widely adopted.

If one puts weight on the analogy between morality(n) and law, one would expect morality(n) to be unpacked in a language of norms, that is, of prescriptions setting out what people are to do or not to do. This is, indeed, the language adopted by the SCAA Forum in its list of statements beginning 'we should . . .' (though I hardly expect that fact in itself to be an argument for such a language). This kind of language is, however, very much under challenge now, as more and more theorists of morality and moral education talk instead about virtues. In this chapter and the next two I shall give some reasons for thinking that, once we recognise that we need a language to perform the kind of function I have picked out, we should not expect a language of virtues to do the job; or at least, we should not think that we can dispense with the language of norms (where norms include both rules and principles). In subsequent chapters I shall give a more direct defence of the language of rules and principles.

Readers who are not acquainted with recent moral philosophy and philosophical writing on moral education may wonder what a language of virtues is — since the actual word 'virtues' is not very common in late-twentieth century evaluative discourse. There is actually no consensus as to just what a virtue is, even among theorists who are currently discussing the issue — and that is one reason, as we shall see, for a certain scepticism about whether the language of virtues can do the job that public moral discourse requires. For the moment, let me say simply, and as minimally as I can, that a virtue is a morally desirable personal quality. Such qualities as courage, honesty and benevolence are standard examples (apart from the standard examples, there is not necessarily much agreement as to which qualities are virtues).

Suppose, then, that we are looking for some sort of public way of talking — which will also provide a vocabulary in which people do much of their own thinking — which will serve the functions of morality(n). Could talk about virtues serve this function? Law, of course, does not for the most part say 'be kind' or 'be honest'; for the most part it lays down rather concrete prescriptions as to what is to be done or (more typically) not done. But if morality(n) shares its function with law, that does not by itself mean that it must share its form. In *The Object of Morality*, G. Warnock (1971), whose account of morality is rightly construed by Mackie as an account of morality(n),[1] criticises the idea that rules are basic to morality and argues instead for virtues as basic.[2]

This is enough to show that the distinction between morality(n) and the wider sphere (however it is designated) is not the same as the distinction between a morality of rules and a morality of virtues. Though it would be true to say that most proponents in recent years (roughly, after MacIntyre's *After Virtue*) of what has come to be known as 'virtue ethics' are aiming at a characterisation of the wider sphere rather than of morality(n), a morality or ethics of virtues can itself come in narrow or wide versions.

Mackie (1977, p. 106) defines morality(n) as follows: 'In the narrow sense, a morality is a system of a particular sort of constraints on conduct — ones whose central task is to protect the interests of persons other than the agent and which present themselves to an agent as checks on his natural inclinations or spontaneous tendencies to act.' It is perfectly possible to interpret virtues as functioning as such checks. This is what Warnock does, and it was also a major element, for instance, of a seminal paper on virtues by Philippa Foot: 'they are corrective, each one standing at a point at which there is some temptation to be resisted or deficiency of motivation to be made good' (Foot, 1978, p. 8). On such a basis, it is possible for an account of virtues to be offered as an account of morality(n); the qualities picked out as virtues will be ones which are seen as minimally necessary as a basis for life in society.

Why might it be thought that a language of virtues is suitable, not only for the broader area of concern, but also for serving the function of morality(n)? Someone might think this on the basis of an argument that dispositions are basic to morality, which is the position taken by Warnock. A similar general point, though not specifically in relation to morality(n), is argued by Williams (1987), in a passage which Patricia White (1996) quotes at the beginning of her exploration of civic virtues. However, it does not follow from a recognition that dispositions are fundamental that a language of dispositions is the best language in which to talk about morality(n), especially where we have public understanding in mind. This would be a little like arguing that because chemical changes in cells are fundamental in human health and fitness, the language of biochemistry is the best language for public-health policy. But this is certainly not an exact analogy. Instead of analogy, we need to think directly about the job that a public language of evaluation has to do, and what kind of language is suited to this job.

A first point is that when we think about a language of virtues as a public language, our focus is rather different from the focus of the writers who have been arguing recently for conceiving of moral education as the development of virtue. An upbringing which develops virtues in individuals does not in itself constitute an education for a shared public conception of morality. One of the features of virtue ethics, as a strand within the literature of moral philosophy, is that it puts rather more weight than do rule-and-principle based theories on tacit elements of morality.[3] For some purposes, for instance in thinking about the moral upbringing of one child by its parents, this emphasis on the tacit is important. Early moral upbringing may be to a considerable extent a matter of the child learning by example with little having to be verbalised at a general and abstract level — 'abstract' in the sense of being abstracted from the particular circumstances. And so it is possible, at least to a degree, for a child to grow up with the virtues, say, of consideration and sensitivity to others, without actually having the terms 'consideration' and 'sensitivity' in his or her vocabulary.

But for a mass education system hoping to promote a shared morality, verbalisation is inevitable, as regards both means and ends. As regards means, even if the attempt to develop certain virtues in pupils were to be carried out in ways that did not involve actually talking to the pupils about the virtues, the teachers would need to have a way of articulating amongst themselves what they were doing, and any educationalists or public bodies concerned with education would need a language in which to talk to teachers about their task.

Then as regards ends, a shared morality requires that citizens have a common language in which they can talk about matters of morality: about what kind of moral education they are going to give their children, about the kind of behaviour they expect from each other, and about public moral problems. Since possessing a virtue does not necessarily mean that one can oneself articulate it, then even if we could suppose that across a modern diverse society all citizens developed certain virtues in common, this would not by itself mean that they had a shared language of moral evaluation. To some degree this point is recognised, for instance, by Patricia White (1996, p. 6) when she argues that as well as fostering dispositions (which might by itself seem manipulative) education needs to promote understanding of the dispositions. But she does not in my view go far enough in asking whether this understanding, even when shared, provides a suitable language for public discussion of morality and moral issues.

There are several reasons for a degree of caution about this. Most pragmatically, consideration of the language to be used in education has to start, not with a clean slate, but from where we are now. And where we are now is that while words for virtues and their negative counterparts — what some philosophers have called 'thick' terms of moral evaluation, such as 'generous', 'decent', 'caring', 'self-centred', 'dishonest' and the like — are very common in everyday discourse, reflection on such qualities, and their labelling by a general term such as 'virtues' — let alone a shared conception of what kind of quality a virtue is — are not everyday parts of ordinary discourse.

This may sometimes be forgotten now by moral philosophers and philosophers of education, since in recent years the word 'virtue' has come into common use in these circles. This does not mean that it would be easy to get the general public to make explicit use of the notion of virtues. The notion of a virtue to the layperson can carry a connotation of an ideal, even of saintliness, that is of a quality which could hardly serve as an everyday standard of evaluation or a public expectation.[4]

If the general public were aware of some of the remarks of philosophers on virtues this connotation could only be strengthened. Thus Hursthouse (1997, p. 235) says (referring to a woman because she is discussing abortion, but making it clear that she intends the gist of her remarks to apply to males also):

> The virtuous woman (which here of course does not mean simply 'chaste woman' but 'woman with the virtues') has such character traits as strength, independence, resoluteness, decisiveness, self-confidence, responsibility, serious-mindedness, and self-determination . . .

If the language of virtues is to be understood as putting forward such an ideal, (a 'paragon of virtue', in a phrase which significantly seems still to be in the everyday language) it may well be widely seen as barely relevant to ordinary mortals. No doubt, however, this is partly a matter of style; Patricia White (1996) uses the language of virtues without giving the impression that being virtuous would be beyond the ordinary democratic citizen. And if there are good arguments for trying to promote a language of virtues as a language of common currency and moral reflection and debate, then education will have to take on this task, even if it does mean, over a generation or so, changing the way people talk.

A THIN LANGUAGE OF VIRTUES

There are problems, though, about which language of virtues we are to choose — for there is more than one. While philosophers often refer to the words for virtues as 'thick' terms of evaluation, there are many possible, overlapping, languages of virtues, consisting of different sets of virtue terms; and there is also at least one possible language of virtues, with a certain plausibility, which does not consist of 'thick' terms at all, but of rather thin ones, and only a few of them. I shall consider this 'thin' language of virtues first, before looking at thicker ones.

The 'thin' language of virtues which I have in mind is that used by G. Warnock (1971). In his own account of morality he introduces what I have called elsewhere (*Teaching about Values*, p. 42) 'an all-purpose set of virtues': non-maleficence, beneficence, fairness and non-deception. He may well be right that these are the basic dispositions people need to have if human affairs are to go better than they would in the absence of morality. But he does not attempt, as many other writers on virtues have, to cash out these dispositions in terms of underlying qualities of character. To refer to these virtues seems to be little different, in its practical effect, from referring to the norms 'don't cause harm', 'do good', 'be fair' and 'don't deceive' — and so the language remains thin. These four virtues of Warnock's in themselves seem to go little way in enabling people to guide their conduct and organise their affairs in society.

Recall that the function of morality(n) is partly one of enabling co-operation and co-ordination.[5] Warnock's basic virtues might be sufficient to overcome some self-interested motivations, and even to motivate co-operation, but will not by themselves give a sufficiently substantial form to co-ordination. To do that, norms appear to be needed. Fairness is presumably close to Hume's artificial virtue of justice, but justice as a virtue needs standards of justice; that is, the just person, who is sensitive to injustice and strives to be just, still needs some standards by which to judge what is just. Non-deception is a disposition which Warnock stretches to account for the obligation to keep one's promises, but an account of that in terms of the norms of the practice and the underlying function of the practice seems more natural. As for non-maleficence and benefi-cence, I shall say a little more about them in the next chapter.

In short, though Warnock speaks of virtues, he is not really propounding (what would now be counted as) a 'virtue ethics' at all.[6] Many writers have been willing to speak of virtues and to recognise their importance; but for some, the notion of a virtue has been secondary to, and parasitic on, certain norms. That is to say, virtues have sometimes been defined just as the dispositions to adhere to certain norms (Warnock himself comes close to this: *ibid.*, p. 86). Honesty will be the disposition to adhere to norms of truth-telling, benevolence the disposition to adhere to norms of helping others, and so on. In this way of talking the reference to virtues becomes just a rhetorical variation on talking directly in terms of norms; it says nothing distinctive about character or motivation.

THREE KINDS OF THICKNESS

What of the thicker languages of virtues? These can actually differ from a thin language like Warnock's in more than one way; there are at least three relevant dimensions of 'thickness'. First, the meaning of each virtue-term in the language will be 'thick': to ascribe benevolence to someone, for instance, will not be just to say that the person has a tendency to help others. It will be to say something about the person's character. Different theorists will unpack just what it is saying in somewhat different ways, but something like the following would be fairly widely agreed. The benevolent person will differ from the non-benevolent first in what he or she notices: she will notice when other people are in need of comfort or help, where another person might not notice at all. Then, the benevolent person will feel differently from the non-benevolent; she will be pained at the other's suffering and pleased at the other's well-being, where a non-benevolent person might be indifferent either way (while a sadistic person might be pleased at the other's suffering). Third, the benevolent person will be moved to act where the non-benevolent person would not be; the benevolent person's feelings will not be inert. If she felt upset by the other's suffering and wished she could help, but when situations like this happened again and again never actually did anything to help, then she would not be benevolent.

This begins to show the way in which terms like 'benevolence', and other virtue terms, are 'thick'. There is much more to be said about what the virtues involve, but to some extent it has to be said for each virtue one by one. In the next two chapters, I shall say something about one or two qualities which may be particularly relevant to violence and non-violence.

A second dimension in which a language of virtues may differ from Warnock's is in simply containing a larger vocabulary of virtue terms. Suppose virtues are listed in a glossary: then Warnock's glossary of moral virtues would be the thinnest of leaflets, but the Aristotelian or the Christian glossaries would be thick pamphlets (with important differences between them); and a glossary of all the words in English which could be the names of virtues would be a substantial volume.

The fact that there could be these different glossaries — in effect different, though overlapping, languages of virtues — creates problems for the use of a language of virtues as a public language of discourse. Which glossary is to be used, in a plural society? The thinnest available, which could provide a *lingua franca* of virtues? But Warnock's is surely so thin that it brings us little benefit from using a language of virtues at all; it seems to enable us to say little or nothing that could not be said in a language of norms. Notice, for instance, that Warnock's set of moral virtues does not even contain courage, one of the qualities most often in the past, across many traditions, considered to be a virtue. Actually, Warnock deliberately excludes courage from his list of *moral* virtues, while recognising that it is a virtue of a kind (1971, p. 78). For Alasdair MacIntyre (1981, p. 179), in contrast, courage is one of three virtues (the others being truthfulness and justice) which will be essential for the pursuit of any human practice. If we recognise that glossaries of virtues might be subdivided, into sections headed 'moral' and 'other', or 'central' and 'minor', or whatever, then there will be still more variation between one glossary and another; and even where two glossaries coincide in the terms they include, they may differ in their definitions because they draw on understandings derived from different traditions.

If there is to be public agreement on some set of virtues within a plural society, that agreement must not be on a glossary which is that of a specific culture or tradition; at the same time the agreement must extend far enough to facilitate at least some workable level of agreement on the application of particular terms. One way of trying to find agreement on a common glossary would be to work from some single underlying rationale which would tell us which qualities are to be counted as virtues. But this is another matter on which we find no agreement among theorists. To some, there has to be something intuitively admirable about a virtue, in a way that is perhaps more a matter of aesthetic than of moral evaluation (e.g. Slote, 1992). To others, a virtue can be any personal quality which contributes to general human well-being (essentially an utilitarian identification of virtues, e.g. Driver, 1996). To others again, a quality is not to be counted as a virtue unless it tends towards the good of *its possessor* (Philippa Foot held this view at one time). Many now would say that to be counted as a virtue a quality must contribute to human *flourishing* or *the good life*, but will interpret that notion in some non-utilitarian way.[7]

Here we come to yet a third way in which languages of virtues can be thicker than Warnock's minimal one. A minimal language of virtues will pick out qualities which can be expected to contribute to human good, where that good is interpreted in a way which we could expect everyone across a plural society to agree on. This will be an agreement on the level of Rawls's (1972) 'thin theory of the good'.

But actual languages of virtues have seen the qualities they pick out as contributing to human flourishing, where this is interpreted in some particular, 'thick', way. Thus the Christian and Aristotelian glossaries of virtues were different largely because their conceptions of human flourishing were different. A language of virtues rooted in a particular tradition with its thick notion of flourishing is a much richer language; but by the same token it is a language for talking about morality, or ethics, in the broader sense, not about morality(n).

VIRTUES AND PUBLIC AGREEMENT

One last point, for this chapter, concerns what would follow from public agreement on a list of virtues, even if that were achieved. There are two kinds of agreement that people can have on norms for conduct: they can agree that certain norms are the ones to be followed; and they can also personally agree to — that is, commit themselves to — follow the norms. Agreement of the first kind gives a common reference point by which actions and policies can be evaluated — a matter I shall return to in Chapter 10. Does agreement on a list of virtues do the same?

It has been a common complaint against virtue ethics that it does not give guidance on conduct where there is doubt about what should be done. According to Louden (1997, p. 206):

> Owing to the very nature of the moral virtues, there is . . . a very limited amount of advice on moral quandaries that one can reasonably expect from the virtue-oriented approach. We ought, of course, to do what the virtuous person would do, but it is not always easy to fathom what the hypothetical moral exemplar would do were he in our shoes.

So far as individual behaviour is concerned, this may be too harsh. Hursthouse in several articles (1995, 1996, 1997) has shown that 'doing what the virtuous person would do' does go further than one might think in giving one guidance. But she does not go far in considering whether it can guide citizens in public quandaries. Recall that MacIntyre (1981) begins *After Virtue* by calling attention to interminable disagreement over issues such as abortion and nuclear deterrence. His arguments in that book do nothing to show (and he would not claim that they do) that talking in terms of virtues, in itself, would enable the citizens of a modern, plural, liberal democracy to resolve such issues. It is the lack of a shared tradition, not the fact of using a language of norms rather than a language of virtues, that keeps the disagreements irresolvable.[8]

Then there is the second kind of agreement: agreeing to (be bound by) certain norms in the sense of agreeing to (try to) follow them. If I agree with you, and you with me, that we will both follow certain rules, we are doing more than agreeing that it would be a good thing if we both acted in such-and-such a way. We are committing ourselves to act in this way, and we are doing this mutually, so that each of us knows that the other expects us to act in this way. We have each made a commitment to the other, and will not want to be seen as going back on it. This gives each of us an additional motivation for so acting, over and above our thinking that it would be a good thing if we both did so. The equivalent understanding between citizens, who agree to follow certain norms, will be important when we consider in Chapter 12 what kind of authority morality(n) can have.

Is there an equivalent in the language of virtues? What could correspond to each of us agreeing to act in a certain way? That each of us agrees to be virtuous? That would leave a great deal open to interpretation, and would raise the problem highlighted by the quotation from Hursthouse above: just how high a standard are people to be taken as setting for themselves?

I do not think that the considerations I have brought forward in this chapter constitute a knock-down argument against a language of virtues as a public language of moral evaluation. But I do think these considerations show that some writers have been rather too sanguine in supposing that somehow talking about virtues rather than talking about rules and principles is going to show us how to get moral education right. The likelihood seems to be that either a language of virtues is going to be a thin one which does not enable us to do anything we could not do with a language of norms, or that it is going to be a thick one, in which case its very thickness will disqualify it as a language for morality in the narrow sense. Since I have not conclusively established this, it is possible that someone will still develop a language of virtues that will serve the purposes of public moral discourse.[9] But if I am right that we do not yet have that language, there is still point in working with the strengths that a language of norms can offer. Before turning to that, I want to see whether there are any special factors that might incline us to use a language of virtues when talking about violence.

NOTES

1. This is shown by the rationale that Warnock gives for morality; and by the fact that he makes a sharp distinction between the topic of morality and that of 'the Good Life' (e.g. *ibid.*, p. 92).
2. In Chapter 8 I shall agree with at least one of Warnock's points about rules.
3. The work of Peters, of which I shall say more below, especially in Chapters 9 and 10, is something of an exception.
4. I have only anecdotal evidence. But in the first draft of a glossary of terms which I was asked to prepare for the SCAA Forum I included the term 'virtue'. The teachers in the group with

which I discussed the draft saw no point in including this term in something intended to be usable in schools; they did not see the idea of a virtue as being relevant to the standards expected of students in schools.

5. On this point cf. Griffin, 1996, p. 93 with particular reference to morality, and using the terminology of 'norms'; also Campbell, 1983, Chapter 3 with particular reference to law, and using the terminology of 'rules'.

6. A conclusion supported by the fact that Warnock is rarely referred to in debate on virtues in the last fifteen years or so.

7. MacIntyre (1981) has his own way of picking out the qualities that are virtues — a way that requires reference to the interrelated concepts of practice, narrative and tradition. Though MacIntyre may still be, after Aristotle, the most widely cited writer in contemporary virtue ethics, it is not clear that many writers actually follow his account in all its details. A good corrective to confidence that we know how to use the language of virtues would be a perusal of three recent philosophical collections on virtue ethics: Crisp and Slote, 1997; Crisp, 1996; and Statman, 1997. These collections show that even philosophers who see themselves as contributing to virtue ethics are by no means agreed on what makes a quality a virtue.

8. A point which becomes all the clearer in MacIntyre's later writings.

9. The recent writings of Patricia White could be read as an exercise in this direction.

Chapter 6 Virtue-talk about Violence

ARCHIE (about McFee): Oh, he could be very violent you know. . . . In fact we had a furious row last night — perhaps the Inspector had asked you about that . . .? (*Jumpers*, p. 68)

BONES (about Dotty): 'No wonder she broke under the strain. And you don't get over it, just like that. It can go on for years, the effect, afterwards — building up again, underneath, until, one day — *Snap!* — do something violent perhaps, quite out of character, you know what I mean?' (p. 58)

VIOLENCE AND CHARACTER

I have given some reasons for doubting whether a language of virtues can do the job which a publicly shared understanding of morality, in modern conditions, requires. It might be, however, that there is a particular role for the language of virtues where violence is the focus; in this chapter I shall consider that possibility. In the philosophical literature on moral education there seems to be little to draw on in this respect. That may be because writers using a language of virtues are interested in some thicker notion of flourishing rather than in establishing preconditions for a minimally good life; but the same point also illustrates the way in which some of the philosophical literature about moral education has become rather detached from certain public concerns.

Consider the first of the *Jumpers* quotations above. It is ambiguous in a way that illustrates the complexity of our languages of evaluation. Is Archie saying that McFee would occasionally act in a violent way? That would be compatible with his occasional violent actions being out of character. Or is the point that McFee was a violent person (unlike Dotty, in Bones's estimation)? On the first interpretation, Archie is not ascribing any underlying vice of character to McFee; he is not talking a language of virtues at all. He is using the term 'violent' to refer to a certain sort of action. But on the second interpretation Archie is talking a language of virtues, in which violence is a character trait.

Even putting aside the use of the term 'violence' itself, there is no doubt that in public contexts the language of virtues is often used in connection with violence. British readers will be able to recall many occasions when politicians have condemned politically-motivated bombings in Northern Ireland. What are the terms of the condemnation? More often than not, at least one description under which the act is condemned is that it is 'cowardly'. Since cowardice is seen as the opposite of, or the lack of, courage, this is part of the language of virtues. To call an act cowardly is to describe the *act*, not directly the person doing it, but the description refers to the motivation of the action and through that to the character of the agent (whereas the description of an action as violent will not necessarily refer to character). The act is being described as the kind of act a cowardly person would do, and implicitly as the kind of act *only* a cowardly person would do.

I shall come back to cowardice, but first I shall try to approach more systematically the ways we may use a language of virtues to talk about violence. As in the previous chapter, we can start by looking briefly at the inadequacies of too thin a language. In Warnock's vocabulary of virtues, the terms which have a fairly direct bearing on violence are non-maleficence and beneficence. On the minimal assumption that violence does generally cause pain or harm, or at least has a tendency to do so, people with the virtue of non-maleficence would not be violent. For non-maleficence, in Warnock's terms, is just the disposition to refrain from (deliberate, unjustified) maleficence. But this shows up the thinness of the language, in several ways. For one, it puts all the weight on whether someone sees the causing of certain harm as unjustified; it does not say that non-maleficence is the disposition to avoid causing any harm at all. The person who has the virtue of non-maleficence, then, must have some basis for seeing (or 'judging', where the latter term suggests a greater degree of explicit thought) whether the causing of certain harm would be unjustified. And that is the sort of judgement we generally make by reference to norms.

This thin language of virtues, too, does nothing to help us distinguish violence from other forms of maleficence, or to see what, if anything, is specially bad about violence. Though Warnock himself rejects utilitarianism, non-maleficence and its positive counterpart beneficence are the virtues that one would expect to be central to utilitarianism. Non-maleficence and beneficence need, if they are to be put into operation, some understanding of what counts as harm and benefit, just as does utilitarianism; they need a degree of inter-subjective understanding of harm and benefit such as might be supplied by shared norms. This reference to harm and benefit is a reference to consequences, and thus turns attention away from motivation and intention. Thus if the consequences overall of a certain way of organising a school appear as bad as the consequences of a physical attack by one person on another, the beneficent person will see both of these as demanding to be avoided. Like the utilitarian, he or she will have a reason for counting the school organisation as a case of 'systemic violence'. If we want to find reasons for counting physical violence (or perhaps physical and in certain respects psychological violence) as in some way morally distinctive, we will not find it by using a thin language of virtues like Warnock's.

RELATIVITY OF VIRTUES

Let us turn, then, to thicker languages of virtues in relation to violence. We immediately have to recall that there is more than one thick language of virtues; and some such languages (or conceptual schemes), such as the language of martial valour in heroic societies (cf. MacIntyre, 1981, Chapter 10) would by no means tend to function to reduce violence. Though none of us now lives in an heroic society, we do, in a plural society, inherit different traditions of virtues. Different religions and different cultures do not necessarily agree on circumstances in which the resort to violence (in response, say, to violence from another) is admirable or deplorable. Turning the other cheek can be admirable moral courage to one and reprehensible timidity or servility to another; hitting back can be reprehensible irascibility or admirable manliness (some parts of virtue language are gender-specific). Using a language of virtues to talk about violence and public responses to violence is by no means unproblematic.

It is not only that as a culture we are heirs to a number of traditions; it is also that there can be subcultures within a culture, and subcultures will not necessarily have the same glossary of virtues as the main culture. Consider this sociologist's description of the kind of 'subculture of violence' already referred to in Chapter 2:

> In this subculture, generated primarily in a lower socioeconomic class disadvantaged in all the traditionally known ways, the use of violence is either tolerated and permitted or specifically encouraged from infancy through adulthood. From child-rearing practices that commonly use physical punishment and that contain many elements of child abuse, to childhood and adolescent play and street gang and group behaviour, to domestic quarrels and bar-room brawls, physically assaultive conduct is condoned and is even part of the expected response to many interpersonal relationships. Machismo, but more than this, is involved in the value system that promotes the ready resort to violence upon the appearance of relatively weak provoking stimuli...
>
> Within the subculture of violence the cues and clues of this stimulus/response mechanism are well known to the culture carriers and thus promote social situations that quickly escalate arguments to altercations and apparently

> quick-tempered aggression from seemingly trivial encounters. This subculture of violence is culturally transmitted from generation to generation and is shared across cohorts of youth who will fight instead of flee, assault instead of articulate, and kill rather than control their aggression. (Wolfgang, 1977, pp. 37–38)

Many readers, not part of such a culture themselves, may have no independent way of verifying its accuracy. (But some teachers in certain urban areas may have relevant experience.) Readers who share in a more literary culture (not that the two are necessarily mutually exclusive) may nevertheless find the description of the 'cohorts of youth' in the last sentence not entirely unfamiliar. Does it not fit the young Montague and Capulet men in *Romeo and Juliet*? (No doubt that is why it has not been difficult for twentieth-century interpretations of the play to be transposed into urban gangland settings.) We can all recognise something of the description, even if only as mediated though more or less 'high' culture.

The subculture as described is clearly distinguished in part by its norms. But we could also describe it as recognising certain qualities as virtues which would not be so recognised in other subcultures. These qualities are variously named: machismo is one name, being 'hard' is another (cf. Shostak, 1986), and so on.

If in relation to violence different qualities may be recognised as virtues in different cultures and subcultures, it is also true that there are different virtues for different roles. Writers on professional ethics, influenced by the wider turn in moral philosophy towards virtue ethics, have begun to discuss, for example, the virtues of nurses. What of the virtues of soldiers? Annette Baier (1997, p. 269) writes that 'the easy willingness to go out and kill when ordered to do so by authorities' does not seem to her 'to be a character trait a decent morality will encourage by labelling it a virtue'. That may be so, but a society may nevertheless consider that it needs people with that willingness, and to that extent it may have to recognise that this trait is a virtue in soldiers. (Whether a decent liberal society can recognise this is one of Baier's questions; we can add the question whether it is a trait that a decent liberal society could encourage through education.)

WHY NON-VIOLENCE IS NOT A VIRTUE

In relation to violence, then, a society speaking a language of virtues may have to accept a certain relativity within that language. It will also have to recognise that a variety of virtues may be relevant to its concerns about violence. There is no single virtue uniquely relevant to violence; hence there is no virtue of non-violence as such. That is, *non-violence is not a virtue*. This does not mean that non-violence is not a good thing. It means that 'non-violence' does not label the sort of quality which a thick language of virtues picks out as a virtue.

The reason for this is that a thick language of virtues always has reference in some way to underlying emotions and motivations. When it evaluates actions as courageous or generous or fair, and so on, it is categorising and evaluating these actions by reference to their underlying motivational basis, rather than by the nature or consequences of the action itself. Consider the kind of account of the virtues which Aristotle gives (and which many recent writers on virtues see themselves as following to some degree, albeit perhaps loosely). Different virtues relate to different sectors of the total human range of motivation. Courage relates to the human tendency to be fearful and also to the tendency towards over-confidence: it gets the balance right. Temperance relates to the appetite for pleasure, especially sensual pleasure: it involves not going overboard in the pursuit of such pleasures, but not being entirely indifferent to them either. Proper pride relates to the human tendency to be pleased at one's own achievement and to take pleasure in the approbation of others: it is a matter of not being too full of oneself, but not being too modest or self-effacing either.

I do not intend my rough characterisations here to represent exactly Aristotle's own account of particular virtues. I am more interested in his general view that we can distinguish a number of different human tendencies in feeling and motivation, and that it is possible for each of these to be manifested to excess, or insufficiently. (This is the point of Aristotle's 'doctrine of the mean', but the general point does not depend on the specifics of Aristotle's treatment.) It is questionable whether this notion that there can be both excess and deficiency will work for all the qualities we may count as virtues, but there seems to me little doubt that it does apply to some important ones.

Within Aristotle's own categorisation of virtues, there is one which has a particular, though indirect, relationship to violence. This is the virtue which relates to anger, because anger can lead to violence. I shall say more about this in the next chapter. If violence always and only stemmed from anger then the virtue which relates especially to anger might be the only virtue we would need to consider in relation to violence. But clearly there can be other motivational bases for violence. Consider professional thieves who in planning a bank robbery are prepared to use violence if they need to. If during the robbery they were to become angry this would be unlikely to further their goals. They need to stay calm and collected. Their underlying motivation might be the desire for money: in classical terms, the vice of greed. A lesser desire for material goods, or greater benevolence, or greater law-abidingness, might all have prevented the action which may lead to violence; a lesser tendency to be angry would here be irrelevant.

Or consider politically-motivated violence. Much violence (including some political protest, and some warfare) has been motivated by a desire for justice. I do not take that to show that all such violence has been justified, even though a desire for justice is surely in general a good motivation for people to have. (The notion of justice is not in modern times usually considered a part of a language of virtues,[1] but to talk about someone's desire for justice and commitment to work for it is to speak of a virtue.) It is also true that people can be angry about injustice, and it will sometimes be that violence flows from the anger, directly expressing the anger, rather than being undertaken, instrumentally and with a cool head, from the desire to achieve justice. But there must have been cases in which it is a commitment to justice which underlies the violence, where the violence would not have happened had the commitment been weaker.

Or consider courage and cowardice again. Traditionally, from Aristotle until quite recently, courage was associated especially with martial valour (and still is in many films). The courageous person was the one who would, in general, be fairly successful in his (it would usually be 'his') violence, where the violence itself is aimed at some goal considered admirable (which might be self-defence or protecting the vulnerable). The person more likely to refrain from violence would be the cowardly person. The reactions to terrorist violence which I mentioned at the beginning of this chapter suggest a reversal of this evaluative scheme. But the appearance of this reversal is often, I suspect, no more than a rhetorical effect.

Many of us (I say 'of us' because the people who read books like this are not in general going to be among the action heroes of this world), even if we were convinced that some political cause justified the planting of bombs, might be too timid to carry this out. Perhaps even that sort of action requires some degree of courage; the terrorists face some personal risk of injury or capture. They could have given up their cause and stayed at home, which would not have been a display of courage.

Do I intend this as a defence of terrorist bombing? Not at all. I intend it to show that the language of virtues is far from settling what we are to say about acts of violence. As Williams (1993, p. 92) remarks in a quite different context, 'the action stands between the inner world of disposition, feeling and decision and an outer world of harm and wrong. *What I have done* points in one direction towards what has happened to others, in another direction to what I am'. I do not know whether I am idiosyncratic in finding — and having found, for as long as I can remember — the description of a terrorist bombing as 'cowardly' oddly weak and off the point. What is wrong with planting a car bomb in a crowded shopping centre? Surely what is wrong with this is that people are going to be — or are put in danger of being — killed or maimed, and other people as a result are going to be left bereaved and grieving. (Some would add to this description that the people are 'innocent' — but that hardly seems to me to be the central point either.) Is *that* not why the act should be condemned? Of how much moment is it that the action is cowardly? To apply that label to it seems to be, not so much to condemn the atrocity, as to utter a personal insult to the perpetrator. Even if the insult is richly deserved, it still seems to me rather beside the point.

DIFFERENT EVALUATIONS

Here I do not expect everyone to agree with me. I can believe that for some people, perhaps many (including many readers), the thought 'What kind of person could do that?' really does point to what is most horrible about the action. To me, what is most horrible about it is the pain and suffering the action causes. (I recognise that the consequences of the bombing might in themselves be similar to the accidental explosion of a gas main or even to the consequences of an earthquake. And I recognise that the fact that the consequences of the bombing stem from the deliberate action of a human being does make the whole event more horrible. But how much more?) Most of us, I imagine, are capable of making both kinds of evaluation, but we may differ in our tendency to make one or the other, or in which we give priority to.

I have no wish to deny the richness of the language of evaluation which our vocabulary and our inherited ways of thinking make available to us. Indeed I would argue that a person's education would be deficient if it left the person able to operate only with some narrow range of evaluative terms. It is worth noting too that the different theoretical accounts of morality and ethics which philosophers have developed do to a considerable extent reflect the different languages of evaluation which we have. To some of us it is the consequences of the bombing which constitute the real horror of it. If we are philosophers, it is likely to be consequentialist schemes that we develop. To others of us, it is the character — as some would say, the evil character — of the perpetrators that is the real horror. The philosophers within this school of thought will develop forms of virtue ethics. That is no doubt an over-simplification, but it does seem to me that the most important distinction to be drawn within contemporary debate between virtue ethics and its rivals is that — while no view need deny that we can and do evaluate both actions and agents — different approaches give the priority to the different kinds of evaluation.

Consider an issue which in itself is trivial compared to terrorist bombings (of course, in calling it trivial I am myself making an evaluation, and making it largely by consideration of consequences). Consider boys (because experience and some reported research suggest that it is more likely to be boys) who pass their time by playing war games, e.g. alien-zapping computer games, or board games on which plastic pieces representing warriors are moved around and 'destroyed' (or not) according to the throw of dice.[2]

No doubt a boy spending hours doing this (with or without live competitors in the game) could be spending his time in something more useful (like homework, perhaps). But what is the activity in itself? It is a quiet, peaceful way of passing the time (quieter and more peaceful, and much less likely to lead to injury, than playing football, say). What objection, then, is there to it? Are such games likely to lead to violence? Hardly in a very direct sense; there is no more intrinsic reason for a fight to break out over one of these mock battles than over a game of chess (which also represents a mock battle in its original symbolism). But perhaps less directly and over the longer term?

There is little research evidence that I know of on this. It seems not quite the same issue as that of violent films and videos to which I referred in Chapter 2, given the greater vividness and immediacy of the images of violence available in films (though as the sophistication of computer graphics increases the difference will narrow). In advance of evidence, it hardly seems likely that boys who spend their time in such pursuits are going to be causing trouble through violence on the streets; if anything, one would expect the reverse. Our contemporary language of combined description and evaluation includes terms like 'nerd' for people who spend their time playing (or indeed writing) computer games. The nerds are not the people one imagines fighting on the streets, or for that matter going into the army.

I suspect, though, that some readers will not see war games as a peaceful harmless occupation, and would not, even if there were evidence which could establish that they were harmless. These readers will view the activity with distaste, and in doing so they will be using a language of virtues. For Aristotle a virtue is partly a matter of what a person takes pleasure in or is pained by (a point I used in my brief discussion of benevolence in the previous chapter). Is pleasure taken in zapping aliens (or anyone else) on a computer screen a good, desirable, kind of pleasure? I shall not try to decide the issue here. My intuition is that this pleasure is qualitatively different from the cruel, sadistic pleasure which some people — one hopes only a few — might take in actually torturing another sentient creature (cf. McGinn, 1997). I would need some plausible evidence before believing that there is likely to be a causal connection between one and the other. Short of that, there is surely something to be said for the liberal pluralist value of leaving people to their own pleasures provided they do not interfere with others.

Perhaps indeed we should be pluralist about our forms of evaluation, and even about our philosophical approaches to ethics, if these reflect different languages of evaluation. But there are limits to pluralism when we are asking what kind of evaluative language can best serve the public purposes of morality in the narrow sense, especially, for the moment, the reduction of violence. The considerations of the last few paragraphs show some of the problems in using a language of virtues to pick out publicly actions or patterns of behaviour that are going to be condemned. We need also to use a language which refers to the nature of actions and their consequences for others.

This is especially the case if we are thinking about whether violence can ever be justified (as a means to ends such as self-defence or the promotion of justice). Here I have not directly engaged in that question. That may seem surprising, given the topic of the book. But whether violence can ever be justified is a public question to which my own contribution would be only one voice. As a philosopher, I am saying that it makes a difference what kind of language we use in talking about that question. This is a question of pertinence to philosophers of education, because it will be for schools to encourage people to discuss that kind of question, and people's experience of thinking and talking about these questions in school will influence the nature of the ongoing debate within society. One of the problems of moral education and education in citizenship is that teachers themselves — having had no more grounding in the languages available than any other citizen — are not sure what kind of language to use.

NOTES

1. Though both Foot (1978) and MacIntyre (1981) have interesting discussions of justice as a virtue.
2. There is a national chain of shops, under the name *Games Workshop*, devoted to this sort of thing.

Chapter 7   Is there Virtue in Anger?

GEORGE: Are you still going on about that? — for goodness sake, I just lost my temper for a moment, that's all, and took matters into my own hands.
BONES: Because of the noise?
GEORGE: Exactly.
BONES: Don't you think it was a bit extreme?
GEORGE: Yes, yes, I suppose it was a bit. (*Jumpers*, p. 59)

UNAVOIDABLE VIRTUE-TALK

Though talking a language of virtues — and doing so with consistency and clarity — may well be more challenging for teachers — as for all of us — than talking a language of norms, there is one area, relevant to violence, where it is unlikely to be avoidable in schools. People get angry, and sometimes anger leads to violence. Though there is also much violence that does not stem from anger, as I have acknowledged in the previous chapter, anger is surely an important element in much of the almost 'casual' violence that can break out in homes, in the playground or classroom, and in the streets.

When someone is angry, reference to a rule such as 'don't be violent' is not necessarily going to stop them being violent; and when someone is beginning to get angry, reference to a rule like 'don't lose your temper' is not necessarily going to stop their anger escalating. In such cases it would very often be better if the person concerned had not got angry at all; yet a rule that said simply 'don't get angry' would probably not be the right rule, since anger is not always bad, and may not always be within a person's control. And a rule which said 'always suppress your anger' would seem to many to be mistaken. The following, for instance, is a not untypical expression of that general suspicion of moral rules which we have already encountered, applied in this case to anger in the classroom (notice the scare quotes, indicating a reluctance to use specifically moral language which I shall take up in later chapters):

Children are taught that it's 'wrong' to be seriously angry with others and to express that anger physically or verbally. The conflict over what they feel and what they are 'supposed' to feel creates a sense of isolation as they move further and further away from their instinctual selves (Leseho and Howard-Rose, 1994, p. 8).

We need to think about the relationship between anger and violence. At this point, particularly if you are familiar with psychological discussions of violence, you may expect some reference to aggression. But 'aggression' is one of those terms which, because of its ambiguities, tends to obfuscate rather than clarify. While in a biological context 'aggression' may be used of a certain sort of motivation, in much everyday discourse about human conduct the term picks out a kind of behaviour — attacking behaviour — rather than any specific motive. There is no single necessary motivation, for instance, behind the aggression of one state against another. In this way the notion of aggression is rather like that of violence itself: violence too may be picked out by reference to motivation or by reference to other characteristics of action.

Where there is reference to motivation we might expect that the term 'aggressive' — partly because aggression can be associated with violence — would be uniformly negative in its evaluative tone. Yet 'aggressive' can function as a positive description in a language of virtues: to call a business executive aggressive is to praise him or her (one wonders whether the same is coming to be true of university vice-chancellors and heads of department). Given the ambiguities around the notion of aggression, I shall concentrate here on anger, an emotion which is typically, though not invariably, associated with aggression in the sense of attacking behaviour.[1] Midgley refers to anger as 'the appropriate motive for attack — not that it must always lead to attack, nor that all attacks are due to it, but that it is the feeling which makes attack intelligible, even without extra background conditions' (1986, pp. 76–77). Where there is anger, it is natural to expect some sort of attacking behaviour (which may be only verbal), though this is by no means inevitable; and if we ask why one person attacked another (physically or verbally), a reference to anger will generally be intelligible as part of an explanation, though it will need to be supplemented by some explanation of the anger itself.

Anger is not the only relevant emotion where attacking behaviour, including violence, is concerned. Hatred and contempt must be relevant, though we may doubt how often it happens that one person is violent against another directly out of hatred or contempt, without anger entering in. And in many violent sexual offences, usually by men against women, sexual desire must enter the picture, though again, as many feminists have argued, hatred or contempt or sheer anger, perhaps at some imagined offence, is likely to enter into the motivation of the rapist. Here I shall not attempt to review all the possible emotional states which can lead to violence, and the relevant virtue in each case. I shall concentrate on anger, partly because some of the points made could be generalised to other cases, but also because, given its particular connection with attacking behaviour, anger seems to be the central case.

We commonly think that anger is an emotion that can get out of control, and that it is when it does get out of control that it is especially likely to lead to violence. It would be possible in a language of norms to give only minimal recognition to this point. If we firmly insist on the rule 'don't be violent', then we could say that it matters little whether people get angry or not: what is important is that they do not actually behave violently. We can even say that it does not matter if you feel like hitting someone, so long as you do not actually hit them (perhaps instead you *say* 'I'm so angry, I feel like hitting you'; cf. Houghton, 1998, p. 47). But a view which depends in this way on a sharp distinction between feeling and action can well seem over-sanguine. If part of the trouble with anger is that it can be difficult to control, and that it tends to lead to violence, it makes sense to look at ways of limiting anger in the first place. Since anger is an emotion which can motivate behaviour, and since some people seem to be more prone to anger than others, this way of thinking is going to lead us into using a language of virtues.

Part of the problem with limiting ourselves, in contexts of personal violence, to a language of norms referring to outward behaviour is brought out by Larry May (1998), in a passage in which he is considering the way that some men (this does mean *men*, not 'persons') try to excuse their violence by pleading that their anger or their sexual desire was too much for them:

> Morality should not be diminished when the going gets tough. Indeed, it is just at that point that morality should clearly come to view. Those people who are already inclined to act in a morally responsible manner do not have as much need for the social institutions that constitute morality's public expression. In a sense, the public sanctions that attach to morality are there for those who would not normally act in a morally responsible manner. Of course, they also play a role for everyone else, since few people are always inclined to do what they should do. But the main function of such public sanctions would be defeated if people thought that morality applied less to those who had a hard time following it.[2]

In other words, a morality of public norms, telling people not to act in certain ways, would be of little effect if people (and, where violence is concerned, males especially) could too easily excuse themselves from it by saying 'my anger (or my sexual desire, or both) got the better of me'. If in at least some of these cases anger really does get the better of the perpetrator, this is in some sense a deficiency in the person concerned; in some sense he would be a better person if this did not happen to him. Here we are beginning to talk the language of virtues. There is some virtue relevant to anger, and the person who has this virtue is a person whose anger will not be excessive, whatever happens.

How are we to characterise this virtue? One common answer is that given by John White in his contribution to *Teaching Right and Wrong* (p. 22): 'The virtue of temperance, which regulates our bodily appetites, or the virtue of self-control, which does the same for anger . . . control the temptations, or inclinations, we all have when we are young to follow easier paths.'

I do not want to read too much into remarks made in passing. But notice how odd it would be if someone were to suggest (though I do not think White meant to) that but for the development of temperance all boys would grow up as rapists, or that but for the development of self-control all children would grow up subject to uncontrollable fits of anger. This does, though, roughly represent a common picture of the virtue that relates to anger: it is the ability to control oneself, so that one's anger does not flow over into violence.

Self-control seems a precarious basis for the avoidance of violence. Self-control sometimes may slip. Would it not be better if a person were not inclined to get angry in the first place, so that the ability to control one's anger was not necessary? This suggests that, rather than the important virtue here being the ability to control the expression of one's anger, it would be the tendency not to get angry at all. Is this what education should be trying to cultivate?

ON BEING PEACEABLE AND GOOD-TEMPERED

Consider the following scene, in which a small boy is observed wandering in the grounds of a sanatorium or clinic in which a number of elderly people are sitting. His elders 'did not appear to take much interest in him, but what interest they took was wholly benevolent' (so they possessed that virtue, apparently). To the boy, this abstracted benevolence appeared as indifference — he was clearly trying to get some reaction out of them:

> He had gone up to an elderly lady apparently engaged upon a cross-word puzzle and unsufferably snatched her paper from her. The lady had merely smiled and made a small, resigned gesture. And at this the boy had lost control of himself. Darting forward again, he had dealt her a stinging blow across the face. And — once more — the lady simply smiled. . . . The boy had drawn back. He was very frightened. He looked from face to face of the people scattered around him. Some of them had seen his act; others were preoccupied. But nobody made any move. He gave a choking cry and rushed at a tall man with a pipe in his mouth who was sitting in idle contemplation of the garden. The boy knocked the pipe to the ground and clawed, battered at the tall man's

face. The man smiled, slightly shook his head, got up and moved to another seat. Most of the people were now watching. They watched as if nothing abnormal was occurring. But this was itself the only abnormal thing about them. (Innes, 1964, p. 221)

These adults showed no anger at the boy's behaviour. This was not because they felt it but controlled themselves; they did not *feel* any anger (I shall come to the explanation of this in a moment). Does this lack of anger constitute a virtue on their part? It does not. This answer is not unconnected with the fact that their lack of reaction is indeed thoroughly abnormal. In Aristotle's understanding of a virtue, even though the possession of a virtue might be statistically abnormal, it would not be abnormal in the sense of running counter to human nature. The abnormal reaction observed here is a deficiency in the usual human tendency to respond with anger, or at least with something milder like annoyance or irritation, to injuries and insults. In failing to respond at all in any such way, these people are not only showing indifference, they are showing a lack of self-respect.

A virtue, on the Aristotelian model, is a quality which contributes to, or is partly constitutive of, human flourishing. Does this lack of reaction to injury or irritation contribute to human flourishing? It does not, because it renders the people concerned far too passive; we could even say that in a sense they are being less than human. Does this deficiency count as a vice? In this particular case it does not, because it is in no way the fault of the people concerned; in fact it is drug-induced (the scene comes from a novel by Michael Innes about a highly improbable plot to take over the world by rendering people incapable of active resistance — making them, in fact, peaceable, or peaceful in at least one sense of the term). But if the people had knowingly allowed their normal human responses to become atrophied, through habitually failing to stand up for themselves when they could have done so, then they would, on the Aristotelian model, be manifesting a vice, a culpable deficiency in an important human capacity.

To the sort of provocation experienced here there can be, then, under-reaction as well as overreaction. What would overreaction be? Well, suppose the tall man, roused to fury, had jumped up, pushed the five-year-old boy to the ground, and jumped on his head. He would be angry to an unreasonable degree. Somewhere between the extremes is the reaction of the person who has the relevant virtue in an Aristotelian scheme. Translators sometimes render the name of this virtue as 'good temper'. (Annette Baier, 1985, p. 219, speaks of a virtue she names 'gentleness' which is similar, though probably not identical, to Aristotle's.)

It is important that there can be a deficiency in anger as well as an excess. While it is clearly possible to be too angry, and hence too violent, it is also possible to be too little angry, and hence, *in a sense*, too peaceable. (Deliberate policies of non-violence, as in Gandhi's case, are quite different from passivity; they are policies actively engaged in.) As Aristotle is careful to point out, this does not mean that we can mathematically calculate where the mean will be; and we can now see, as perhaps Aristotle could not, that there is scope for cultural and even subcultural differences as to where the mean should be. As a matter of public discourse in modern plural societies we face the challenges of seeing how far we can agree on an understanding of this mean.

ANGER AND JUDGEMENT

For Aristotle, the good-tempered person 'tends to be unperturbed and not to be led by passion, but to be angry in the manner, at the thing, and for the length of time, that the rule dictates' (*Nicomachean Ethics* IV. 5, Ross translation pp. 96–97). This phrase 'the rule dictates' (where 'rule' translates *logos*) can be puzzling, but is typical of Aristotle's treatment of the virtues generally. There are right and wrong ways of responding to situations and other people, hence there are judgements to be made. The judgements cannot be made just by following a rule which could be set out in advance: that is why for Aristotle ethics could not be just a matter of rule-following, and why the notion of the person of practical wisdom (the *phronimos*, the person who has *phronesis*) is central to his ethics. The person who has practical wisdom will, from situation to situation, in effect be following a rule or principle (both of which terms are sometimes used to translate *logos*) but not one that could be set out by others, or perhaps that this person himself could articulate in words. The mean between excess and deficiency will be determined by the principle by which the *phronimos* would determine it; and that may be as much as can be said, *in completely general terms*.

There is, however, more that can be said about the nature of the judgements involved in particular virtues. Anger is a response to a perceived injury or offence of some kind. (Some writers treat anger as always a response to some perceived injury *to oneself*, but that is too narrow: one can be angry at the way one person is treating another, or angry about injustice, even where one is only an observer.) Part of the judgement to be made is about what sort and degree of active response is appropriate (e.g. in the example of the small boy the good-tempered person would perhaps have judged some verbal rebuke, but not physical violence, appropriate). But prior to that there is a judgement or perception that an offence has indeed been committed. This judgement is in a certain way internal to the emotion of anger itself.

It is a familiar philosophical thesis that any emotion involves a cognitive element which is a judgement or perception. Thus fear is in part constituted by the sense that something in the environment is dangerous, and so on. Anger is in part constituted by the judgement or perception that the person one is angry with has offended in some way; without this perception it would not be anger that one feels (whatever the physiological concomitants may be). If this seems implausible, try a thought experiment. See if you can feel angry — here and now, while reading this — with some particular person that you normally get on well with. If you can succeed at all, it will be by recalling, or even imagining, something that person has done, or might do, or some characteristic of that person, that hurts you or offends against your values in some way.

Since a judgement that some sort of offence has been committed is inherent in anger, anger carries with it the sense that it is justified. While we are actually angry with someone we think that they deserve our anger. This seems to be true of anger against persons, which we should treat as the standard case. It does seem to be possible to be angry with things — like the computer printer when you cannot get it to work — but when this happens it seems as if we are to some degree personifying the object, treating it *as if* it were a person and hence a deserving object of our anger (cf. Sabini and Silver, 1982, Chapter 9).

There is certainly such a thing as unjustified anger, but there is hardly such a thing as anger which the angry person, with a clear head, considers to be unjustified at the very same time as feeling it. This is not quite true, because feelings, once aroused, do tend to last for a while, probably because their physiological concomitants of increased heart rate, flushed skin, or whatever, cannot instantly subside. So it is possible to continue to feel angry with someone — for a while — even after one has consciously realised that there is no good reason for one's anger (perhaps one only imagined the slight; perhaps one had been misinformed, or misunderstood, or whatever). But once one consciously judges that one's sense of an insult or injury is misplaced, hence that one's anger is unjustified, the anger is on the way to evaporating.

But while the anger lasts, and whatever may have occasioned it, we typically feel — the word 'think' may suggest something too rational for such occasions — that the person we are angry with deserves our anger. Indeed our anger inclines us to interpret whatever the other is doing in a negative light. Harré (1986, p. 7) has a good description of this:

The anger 'felt' by the apparently injured party (A) is the (almost) exclusive basis for A's interpretation of the actions of B as transgressions against A's rights, dignity or the like. If A feels annoyed, then this is the best ground for holding that B's actions must have been offensive. Furthermore, if B tries to escape from the 'no win' situation by denying an intention to offend, then A has further cause for complaint and ground for indignation. B's defence implies that B (offensively) believes that A is the kind of person who would impose unjust interpretations on B's actions or facial expressions, just to nourish his or her anger.

Indeed it is not just B's anger that A thinks B deserves — typically A wants to hurt or punish or humiliate B in some way, and this too A thinks B deserves. It is, then, all too easy for anger to slip into violence, accompanied by the sense that the violence is just what the person had coming to them.

This kind of analysis gives us a way of unpacking what is involved in the differential tendencies, in line with Aristotle's account, to feel anger too little, or appropriately, or too much. The person who is too little inclined to anger is likely to be someone who has no self-respect or who does not think anything is worth feeling strongly about. The person who is too much inclined to anger is likely to be someone who is in a certain way over-sensitive, perceiving slights or offences where there are none, or reacting disproportionately to those which are there, even at times to the point of violence. The person whose tendency to anger is neither defective or excessive gets his or her judgements right.

The person who has the genuinely Aristotelian virtue — who will also be a person of practical wisdom, since for Aristotle this is essential to any genuine virtue — will get these judgements right without particularly having to think about it. Having consciously to review one's judgement and perception is in that way a second best; nevertheless, it may be very desirable. Suppose a person is in the habit of asking herself 'am I right to take this as an insult, or am I overreacting?' This person will be slower to anger than one who does not reflect on her own reactions in this way; and even where her anger survives her self-reflection, she will be less likely to feel that violence is a deserved expression of her anger.

This shows a way in which education should be able to get a grip even on something often as apparently non-rational as anger (cf. Dent, 1984; anger is one of his main examples). There is a sort of reasoning inherent in anger, and it is an educational task to try to see that people are aware of the reasoning which they would otherwise not articulate to themselves, and that they are concerned about the validity of their own reasoning. This also shows that the language of virtues can lead us back to the language of norms, in which we ask ourselves whether our responses and our feelings are justified. 'Has this person actually offended against some moral norm? (Maybe he has upset me, but that is not the same thing). Should I blame him? Or was he only doing what one would expect of anyone in that situation?' And so on.

None of this is saying that we should belittle our own feelings or ignore those of others. There is point in the idea, often found in suggestions for conflict resolution, and in the book about *Anger in the Classroom* (Leseho and Howard-Rose, 1994) from which I quoted above, that acknowledging our feelings, to ourselves and to others, can be a step in preventing negative feelings from escalating into anger and beyond that into violence. But part of the point of this is that acknowledging our feelings brings them into the open and hence up against public norms. Our feelings are not self-validating; the fact that I feel angry cannot by itself show my anger to be justified. Yet that *is* just the way it feels at the time; so I need the reference to something external to my feelings — which can include public norms — to bring me to question my own feelings. Recognition of a clear prohibition on violence, for instance, could be the factor which makes the difference between anger turning and not turning to violence.

This chapter has reinforced the conclusion of the previous two chapters, that the public concern about violence cannot without remainder be unpacked into talk about the virtues that are to be developed or the vices to be avoided. We need to recognise, with MacIntyre (1981, p. 141), that a community needs a table of offences — of kinds of act which are intolerable — as well as a table of virtues. In other words, we cannot avoid thinking in terms of norms which prohibit certain types of action. At the same time we can recognise that the two ways of talking need not be opposed to each other. As we shall see again below, the contrast can easily be overdrawn.

NOTES

1. There are interesting discussions of anger and its relation to aggression in Midgley (1986) Chapter 4, and Sabini and Silver (1982) Chapter 9.
2. Some strands of feminist thought and research point to the possibility that males may be more inclined than are females to think in terms of a morality of norms which constrain 'natural' appetites. May's discussion suggests that males may be more in need of such a morality; or rather, that females may need such a morality in males.

Chapter 8 What is Wrong with Rules?

GEORGE: All I know is that I think that I know that I know that . . . my moral conscience is different from the rules of my tribe . . . (*Jumpers*, p. 67)

OBJECTIONS TO MORAL RULES

We have as yet seen no reason to think that the language of virtues can replace a language of norms for purposes of public moral discourse (though the one may exist alongside and interact with the other). The language of norms is likely to have a certain priority for the articulation of morality(n), particularly if the role of morality(n) is seen as analogous to the role of law. If the analogy is extended to cover not only the role of morality(n) but its form, then morality(n) will be seen as a system of norms, as law often is.

For morality, however, it may be better to use the term 'set' rather than 'system'. Ethical *theories*, such as utilitarianism and Kantianism, have been presented as *systems* of norms, in which there is a hierarchy of lower-level norms deriving from higher ones, but the notion of morality as consisting of norms does not have to subscribe to this (see Griffin, 1996, for a view of morality as consisting of norms with no particular system to them). To the extent that the norms of morality are seen as unsystematic, with, for instance, no particular criteria or procedures for determining which are dominant over others, this may be a disanalogy between morality and law.

For the moment I am taking 'norms' to be a broad term referring to standards for conduct which are taken to be prescriptive (rather than just ideals or aspirations), which can either be followed or not followed on particular occasions of action, and which can be, though they are not necessarily, expressed verbally as imperatives. For example, two of the norms to which Griffin (1996) gives a good deal of attention are 'don't take innocent life' and 'limit the damage'. Like these two, norms commonly pick out actions by reference to their external features. What these two tell us to avoid are the taking of innocent life, or unnecessary damage; they say nothing about feeling or motivation. But there can also be norms which do refer to feeling and motivation, like another example from Griffin, 'don't be cruel', or, an example from the last chapter 'don't lose your temper'.[1] Even, though, where norms like these two are referring to feeling and motivation, they are norms that can be followed or not followed on particular occasions of action. Griffin's example means 'don't act in a cruel way', not 'don't be a cruel person'. The latter, though expressed as a norm, would be part of a language of virtues.

Norms which refer to actions by their externally observable features or consequences (though possibly not only such norms) are often referred to as rules. I pointed out in Chapter 2 that rules have had a bad press in recent philosophical writing about moral education. Here and in the following chapter I shall reply to some of the objections. In the latter part of the next chapter and in Chapter 10 I shall give a more positive account of the role of rules, and will need an explicit distinction between rules and principles.

Criticisms of the role of rules in the literature do not necessarily take account of the distinction between morality(n) and the broader field. An argument, then, which says in general terms 'there is more to morality than rules' may turn out in effect to be an argument that there is more to ethics than morality(n); and this, of course, is something that the case for morality(n) is already committed to. On the other hand, objections to the role of rules in morality may turn out to have a bearing on how we interpret morality(n); it would be pointless to insulate morality(n) from criticism by defining it in advance as a set of rules and thereby interpreting all objections to the role of rules as being objections against something other than morality(n). Here, then, I shall not try to select out in advance points which bear only on morality(n), but will consider what seem to me to be the main lines of attack in the literature on the role of rules in morality (there may, of course, be some that I have missed). These attacks are not necessarily all found in the same writers and they do not necessarily form a consistent set.

(a) Some objections to a morality of rules are objections to the idea of *absolute* rules.
(b) Some are objections to the idea of *unchanging* rules (cf. the passage from Cox, quoted in Chapter 2, denying that there are tablets of stone on which the rules are written).
(c) Some are objections to the idea of universal rules.
(d) Some objections turn on the fundamental matter of what it is that makes something right or wrong: the objection is to the idea that something is right or wrong *because it is against the rules*.
(e) Some objections turn on the role that rules have — or may be thought to have — in moral reasoning, judgement and perception. In particular, such objections often involve the rejection of a model by which moral reasoning consists in seeing that a particular instance falls under a general rule.

(f) Some objections turn on the question of motivation: it is argued that doing something *because the rule demands it* is not an appropriate or desirable form of motivation.

(g) Some objections concern the kind of *authority* that rules can have: why should moral rules be taken to be in any way authoritative? (Cf. Anscombe's argument against the idea of moral law, mentioned in Chapter 4.)

Of these types of objection, the last two seem quite closely interrelated: if someone does something because a rule demands it, then what moves them to obey the rule may be that they recognise the rule as having authority. At the same time, the questions about motivation and authority are not ones that arise only about morality construed as a set of rules; they arise more generally about morality(n), so that even if we were persuaded that we should think of morality(n) in some way other than as a set of rules, we would still have the questions 'is it a desirable form of motivation that a person does something because it is what morality(n) requires?' and 'what kind of authority does morality(n) have?' These are questions I shall take up in Chapters 11 and 12.

In the remainder of this chapter I shall start with the earlier objections. I shall treat (a) to (c) as matters of clarification to be cleared out of the way fairly briskly. Objection (d) will turn out to raise more fundamental issues, and will lead into consideration of (e), which will be the topic of the next chapter.

ABSOLUTE, UNCHANGING AND UNIVERSAL?

a) A full response to this objection would require consideration of whether there can be absolute moral rules, and this in turn would require a distinction between what seem to me to be two rather different (though not unrelated) construals of 'absolute' (cf. *Teaching about Values*, pp. 38–39). 'Absolute' can mean 'not relative to anything': this is, I think, the sense in which Kant conceives the categorical imperative as absolute (though the term, so far as I am aware, is not his). The categorical imperative is not even relative to human nature, since it would apply to any rational beings. More often perhaps, in ordinary speech, 'absolute' is used to mean 'without exception'.[2] Some people who want to defend a morality of rules may want to defend exceptionless rules along with this, but I see no need to. Our ordinary concept of rules does not imply that they are absolute: this is shown by the fact that we have in common usage the idea of an exception to a rule (as opposed to a violation). Without further argument as to why morality must be special in this respect, it is possible that morality(n) is a set of rules to which there can in special circumstances be exceptions. And this too is an idea that is common in ordinary conceptions of morality (one of the commonest reactions of students to a presentation of Kantian ethics is to point out circumstances in which it seems that there might be a justified exception to, for instance, the rule that one must not tell a lie).

b)   That rules can change is a familiar fact in many contexts. So the idea of morality(n) as a set of rules is not (without further argument) committed to these rules being unchanging. Indeed *prima facie* there is reason to think (with Cupitt in the passage quoted in Chapter 2) that they are likely to change. The root idea of morality(n) was of checks on tendencies which in some sense 'come naturally' (the scare quotes are essential). But human beings, as part of nature, live in an environment, both natural and humanly manipulated, which is changing. If the environment changes so much that 'natural' tendencies which once would have been dangerous are no longer dangerous then (I am tempted to say 'naturally') one would expect the elements of morality(n) to change. (This is roughly the kind of account which many people would give of the way in which contraception has changed the rules of 'sexual morality'.)[3]

Of course, if moral rules can change we need some account of how they can change. Since this question is closely bound up with the question of the authority of morality(n), I shall defer it until I discuss that.

c)   The idea that moral rules are universal often comes in the same package (labelled 'Kantian') with the ideas 'absolute' and 'unchanging'.[4] No more than the other ideas is it a necessary part of the notion of morality as a set of rules. Remember that morality(n) has a similar function to that of law. The idea of law (the positive law of states) is clearly not undermined by the fact that it is not universal.

Of course, to return to a distinction made in Chapter 4, the Kantian (and in many respects the Christian) conception is that the moral law is universal, and this idea is held in conscious distinction from the idea of the positive law of states. But the notion of morality(n) as such is not committed to this.

Interestingly, it is also possible to see morality, on the dimension of local to universal, as closer to the *local* than positive law is. This is because in a modern plural state, the law at least applies to everyone under the jurisdiction of that state,[5] whereas (on certain relativist views) morality may vary from culture to culture within one state, or (on certain sorts of subjectivist view) it may even vary from one individual to another.

The most viable conception of moral norms in the foreseeable future, fitting with the notion of morality(n), may well see them as not very different in scope from actual law. That is, any set of moral norms will be the norms of a society, though its elements will often in fact, but not necessarily, be universally held. It is a communitarian truism, now increasingly recognised by liberals, that human beings are not brought up (merely) as members of the human race, but as members of a particular society. It is the norms of a society, whether moral or legal, which they are, first and foremost, initiated into. Some moral norms may indeed be widely, and progressively more widely, shared across many societies, for intelligible reasons (just as legal systems also, with increasing globalisation, may tend towards increasing similarities); but it will still be true that what the child first learns is 'this is what we do (here)' or 'this is not done (here)' rather than 'this is how anybody, anywhere should behave towards anybody, anywhere'.[6]

RULES AND REASONS

From the point of view of recent mainstream moral philosophy (at least in the Anglo-American tradition), objection (d) probably raises the most fundamental issues. Does reference to a rule tell us *why* something is wrong (or right)? If not, what are the rules for?

The basic point behind the objection can be put like this. If something is wrong, there are reasons why it is wrong. These reasons may or may not apply also to any other instances which are similar in certain ways (many philosophers, including myself, think that reasons have an inherent generality; but Dancy (1993) argues against this, and some feminist positions perhaps reject it without a great deal of argument). If there is a rule against something then, if the rule is not simply ungrounded, like the taboos to which MacIntyre (1981, pp. 105–16) refers, there will be this rule *because* the kind of conduct to which it refers is wrong; the conduct will not be wrong *because* of the rule. Any reasons we can give for the wrongness of killing will be reasons against killing in any individual case, and will also be reasons for a rule against killing; but 'because there is a rule against it' will not itself be a reason why killing is wrong.

Mary Warnock (1977, p. 138) goes so far as to say 'a rule against bullying or theft would be an absurdity'. In the context, she means that it would be absurd for a school to put in its list of rules 'there is to be no bullying' or 'there is to be no theft'. To me, this is not obviously absurd, but that is a point I shall eventually return to in Chapter 13. Warnock's underlying point is the one we are concerned with now, and this relates to morality(n), whether or not it applies to school rules: 'A rule against bullying or theft . . . would suggest that . . . apart from the existence of the rule, there might be nothing against bullying or theft' (*ibid.*).

Geoffrey Warnock makes much the same point, explicitly referring to a putative analogy between morality and law. On a certain interpretation of this analogy 'just as something illegal would not *be* illegal if the legal rule in question did not exist, so something morally wrong would not *be* morally wrong if the moral rule in question did not exist' (1971, p. 57).[7] This, as he says, does not seem right. But while Warnock has shown here a point at which the analogy between law and morality breaks down, this seems to me not to undermine a possible deeper analogy: that both morality and law might involve rules *which can be seen to have a certain kind of underlying rationale.*

The disanalogy perhaps occurs because there is a distinct process by which laws are made but no such process by which moral rules can be made (this point will be relevant again in Chapter 12 when I am discussing the kind of authority that rules can have). So although the same reasons which could underpin a moral rule might also in many cases be able to underpin a law, it is not possible to say that the law exists until it has been made, and if a law has been made for quite other reasons, it still exists. In the case of morality, if we are to speak of moral rules at all, we will want both to look at actual practice — what is recognised, taught and so on within a given society — to establish whether certain rules exist, and also to look at the reasons behind the rules, to know whether they are to be counted as *moral* rules.[8]

If the analogy between law and morality(n) still holds in terms of the underlying functions they serve, then the essential point which I take both Warnocks to be making still holds. There will be no reason for counting certain rules as part of morality(n) if they cannot be seen as serving the underlying values and interests which morality(n) protects and promotes; when something is wrong, in the context of morality(n), it will not be wrong *because it breaks a rule* but because of its relation to the values and interests which underlie morality(n).

There are complications to be considered. One concerns the difference between regulative and constitutive rules; another concerns the extent to which the reason for a rule has to be understood.

REGULATIVE AND CONSTITUTIVE

Discussions of morality(n) commonly treat moral rules as regulative, that is, as regulating, directing and putting constraints on conduct which could go on independently of the rules. To put it crudely, it is possible, prior to or independently of the existence of the moral rules, for people to ignore others, aid others, injure others, and so on. The rules come in to tell people whether or not they should do these things.

Standish in *Teaching Right and Wrong* (p. 52), referring to the distinction between regulative and constitutive rules,[9] says 'to imagine that morality is centrally a matter of regulative rules gets the whole landscape wrong. The regulative comes to usurp the place of meaning in our moral geography, covering it over with abstract grid lines of control'.

The point that Standish expresses in terms of 'meaning in our moral geography' is an important one. A lot of morality, or ethics, is a matter of giving shape to lives. The biological make-up of human beings by itself leaves open a vast range of ways of behaviour. Even if evolutionary psychology succeeds in explaining some of the ways in which patterns of behaviour emerge, it cannot by itself explain just which particular forms of life will emerge within the range of possibilities. And we know that the range of possibilities is considerable, because all the human forms of life which ever have existed must be compatible with human biological make-up, and it would be implausible to suppose that what has existed so far has already exhausted the possibilities.

Within this vast range, then, what would otherwise be an almost formless landscape is shaped into meaningful contours by the moral geography of particular ways of doing things and particular norms saying what is to be avoided.[10] Standish, then, wants to treat morality essentially as constitutive of forms of life rather than as regulative of basic human behaviour.

It is tempting to think that the distinction between regulative and constitutive rules lines up with the distinction between morality(n) and other areas of morality or ethics. Regulative rules for human conduct would constitute morality(n); lots of constitutive rules, giving particular shapes to human activities, would exist in the wider ethical space. It is not, however, possible to collapse the two distinctions into one; nor does there seem any particular reason, other than a desire for neatness, for trying to do so.

There may be some clear cases of constitutive rules (though the obvious ones, like the rules constituting the games of chess or football, seem to fall outside morality even in the broadest sense); and there may be some clear cases of regulative rules ('do not let your weapon get blunt' in the case of the hunter–gatherer band?). But in many cases between the clear ones it appears that norms regulate human behaviour precisely by constituting one practice rather than another possible practice. Thus as Hampshire (1983) and Nussbaum (1993), for instance, have argued there will always be some norms regulating sexual relationships. In many societies there have been norms constituting the relationship, and institution, of marriage. It is plausible to see the rule against adultery, for instance, as constitutive of the institution; but the whole institution has itself performed a regulative function.

Similarly, the rule 'don't break promises' is not plausibly seen as a rule regulating the activities of people who happen to have made promises: it is rather a constitutive element of the practice of promising. At the same time, the whole practice of promising serves a regulative function in human affairs, bringing a degree of structure and predictability where these would otherwise be lacking. Thus it can be seen as contributing to the function of morality(n) just as surely as a norm against killing.[11]

A significant difference between the two cases just considered seems to be, not the distinction between the regulative and the constitutive, but the difference of degree in how much scope for variation there is, compatibly with the function of morality(n). It seems unlikely that any set of norms which had developed to serve the functions of morality(n) would not incorporate in some form the practice of promising. There seems, in contrast, scope for considerable variation in what sort of practices relating to sexual relations might be incorporated into a set of norms.

To be more systematic, I would suggest that among the prevailing norms of a given society we might find at least the following four kinds of relationship which a norm might hold to underlying reasons for the norm.

There are cases (1) like the norms against killing and assault causing serious injury, where there are generally clear enough considerations against the action itself which would hold even if no general rule had been formulated.

At the opposite end of the spectrum, hence numbered (4), there are norms which, viewed in relation to the underlying point of morality(n), will seem no more than taboos. (I am old enough to remember a time when many people in England viewed the length of a man's hair with something tantamount to moral fervour.)

The awkward cases are between the ends of the spectrum. Closer to (4) are cases where wide variation in the norms between one culture and another seems possible, since morality(n) does not dictate any particular set, but some set of norms rather than none at all may be necessary. Many people have viewed norms about sexual relationships in this way (whereas on hair length there probably does not have to be any norm at all). This will be category (3).

Similar in some ways to category (3) will be cases in category (2) where there actually seem to be good reasons, of a consequentialist kind, for one particular set of norms (or some set within a narrow range), but where the connection between individual acts and the underlying purposes of morality(n) is looser than in (1). Some people have argued that, rather than monogamous marriage being just one among many possible sets of norms for sexual relationships, it is the best available on consequentialist grounds, because of the effects regarding stability in the upbringing of children and so on. My own argument does not require me to take a view on this, but suppose for the moment that it is right. Then a society has reason to try to uphold norms of monogamy. But that fact itself seems to give only a weak reason to any individual for going along with the norms. I shall come back to this point in Chapter 13 when considering the ways in which norms can be criticised and changed.

As regards norms against violence, it is tempting to put all of them in category (1), along with rules against killing and against assault which causes serious injury. But perhaps this can only be done if the concept of violence is normatively defined so that '(physical) violence' stands to 'forceful physical contact' rather as 'murder' stands to 'taking human life': that is, violence will be forceful physical contact which is wrong, as murder is wrongful taking of life (the word 'killing' has itself come often to carry the normative connotations of 'murder', but not invariably so).

If violence, then, is normatively defined, any culture will have norms against it. But we cannot say that any culture must have norms ruling out any kind of forceful physical contact between one person and another. Some cultures or subcultures may be more 'physical' in their interactions (especially perhaps between young males) than others; some cultures may look benignly on play-fighting between young children which arguably is analogous to the play-fighting of the young of many mammalian species (including kittens and puppies). The culture which has in its language a term like 'rough and tumble' is a culture which at least in the past has taken that sort of benign view.

My argument here is *not* that because certain cultures take a benign view of certain activities, these activities must be all right morally. My argument is that the fact that there are cultural variations shows that it is not *obvious* what the rules should be: hence that there is scope for an attempt consciously to work out the rules, a point to which I shall return in Chapter 14.

RULES AND UNDERSTANDING

That a rule serves the general function of morality(n) does not by itself imply that the rule must be understood *as serving that function* by all those (or even any of those) who follow it. Rather in the way that religious rules prohibiting certain dietary practices might in fact serve functions of nutrition or hygiene, rules which are understood as commands of God or even rules which are simply seen as taboos (cf. MacIntyre, 1981, pp. 105–106) could be part of morality(n) if they in fact serve its functions. In that case, the fact that an act is against the rule (or is *taboo*) might be all the reason against the act which those following the rule could actually offer.

In such a case, although the existence of the rule, and the fact that the rule is followed (whatever the reasons for people's following it) may together serve a social function, the extent of understanding of the rule (within the community concerned) is clearly limited. But if a society is to have a shared morality which incorporates a shared understanding of the nature of that morality, we can hardly include *rules whose rationale is not understood* among the contents of that understanding. (If we did, we would be going for something like Plato's noble lie; I shall in effect be arguing in Chapter 12 that in such a case the rule could not be granted the kind of authority that a moral rule needs.)

In an educational context, we have to consider whether rules whose rationale is not understood can be part of the content of education. Perhaps such rules can be inculcated early on, but an education which in general encourages critical reflection cannot insulate particular rules from reflection. Arguably, it is not just education but the whole cultural climate of late modernity which encourages critical reflection (*pace* the kind of argument associated with Marcuse's (1969) notion of '*repressive toleration*'); in that case, Williams's (1985, Chapter 9) point about there being no route back from reflection applies: we cannot go back to rules unquestioningly accepted, even if we did (on reflection) consider that the purposes of morality(n) would be better served by rules unquestioningly accepted.

So far, I have argued that none of the objections from (a) to (d) gives us much reason for rejecting the role of rules in morality. I shall turn in the next chapter to a consideration of moral reasoning. It is worth remarking here that in recent philosophical thinking about moral education there is an unstable relationship between the idea of rules and the idea of reasoning. Sometimes, both reference to rules and the idea of moral reasoning are lumped together in one package (which might be labelled 'rationalistic' or 'cognitive') which is opposed to the package labelled 'ethics of care' or 'virtue ethics' — where the latter package both puts more emphasis on the affective as against the cognitive or rational, and more emphasis on the particular as against the general. In other contexts, reasoning and rules may be seen as opposed to each other; here rules are linked to the general and reasoning is linked to the particular, the idea being that general rules will not by themselves give answers (or will not give appropriate answers) in all particular cases, so that reasoning about the particular has to be done.

In the next chapter, I shall agree that reasoning about particulars does not have to refer to general rules. Having at that point apparently endorsed the view that rules are not needed at all, I shall still have to show reason why, nevertheless, there is a lot to be said for rules.

NOTES

1. Gibbard (1990) works out a naturalistic account of morality in terms of norms about what it is appropriate to feel. His talk of norms for feeling sometimes reads oddly, but is certainly not inconsistent with the usual use of the word 'norm'.

2. On the matter of absolutes in this sense, it is interesting that Anscombe (who is no Kantian) in her critique of law-like conceptions of ethics and defence of attention to virtues also criticises consequentialist thinking precisely because it does not recognise absolutes. (See Anscombe, 1997, p. 35.)

3. I put this in scare quotes because I think that in a sense there is no such thing as sexual morality. Cf. *Teaching about Values*, pp. 64–65.

4. Cf. A. Baier (1985, p. 235), for whom universality is a 'mere Kantian prejudice'.

5. There is, however, beginning to be increased consideration, both in political practice and political philosophy, of the possibility of culturally-differentiated legal systems: cf. Kymlicka (1995) and Young (1990). In an unpublished paper on children's rights I have considered whether plural societies might have to accept cultural differentiation in this respect.

6. Griffin (1996) also argues that morality is rather like law — meaning positive law — instancing the norms relating to matters such as euthanasia. Though he does not explicitly address the point about scope (using in this context, as is so often done in philosophy, the philosopher's rather unspecified 'we') it is a plausible concomitant of his view that there would be a certain culture-relativity about norms on life and death.

7. Warnock does acknowledge the existence of moral rules in a certain sense, but thinks their existence is of no fundamental status. We shall see this in Chapter 10.

8. In societies in which a firm distinction between law and morality had not emerged, this distinction could not apply; and it might indeed be more likely in such societies that there would be talk of something being unlawful even though no law against it had explicitly been made.

9. The distinction itself is by now a commonplace of philosophical terminology. It was possibly first used by Searle (1967), while a related distinction was used by Rawls (1967).

10. Cf. *Teaching about Values*, p. 45 and Hampshire, 1983, Chapter 6.

11. Cf. my comment in Chapter 5 on Warnock's attempt to construe the practice of promising in terms of the virtue of non-deception.

Chapter 9 Rules and Reasoning

GEORGE: A man who sees that he is about to put his foot down on a beetle in his path, decides to step on it or not to. Why? What process is at work? And what is that quick blind mindless connection suddenly made and lost by the man who didn't see the beetle but only heard the crunch? (*Jumpers*, p. 66)

MORE OBJECTIONS TO RULES

Of all the objections to construing morality(n) in terms of rules, those which turn on the nature of moral reasoning, judgement and perception are perhaps the most directly pertinent to education, since they raise the question of whether people can be taught to think morally. The terms 'reasoning, judgement and perception' cover a wide field (deliberately); below I shall sometimes use the term 'moral thought' as a general term which does not prejudge questions such as how explicit the thinking has to be, or whether there has to be some thinking which *precedes* action.

One quite common objection in recent moral philosophy to the model of morality as a set of rules is an objection to a certain model of moral thought.[1] This model is one of deduction of a conclusion about a particular instance from a general rule. Thus:

- Violence is wrong (a universal premise which is known in advance).
- This would be an act of violence (a particular premise, arrived at by seeing that this particular act can be subsumed within the general category of violence)
- Therefore I should not do this.

Such a form of argument could be expressed formally as a syllogism; indeed it can fit the pattern of practical reasoning used by Aristotle in *Nicomachean Ethics* VI.7. The pattern need not be confined to one syllogism at a time. For instance, if it is not immediately obvious that a certain action is a case of violence, this itself might be deduced:

Acts with such-and-such features are acts of violence.
This act has such-and-such features.
. . . and so on.

I shall call this the deductive/subsumptive model of moral reasoning.

That some moral philosophy and philosophical writing on moral education has used such a model is certainly true: see, for instance, K. Baier (1973). Explicitly using an analogy with legal reasoning, which he construes on the deductive/subsumptive model, he argues that legal reasoning should be taught as an element of moral education.

There are several possible objections to the idea that moral thought works on the deductive/subsumptive model. One would be that it is in all circumstances false, since moral thought never works that way. But that is implausible: it is surely not unknown for someone to avoid taking an action because she realises that it would involve breaking a promise, and she believes that promises ought to be kept. Far more plausible is the objection to construing all moral thought on this model, since some moral thought does not take that form. That seems to me certainly true, as I shall illustrate below. A third objection, which I shall call here the Standish objection, holds that in so far as we do try to follow, and to teach, a deductive/subsumptive model we shall be going wrong by obscuring people's responsibility to exercise their own judgement in the complexities of real life: 'clear rules cover over the difficulty that *responsibility* to our circumstances must face. The regulative can seduce us with its formal appeal, seeming to dissolve the messy complexities of our ordinary experience' (Standish in *Teaching Right and Wrong*, p. 52).[2]

A fourth objection, the Smith objection, is that overemphasis on rules and principles 'acts as a standing invitation not only to conceive of moral thinking as a search for the rigid and unvarying guidance of rules. *but to see that search, and the use of rules, as something for special occasions only*: for when we are confronted with a dilemma, or when we are discussing euthanasia or genetic engineering. It obscures the way that the moral dimension colours the whole of our lives.' [emphasis added] (Smith in *Teaching Right and Wrong*, p. 116).

Here, fully conceding the second objection, I shall argue that while in theory moral reasoning could dispense with rules, we can recognise an important role for rules and principles in actual moral thought, while meeting the Standish and Smith objections.

Consider Blum's everyday example (Blum, 1994, pp. 32–3) of the woman giving up her seat to an older woman laden with shopping: 'when Joan perceives the standing woman's discomfort, her offer to help need not be mediated by a rule, principle or precept; she may be acting out of direct compassion, an emotion-based sentiment in which the woman's discomfort is directly taken as a reason for helping.'

In such a case we do not need to say that no kind of thought whatever is involved. There is after all a perception of the woman as being in discomfort, and the woman's discomfort is taken as a reason;

we are not talking about a pure stimulus-response, automatic piece of behaviour. But certainly there need be no spelt-out step-by-step reasoning procedure going on.

There are in fact two important points illustrated by Blum's example:[3] that there need be no reference to a general rule, and that there need be no conscious reasoning process going on. Sometimes it may be assumed that these two points are effectively one, on the basis that when there is a consciously articulated process of reasoning going on, it must be a matter of deducing the particular conclusion from the rule. But this is not so: *even a consciously articulated piece of reasoning need not refer to a general rule.*

GUIDELINES FOR MORAL REASONING

Consider the following set of guidelines for moral reasoning (deliberately expressed in non-technical language, such as could plausibly be used in schools rather than academic journals):

1. *Be aware of the ways in which what you are doing is going to affect other people. Think about this if it is not obvious.*
2. *Try to think yourself into the position of other people affected by what you are doing: try to see what it is like to be in their shoes.*
3. *Think whether they would be likely to agree to what you are doing. Sometimes, the appropriate way of doing this will be to ask them. If that is not possible, you can still ask yourself 'if I were in their position, would I agree to be on the receiving end of the kind of thing which I, now, am thinking of doing?' (E.g. if you have in mind to do something which involves deceiving another person, ask yourself whether you could agree to be deceived in a situation like this.)*
4. *Having seen what it would be like to be in the position of each of the people affected — seeing it, if you can, as if it were happening to you — ask yourself whether you think it is all right for people, in the sort of situation you are in now, to do the kind of thing you are thinking of doing.*[4]

I formulated this set of guidelines on an earlier occasion to show that it could be done: that it is not difficult to construct guidelines for moral reasoning (it being a further question whether there is good reason for anyone to adopt them). This set of guidelines is not, of course, in any important sense original; indeed to anyone familiar with the literature the influence both of Kantian ethics and of utilitarianism will be clear. It is closest perhaps to the moral philosophy of R. M. Hare, who was himself influenced by both Kant and utilitarianism (and hence it might remind some readers of

Kohlberg, who was in turn influenced by Hare in his discussion of Stage 6 reasoning). But there is also in it (in the move from the 'monologic' to the 'dialogic' in step 3) a reference to Habermas, and to the strand in feminist ethics which stresses conversation as the way for moral problems to be resolved (e.g. Noddings, 1984, pp. 132 ff.). Outside of academic writing there is in it something of the everyday question 'what if everyone did that?' That carries in turn echoes of a tradition stretching back to the Golden Rule of the Bible 'do unto others what you would have them do unto you', while something similar is found in many other traditions. This is not surprising, since a form of reasoning which requires people to think about the effects of their actions on others will tend to serve the functions of morality(n).

I am not concerned here with whether this set of guidelines is in some sense 'the correct' model of moral reasoning. If moral reasoning were to be taught as such, then it might be that individual schools, on their own initiative, would develop their own model, or could follow the model above, or some other which is available.[5] Alternatively, if there were to be a national scheme, and appropriate teacher training to back it up, there would have to be convergence on a single model, whether by consensus or by imposition. But my guess is that any model which would be likely to attract sufficient agreement would have to say something about considering the effects of one's actions on others, and it would have to have an affinity with the 'what if everyone did that?' question; and so it would not look totally different from the version above.

I am interested here in the fact that this model of moral reasoning makes no reference to moral rules.[6] In that way it escapes many of the objections that may commonly be raised against any suggestion that moral reasoning might be taught. Moral reasoning in the form suggested does not, so far as I can see, dilute in any way the *concreteness* of thinking about what to do in a particular situation. Much moral reasoning *is* a matter of attending to the actual situation, seeing how people will be affected in this situation, seeing whether these people in this situation could agree to what you are proposing to do — actually asking them and talking it through when possible — and in all of this paying attention to how people will feel, whether they may be hurt, and so on. This seems to me to be just the sort of contextualised thinking that writers such as Noddings or Gilligan, and many other advocates of an ethic of care, have in mind.

A major plank of the objection to general (let alone universal)[7] rules which we find in such writers is that rules cannot be sensitive to the particularities of the individual case (especially, perhaps, in contexts of personal relationships — cf. Blum, 1994). It should be clear that this objection to rules is not an objection to moral reasoning as such. If anything, the emphasis on how much one situation can differ from another, and the emphasis on response to the 'concrete' rather than the 'generalised' other — to use Benhabib's (1992) terminology — show how important moral reasoning (or 'thinking' if that term carries less baggage) is; we would need it much less if we could mechanically apply rules as algorithms.

Does all this mean that moral thought could dispense with rules altogether? There are various accounts by which this is possible: not only that given by some of the writers on an ethic of care, and not only Dancy's particularism, but also Hare's critical moral thinking. Hare (1981) shows that it is possible to carry through a whole piece of moral reasoning in terms of how far people's preferences are satisfied — the preferences, that is, of all who are or who might be affected by one's action. So with sufficient sensitivity to the particular circumstances one would never need to refer to a moral rule (as conventionally understood) at all. And this is a conclusion which might well be congenial to writers such as Cox (quoted in Chapter 2) who are inclined to dismiss the role of rules altogether. On the other hand, it might well be worrying to others, who might want to say, in effect, that it is all very well for people to do their own moral thinking so long as they only do it within the framework of the rules (the kind of view which Cox was rejecting).

People who think it vital to keep the framework of rules may want this because they are afraid that if people do their own thinking they will go off the rails. In some quarters, existing oddly alongside an insistence on educational standards, there is a suspicion of people *thinking* (very much, or for themselves) when it comes to morality (see Chapter 12 below). But the most fervent critics of 'relativism' or 'subjectivism' would hardly need to worry about people doing their own moral thinking, if they were doing it in something like the way suggested here. Suppose the question were 'Is it all right to assault an old man in the street for fun?' Is there any room for doubt that someone following the kind of reasoning suggested above would come to the answer 'No'? If people had been taught a rule (say, 'don't assault people for fun') could that make it any more certain that the answer would be no?

At this point in my own argument I have tried to answer a number of objections to moral rules; but far from showing that moral rules are necessary, I have granted that there is at least a theoretical possibility of our managing without them altogether. I need, then, to consider in what way, after all there is still a role for them.

HOW RULES AND PRINCIPLES CAN WORK

Consider a person who, about to take some action which in itself seems perfectly innocuous, or even morally desirable, realises that taking this action is going to make it impossible to fulfil some — initially quite unconnected — promise she has made. (In the complexities of real life, it may have been far from obvious that there would turn out to be this incompatibility.) If the deductive/subsumptive model were all there could be to moral thought, the reasoning would have to go: this would be breaking my promise, therefore I must not do it — end of question.

If this really were all there were to it in the particular case, the person could probably have got to the same conclusion — that she ought not to do the action — by a form of reasoning more like that mentioned above, in which a general rule does not figure at all. Does this mean there is no point in a rule? It does not. Rules have a degree of convenience that a more discursive process of reasoning does not have. The advantage this brings is not the saving of labour to the agent as such. If that were all, we could say 'people ought to be prepared to do a bit more thinking', and no doubt often that is right. But people will not always have time to do the extra thinking. If they do, they will not in fact always be prepared to do it; and if they do it, they will sometimes not do it very well or will go in for special pleading (cf. Hare, 1981, p. 38). From the point of view of the function of morality(n), it may well be better that there are recognised rules than that people always have to do their own thinking from scratch (I shall say more on the importance of the rules being socially recognised in the next chapter).

Now suppose that our example of the promise-breaking is more complicated, and that there are more factors to be considered. The person will now have realised a factor which she takes as relevant to her considerations; that may be the beginning of further thinking rather than the end of it. She may take the breaking of the promise to be *prima facie* wrong,[8] she may also think of other moral rules which seem to count in a different direction, and she may be aware of special circumstances which do not fall under any established rule. She will treat the possible breaking of the promise as one factor among others, and will try to think what is the best thing to do overall in the circumstances (this could sound like utilitarian reasoning, but what I have in mind is more the kind of contextual thinking which the proponents of an ethic of care write about; it is interesting that accounts of this can indeed come out sounding like utilitarian reasoning).

This is the point at which it will be helpful to bring in explicitly the terminology of principles as well as that of rules. A distinction between these is not consistently marked in ordinary language, but has been used by some writers in the philosophical literature. The distinction seems to me to be one worth marking, though the difference will be one of degree (I shall return to the terminological points in the next chapter).

I shall say that rules are relatively specific prescriptions for conduct, such as 'don't tell lies' or 'don't hit people'. The more concrete and specific they are, the more it may be possible for them to be used in a way approaching the algorithmic, but such possibilities will always be very limited. If the need for moral thought is granted at all, there are going to be the possibilities both of recognising sometimes that what a rule requires is indeterminate, and of recognising sometimes that it is better to make an exception to the rule. Only further thought will be able to deal with these possibilities, and the further thought is likely to bring in principles.

I shall say that a principle is a more general consideration which is to be treated as relevant in any moral thinking.[9] Examples of principles in this sense are 'respect for persons', 'fairness' and 'consideration of interests'. Clearly these are not rules in the sense of specific prescriptions for action. How, then, could they function? Recall that the model of moral reasoning I proposed above began: *Be aware of the ways in which what you are doing is going to affect other people. Think about this if it is not obvious.*

In thinking about how one's conduct will affect others one needs some basis by which to count the effects on others as relevant or irrelevant, good or bad. After all, some effects on people may simply not matter. If I keep in mind such considerations as fairness and respect, then I have an idea of what I am looking for. This does not necessarily mean that one is rehearsing principles to oneself, let alone trying to deduce determinate conclusions from them. But even where the thinking in question is at its most situated and contextual, as in many of the situations which writers on an ethic of care focus on, the person in the situation has to see some factors as more salient than others. In this way he or she will be at least implicitly using certain principles (cf. Grimshaw, 1986, p. 209). Using principles of fairness, respect and consideration of interests, though it may sound a rather abstract procedure if expressed in this way, may only mean that in any situation one is trying not to be unfair to people, to respect them and not to hurt anyone if possible — and that seems to me compatible with the most situated and contextualised moral thinking. (The fact that many writers on an ethic of care do not use the terminology of principles may be due to their associating that terminology with a rather simplistic deductive/subsumptive model.)[10]

Since this present discussion is framed within a consideration of morality(n) as being in important ways similar to law, it is worth noting that making the distinction between rules and principles does not undermine but rather reinforces the similarity (and in some respects continuity) between morality and law; indeed a very similar distinction between rules and principles is a major plank in Dworkin's (1977, pp. 22 ff.) account of legal reasoning. Dworkin's argument in outline is that in deciding cases judges cannot entirely be applying rules given in legislation; they sometimes have to appeal to principles which they perceive as being part of the morality underlying the legal system. These will be for the most part principles of justice, widely recognised even if not, at a given time, written into statutes, such as the principle that people should not profit from their own wrongdoing (Dworkin, 1977, p. 23; 1986, pp. 15 ff.).[11]

There is yet a further way in which the analogy between moral and legal reasoning can be developed, beyond the deductive/subsumptive model. The idea that law is a system of rules binding on judges has led some commentators to suggest that when judges exercise their discretion in hard cases, not clearly covered by statute law, they are simply making up the law as they go along. This is analogous to the idea that a moral agent, in a dilemma in which the normal rules do not give a clear answer, can only decide subjectively, i.e. arbitrarily. Dworkin's (1986) response in effect is that in legal reasoning the notion of *what the law is* still functions as a regulative idea. When judges have to decide a case to which written rules and recorded precedent give no clear answer, they will appeal (even if they do not themselves describe it this way) to a broader sense of the purpose of the law and of the values inherent in it. In doing this they are engaging in an interpretive, hermeneutical process, which, far from supposing that any answer is equally valid, presupposes that there is some interpretation which is more defensible than others. It is significant, again, that Dworkin makes the kind of use of hermeneutical ideas, in his writing on legal reasoning, which many recent writers on ethics have been making.

Neo-Aristotelians appealing to *phronesis*, proponents of Gadamerian hermeneutics,[12] and proponents of an ethic of care can all agree that ethical thinking has to be situated and contextualised. That it is contextualised does not show that there is no point in seeking what is the right or the best thing to do; this can function as a regulative idea, a notional goal. Someone in a complicated interpersonal situation, having to weigh up all kinds of factors, aware that it is going to be hard for someone not to get hurt, may well say to herself 'I wish I knew what is the right thing to do' or 'I wish I knew if I was acting for the best'. This does not imply that she thinks there is some deductive/subsumptive process that will turn out an answer at the bottom; it does imply that she does not think she is in a situation where any move is as good as any other and she might as well toss a coin. In recognising that this is so, she is implicitly, even if not explicitly, recognising the salience of factors which will inevitably have salience in other cases than this particular one — factors indeed which would be widely recognised to be salient. The language of principles functions to pick out — for certain purposes, when there is actually point in picking them out and looking at them — just this kind of factor.

Perhaps these arguments will reassure those who think that any reference to rules or principles must immediately shift moral thought onto an abstract plane, away from the concrete and particular level where (in the view of these critics) it should be located. The Standish objection has by now been answered: there need be no derogation from the responsibility of individual judgement which takes full account of circumstances. The Smith objection still needs some attention.

THE PERVASIVENESS OF MORALITY

The idea that 'the moral dimension colours the whole of our lives' and is not something which only obtrudes itself from time to time when we come up against a problem, is a common one within *Teaching Right and Wrong*, and indeed in many arguments critical of rules and favourable towards caring or virtue ethics. Another of the contributors to *Teaching Right and Wrong*, Mary Midgley, has in a different place expressed this idea by saying that getting outside morality is like getting outside the atmosphere (Midgley, 1991, p. 8; on the same theme see also Pincoffs, 1983). It is a thought which I fully endorse. But I question the idea that recognising the salience of rules is in any way incompatible with recognising the all-pervasiveness of morality, and hence of moral thought. It is as if rules were thought only to apply from time to time. But moral rules, on any view I am aware of (including, on the theoretical front, both Kantianism and utilitarianism) apply all the time; so far, then, they are perfectly compatible with the all-pervasiveness of morality. If critics think that reference to rules encourages the idea that the moral dimension only becomes salient from time to time, it must be something else about rules which they have in mind.

Perhaps the idea is that it is, for any one agent, only occasionally that any question of following or not following the rule comes up.[13] Here a lot may turn on what is meant by 'the question comes up'. Perhaps the critics have in mind a rule like 'keep your promises'. If one has made a promise to do something at a particular time, then it is at that time that one has to fulfil one's promise; so it might seem that outside of that time the rule has no salience. Even for a rule of promise-keeping, this is a very limited view. The need to keep a promise may have other implications for how the agent lives his or her life, the acknowledgement of the rule may affect how far someone is or is not willing to enter into promises, and some promises do not have the limited temporary character of, say, promising to return a book on a particular day. Consider, though the example is somewhat culture-bound, the promises involved in marriage. Or consider truth-telling as a moral rule. Since most of us rarely go for more than a few hours at a time without communicating something to someone, the possibility of not telling the truth is constantly there. If we need a rule to tell us not to lie, that rule is one that is constantly salient.

But do we need such a rule? Not in the sense that we have to be constantly articulating it to ourselves. But a rule — or again, a principle — can become internalised, so that we do not constantly have to be reciting it to ourselves, but would nevertheless notice if something we might do was liable to go against it. Following a rule, or not breaking a rule, can become in a certain sense a matter of habit.[14] Something that Peters realised and stressed more clearly than most writers on moral education was that the rules can recede into the background, only occasionally having to be brought to mind. But, as a part of the background, they can still be a vital feature of our moral lives. They mean that we do not have to be constantly thinking about every situation anew, trying all the time to be sensitive to all the features of every situation we are in and responding to it *ab initio*. As Peters (1981, p. 98) put it, 'Surely the importance of established habits in the moral life is manifest. Life would be very exhausting if, in moral situations, we always had to reflect, deliberate, and make decisions.'

Adding only that every situation is a moral situation ('every day is judgement day', as Smith puts it: *Teaching Right and Wrong*, p. 116), we can say that it is only the existence of a background of habit capable of taking us through most of these situations, that frees us to respond seriously and even afresh to situations which really do turn out to demand something more than habit.

This means that while an individual agent may only occasionally refer to rules explicitly, reference to rules *within a philosophical account of the moral life*, far from suggesting that morality is only relevant to 'special occasions' (as in Smith's claim above), actually supports the idea that the moral dimension is all-pervasive.

RULES AND VIRTUES

It might be thought that in saying that rules often recede into the background in an individual's moral life I am almost removing them from the moral landscape after all. But this would be to neglect the large role that rules can still have in public, including public educational, contexts — the topic of the next chapter. Here it is worth saying a little about the relationship between two kinds of account of the moral life which can be expressed using the two different sorts of language we have looked at: a language of virtues and a language of rules. There can seem to be two quite different accounts, if they are expressed this way: on a rule-based account, a person goes (or should go) through life constantly referring to certain rules and consciously following them. On a virtue-based account, a person goes (or should go) through life with a set of dispositions which have already been formed, and in the light of which she recognises the salient features of whatever particular situations she is in and responds accordingly.

It is possible now to see that this contrast is overdrawn. If rules often operate as a background factor then they can be operating within the dispositions of the virtuous agent, as we saw in the case of the virtue relating to anger. If we start, in our account of moral life, from rules, then we have to say that rules cannot be applied mechanically; indeed the agent who has internalised certain rules has to have the sensitivity and judgement to see what is compatible with the rules in the particular circumstances. Thus our account begins to move towards a virtue account. If we start, in our account of the moral life, from virtues, then we have to say that the person who possesses certain virtues will be aware of features of situations which are of general relevance, and will be aware of public expectations in relation to these features; the person of virtue is, after all, far from being a subjectivist. Starting from either end, the two accounts may well converge (see also my remarks on Hursthouse in the next chapter).

Thoughts of this nature presumably underlie White's view that 'the distinction between virtues and rules could well be eroded' (*Teaching Right and Wrong*, p. 23). This ought to be no surprise to anyone thinking about moral education without a preconception that rules and virtues can never meet. Certainly there is a strong precedent in Peters, for though, as I have pointed out, he gave a good deal of attention to rules, he also had a lot to say about virtues (in articles written well before *After Virtue*). And Peters saw his account as being in the tradition of Aristotle, whom he read as arguing that virtues have to be developed through first initiating people into rule-following.

This does not mean that there is no distinction to be drawn between an ethic of rules and an ethic of virtues; it does mean that there is not a great gulf between them. As Griffin (1996, p. 113) puts it:

> Most moral views — indeed all plausible ones — make the virtues important. So that is not enough to qualify those views as a form of what we nowadays call 'virtue ethics'. What is definitive of virtue ethics, as I take it, is that it makes virtues not just important to, but in some sense basic in, the moral structure; they are so deep in the structure that they can be said to generate or to animate the rest of it.[15]

A similar point has been made within philosophy of education by Steutel (1997), who argues that virtually any approach to moral education — including Kohlberg's — could be construed as a virtue approach, but that only some are based in virtue ethics. But the distinction between virtue ethics and other forms, as a distinction about what it is that 'generate[s] or animate[s] the whole of an ethical position' is a distinction within moral philosophy. In considering morality(n) — which by definition would not be the whole of anyone's ethical life — we need a language which is susceptible of broad public understanding and agreement. In the light of the last few chapters we can see, I think, that while a language of virtues must have a place, the primary language for public moral discourse is likely to remain one of norms (including both rules and principles), though some of these norms will themselves refer to feeling and motivation. It is time now to attempt something like an overview of the public role of moral norms, beginning with their place in moral education.

NOTES

1. For this objection see, for example, Pincoffs (1983) and Schneewind (1983).
2. By 'responsibility to our circumstances' Standish presumably means something like 'responsiveness to circumstances'. It is a point worth making (in line with Sartre) that no one has responsibility *to* (as opposed to 'for') the rules as such; but to speak of responsibility *to* the circumstances is no better. One has a responsibility *to* other persons, and that responsibility includes both responding to circumstances and also not neglecting to consider, though not slavishly obeying, the rules that the other persons recognise and therefore expect one to follow. Within a religious framework, one might also have responsibility to God. By extension from responsibility to other persons, one may have responsibility to animals, and even conceivably to the environment. But if we speak of our responsibility *to* (as opposed to *for*) the environment, it is as if we are supposing that the environment can call us to account, because responsibility in the present sense is very close to accountability (see Haydon, 1978).
3. Later in the same chapter Blum analyses in detail the elements which make up the moral thought that may be involved even in quite simple exercises of moral appraisal and behaviour.
4. This set of guidelines is taken without alteration (except that I have added numbers) from a conference paper, forthcoming as Haydon (1999d).
5. John Wilson (1990) has provided a much more detailed account, influenced by similar sources.
6. While they do not themselves refer to any first-order moral rules, these guidelines, or something like them, could themselves be seen as constituting a set of moral norms. That is, it could well be considered that thinking morally in something like this way (and taking the trouble to do so) is not optional, but is itself a moral requirement — especially in situations where no clear application of first-order rules is to be had.
7. It is perhaps unfortunate that the distinction between 'general' and 'universal' which Hare (e.g. 1981, p. 41) drew has not been more widely recognised. The distinction will be illustrated in the next chapter (note 3).
8. The use of the term 'prima facie' in this context is owed to Ross (1930, 1939), whose position is discussed by Dancy (1992, 1993).
9. Among writers who have made the distinction in something like this way are Beauchamp and Childress (1989), Grimshaw (1986) and Peters (1966).

10. In developing his particularism, Dancy (1993) gives a role to principles, arguing that 'a moral principle amounts to a reminder of the sort of importance that a property *can* have in suitable circumstances'. Dancy treats this rather as if it is his own suggestion, but it has surely been anticipated by Peters, and indeed by many others: the difference being (only?) that whereas Peters would say that the considerations picked out by principles such as fairness or consideration of interests are always relevant, Dancy wants to say that they are likely to be relevant, but that we cannot know in advance that they will always be relevant. This enables Dancy to stick to his particularism, but rather at the expense of plausibility.

11. Much of the prevalent modern rhetoric of rights, I would suggest, functions in a similar way. While for some purposes it is important to distinguish, as analytic philosophers have been wont to do, between moral and legal rights, the notion of human rights functions at a level of principle in a way that spans both legal and moral thinking. It is worth considering, though I shall not argue the point here, whether considerations of principle at a similar level of generality may not be particularly important in what has come to be known as 'citizenship education'.

12. Gadamerian i.e. of the kind associated with Hans-Georg Gadamer. The best introduction to this, in an educational context, that I know of is the unpublished PhD thesis of Steve Bramall, London University Institute of Education.

13. Even if this were so, it would not diminish the social importance of rules, which will be my concern in the next chapter.

14. Cf. Peters (1981), pp. 95–104.

15. He adds that virtue ethics need not make virtues fundamental in the whole structure of *values*. The point is similar to one I made in Chapter 4 about morality(n). Both our thinking about norms and our thinking about virtues have their point or meaning by their relation to what matters in life.

Chapter 10 The Public Role of Moral Norms

> GEORGE: ... social and psychological conventions which we have evolved in order to make living in groups a practical possibility, in much the same way as we have evolved the rules of tennis, without which Wimbledon Fortnight would be a complete shambles, do you see?
> (*Jumpers*, p. 48)

RULES IN MORAL EDUCATION

The role of rules in moral education has often been recognised by moral philosophers, but sometimes with the implication that this role is rather unimportant from the moral philosopher's point of view. Thus Geoffrey Warnock (1971, p. 51):

> It is often said, reasonably enough, that the moral education of children at any rate may include, at a certain stage, the promulgation to them by parents and teachers of rules for their conduct on certain moral matters.... However, if it is to be admitted that there are moral rules in *this* sense, it must surely be added at once that they are of no great theoretical importance.

They are of no great theoretical importance because, as Warnock goes on to argue, the need for such rules rests only on the contingent fact that children at a certain stage are incapable of appreciating the underlying moral reasons for behaving in one way rather than another.[1] This is perhaps enough to show the relativity of 'theoretical importance'; what is unimportant to the Oxford moral philosopher of a certain era may be rather central to the theorist of moral education. Schneewind's summary of the attitude of some proponents of virtue ethics seems to apply also to Warnock: 'We may educate children into virtue by teaching them some simple rules, but mature moral agents do not need them' (Schneewind, 1997, p. 179).

This invites the obvious riposte 'what about the immature ones?' Even if it were true that a degree of moral maturity removed the need for rules, this can hardly be a matter of only peripheral interest for philosophy of education. Philosophy of education needs to enquire into what might be meant by 'immature' and 'mature' in this context. The term suggests a development over time, and certainly many theorists of moral education have subscribed to the view not only that individuals over time come to be more able to make rational moral judgements, but also that some individuals get further in this development than others. This sort of view may be especially associated with Kohlberg, but Peters also subscribed to it: 'a great number of people do not develop to a rational level of morality' (1981, p. 157). How far one subscribes to this view — how great one thinks the number of people is who do not develop to a rational level — partly depends of course, on how much is written into the notion of 'rational'.

If we are interested in promoting a shared public understanding of morality, we will want the understanding in question to be widely distributed; hence we will also want it to be of such a nature that it can be widely distributed. Some trade-off between depth and breadth of understanding may be unavoidable. Thus if we were to interpret 'the public understanding of morality' in such a way that no one counts as understanding morality who is not able to follow and understand the arguments of Kant's *Groundwork*, we might find that this understanding is very narrowly spread — which would defeat the object of promoting public understanding. At the other extreme, if we were to aim at no more than the ability to recite certain received rules in a standard formulation, while we might find this aim could be achieved across a broad band of the population, there would be little ground for claiming that we were promoting understanding.

There would be no good grounds for trying to limit public understanding to either a language of norms or a language of virtues, particularly given the interactions and overlaps that we have seen between the different forms of evaluation. But it is my contention that a language of norms will have a certain priority if we are to have a way of talking about morality which can be publicly accessible and transparent without being too simplistic. (But the norms will be of a variety of kinds, including some which refer to feeling and motivation.) In my conclusion I shall argue further that as norms come both to be widely shared and *to be seen to be widely shared*, and as people come to be able to realise and articulate just what is shared and where there are differences, these developments will be constitutive of *the moral development of society*.

Given a concern with shared public understanding we can see additional reason for putting some weight on rules, as articulated norms of conduct, in moral education. Whatever the outcome of the debate about how far rules are needed in the moral development and education of each individual (cf. Baier, 1985, pp. 222 ff. for a contrary view to Peters's), they provide a means by which a degree of convergence between the moral education of different individuals can be expected. They may not be the only conceivable means; it is possible that a society making considerable use of a language of virtues could have a publicly-acknowledged consensus on the virtues which it expects parents and other carers to try to engender in children. But as I have already suggested in Chapter 5, there are reasons to think, at any rate in a large and diverse society, that a language of virtues may be less effective in this respect. In any case, if Hursthouse (1996, p. 27) is right, even people thinking primarily in terms of virtues would be likely to use rules of conduct in the moral upbringing of young children.

> Why should a proponent of virtue ethics deny the significance of such mother's-knee rules as 'Don't lie', 'Keep promises', 'Don't take more than your fair share', 'Help others'? . . . Virtue ethicists want to emphasise the fact that, if children are to be taught to be honest, they must be taught to prize the truth, and that *merely* teaching them not to lie will not achieve this end.[2] But they need not deny that to achieve this end teaching them not to lie is useful, even indispensable.

The point, then, about teaching rules to young children is not just that it takes them through a certain necessary stage of development individually; it is that, if the same publicly-acknowledged rules are taught to all children, this makes it more likely that there will, as those children grow up, be a publicly-shared morality. And to the extent that there is a publicly-shared morality at any one time, it will be more likely that parents will bring up their children in that morality, and so on from generation to generation (I have yet to consider the ways in which the rules can change). The society in general, however, has no way of ensuring that all parents will bring up their children in the same set of rules (though parentship classes might make a difference); thus it will fall to formal education to attempt to back up, take forward and supply deficiencies in what parents have done.

It is perhaps not necessary to argue at length about why it is desirable that there should be a publicly-shared morality. If it is desirable that there should be morality(n), it is desirable that it should be widely acknowledged, or it will not be able to do its job. Part of its job is, of course, to counteract various selfish or thoughtless motivations by which individuals might act in ways detrimental to others or to co-operation with others. But this task is not carried out only by individuals responding directly to the requirements of morality(n); it also happens partly through individuals being aware of the expectations of other people — provided those expectations have themselves been formed in accordance with morality(n). The norms of morality(n) may be initially transmitted through education, but they can also be reinforced through being referred to whenever appropriate in the discourse of adult members of the society. Part of the way in which this happens is through criticism.

CRITICISM

Criticism itself, of course, is viewed by many people as suspect; to make any moral criticism of another is viewed as being 'judgmental' or 'moralistic'. The situation is well brought out by Midgley (1991, p. 1):

> '*But surely it's always wrong to make moral judgements?*'
> This . . . was spoken ardently and confidently, with no expectation that it might be questioned . . . a moral platitude, something so obvious that it need only be mentioned to be accepted.

Suppose A criticises B for being moralistic or judgmental in criticising C. A is undeniably making a criticism herself. Can she offer any interpretation of her own conduct by which it escapes from the self-referential application of her own norm that one should not criticise? She might try this: what is wrong with B's criticism of C is that B is appealing to norms which he, B, holds but which other people, including C, may not share. A, however, in criticising B for making this sort of criticism, takes herself to be appealing to a norm which she believes to be publicly shared — namely that one should not make criticisms of others which are based on norms which are *not* publicly shared.

If this kind of analysis is on the right lines, then even someone who is wary of being moralistic or judgmental can acknowledge that there is a role for criticism *which refers to norms which are publicly shared*. And it is hard to see how morality(n) could function without the possibility of such criticism. Morality(n) loses its point if it makes no difference to people's conduct. And one of the ways in which it makes a difference to people's conduct is *via* reference to its norms in interpersonal communication.

Suppose I say to you 'You shouldn't do that; it would be breaking your promise.' This is criticism, albeit criticism of a proposed action which you have not yet taken. It is intended to make a difference to what you do, by appealing to a norm which I assume you already recognise (there is also an assumption here that you might be *moved* by the thought that the action is against the norm — this raises questions about motivation and recognising the authority of norms which I shall take up in the next two chapters). The reason why I can assume that you already recognise this norm — even if I do not have any special knowledge of you personally — is that I take the norm to be publicly recognised.

Suppose instead that I criticise some action you have already taken. Is this pointless, because it can no longer affect your future conduct? Not necessarily, because the fact that one action of yours has been criticised might affect the likelihood of your doing something similar in future. Notice that in making such a criticism, whether of past or possible future action, there are various things I need not be doing. I need not be taking a stance of moral superiority. I am appealing to a norm which I take to be shared; I acknowledge tacitly, and might acknowledge explicitly, that it applies to me as well. I am not claiming that I have never gone against this norm myself. Thus, I am not *necessarily* being hypocritical (the fear of being judged hypocritical may be one common reason for reluctance to criticise). I am also not condemning you as a person. And I am not claiming to have the last word on the matter. I can be willing to listen to your response, 'Yes, I know it's breaking a promise [here you acknowledge that you do recognise the norm], but in the circumstances . . .', and you may well be right.

This is not to say that it is desirable for people to go around constantly criticising each other. And it is not to deny that when criticism is made there are better and worse ways of doing it. To judge when it is appropriate to criticise, and when it is not, to see how to do it and in what words (if in words at all); and if in words, to do it in the right tone of voice, and so on, requires all the *phronesis* and sensitivity which any neo-Aristotelian, particularist or proponent of an ethic of care could wish for. No wonder, then, that some people might prefer to treat 'never criticise anyone' as an exceptionless rule. But the norms of morality(n) not only need to be learned, which will inevitably involve parents and others sometimes saying to children 'You shouldn't do that' or 'You shouldn't have done that' and explaining why; they also, as I suggested above, need to be reinforced, even for adults. And these last two points come together, since if children were never aware of norms being used by adults in criticism of adults, morality could come to seem to children to be an imposition by adults, which they could shake off when they themselves become adults.

There can be no sharp cut-off point here between education and the rest of life. And this in practice means that a willingness both to offer and receive criticism which is intended in a constructive spirit is desirable throughout life. What goes with this is a disposition to consider whether one's own conduct is justifiable in relation to public-acknowledged norms, and to be prepared to discuss with others whether it is or not. One of the problems about anger, as mentioned in Chapter 7, is that the angry person, focusing his or her attention on a perceived slight to himself or herself, can too easily lose sight of the public norms by which the angry reaction might be shown to be or not to be justified.

The *public* aspect of norms, then, is vital as a basis for criticism which is not to be purely 'personal' in the sense of *ad hominem* (which may well be resented as such). The need for a publicly-acknowledged reference point does not rule out an appeal to virtues as a basis for criticism, and we often do criticise in this language. ('That was mean of you'; 'You could have been more generous', and so on.) But there are difficulties in criticising on the basis of virtue-assessments. It may be unclear, and not necessarily publicly agreed, how high a standard is being expected, or where the mean in some quality is (cf. Chapter 7). And we cannot assume that any one virtue is equally easy for one person to acquire as for another; to that extent, criticising a person for not possessing a given virtue can appear unfair. Publicly-acknowledged rules of conduct, on the other hand, set up a standard that we assume everyone is capable of meeting (though we may also acknowledge mitigating circumstances, on which I shall say more in the next chapter).

These points on the role of criticism show part of the sense in which morality(n) is, as it is sometimes put, a matter of public morality. But it is important that this public morality does not apply only in what might be called public life (recall that in the last chapter I endorsed the all-pervasiveness of morality). So publicly-acknowledged norms can provide a basis for criticism even within close personal relationships. This is certainly an area where care is needed. It can become too easy to criticise (why otherwise would it have become 'a moral platitude' that one ought not to?). People can get into the habit of doing it all the time, and that habit can ruin relationships. But it is just because of the dangers of indiscriminate criticism within personal relationships that the distinction between norms which are publicly shared and standards which might be particular to an individual, or to a background the individual shares only with certain others, can be vital. It is, for instance, the distinction between 'You should not have said that because it was a lie' and 'You should not have said that because it's not the sort of thing my parents would have said'.

In a plural society, many relationships, whether entered into through choice or not (the latter for instance will include many relationships between work colleagues), will be between people who do not necessarily share the same background of assumptions about values and goals. It cannot be assumed that they will agree on all issues of values; if we are thinking of morality or ethics in the broadest sense, the sheer range of possibilities is so great that total agreement is likely to be the exception. Part of the role of morality(n) is to provide a set, in effect, of working assumptions which all parties can be assumed to share. In many past societies arguably the existence of such shared working assumptions could be left to look after itself; it would seem rash now to assume that it can be.

NORMS, RULES AND PRINCIPLES

I have been arguing that a language of norms is suitable for the maintenance of a publicly-shared morality(n). I also said above that goals for public understanding should be neither too simplistic nor too ambitious. I shall argue here, and indeed in the rest of this book, that something more than just shared acknowledgement of a list of norms, all on the same level, should be possible — not only because some norms may rightly be seen as more important than others, but also because different sorts of norm stand in a different relationship to people's conduct.

At this point I need to return to some issues of terminology, because education for public understanding of morality will have to address some important distinctions and hence will have to consider the terms in which they may be expressed and by which they may potentially be obscured. It may well be, for example, that if there were greater consistency in the marking of a difference between rules and principles there would be less confusion about whether there can or cannot be *absolute* rules (or principles).

I have been using the word 'norms' as the broadest of the terms 'norms', 'rules' and 'principles', broad enough to include conventions which may not be verbalised. We can imagine, for instance, that in the early human society mentioned in Chapter 4 certain conventions or expectations might have become established before the language had even developed in which it would have been possible to articulate them. Though usage of the terms is probably neither fixed nor consistent, we are more likely to speak of rules when we have in mind norms that can be and sometimes, perhaps often, are articulated in words, particularly if they are expressed grammatically as imperatives. (This may also be why the word 'rule' may be more likely than 'norm' when philosophers are making comparisons with law.)

I also introduced in the last chapter the distinction between rules and principles, where a principle is a broader, more general consideration, while a rule is more specific in its action-guiding force. This distinction is connected, I think, with the fact that we are more likely to speak of a rule when we are dealing with imperative formulations. It is not that the grammatical imperative form cannot be used to express broad principles — for instance, rather than speaking of the principle of non-maleficence (principles are often referred to in this way by a single word or phrase) we can say 'do no harm'; but 'do no harm' is so broad as to give little indication as to what a person is actually to do or not do. In contrast, the imperative 'don't hit anyone' is more specific. There seems more point in the imperative form here, and we are more likely to speak of this prescription as a rule.[3]

I also said that the rule/principle distinction is one of degree. Clearly there are degrees of specificity and generality, and even if we try to use the terms consistently there may well be cases where we are uncertain whether to speak of a rule or a principle (it is also unlikely in such cases that much will hang on which term we use). It also seems possible for the same consideration be treated more as a rule or more as a principle. This can be illustrated by the example used before, of promise-keeping. In simple enough cases, the norm of promise-keeping can function as a rule; it can be straightforwardly followed. In my further development of the example, where the person realised that what she was thinking of doing would amount to breaking a promise, she took this into account as one factor among others. The idea that the breaking of a promise is a negative factor in a situation, something to be avoided if possible, functioned then more in the way I have spoken of principles as operating — it picked out one feature of the situation which was relevant but not conclusive. In other words, it is possible for someone to treat a consideration as a rule or as a principle, depending on how much discretion they see it as allowing.

The linguistic situation, however, is still more complicated, because we have such locutions as 'on principle' (which is different from '*in* principle') and 'as a matter of principle'. If someone says that as a matter of principle they will never do such-and-such, then because of some rather general consideration they are in fact 'making it a rule' (an exceptionless rule) not to do such-and-such. Safety considerations provide an interesting comparison here. Safety in the workplace is a very important principle of great generality. There are times when the chances of safety on a particular occasion will not in fact be compromised if someone does not wear a hard hat on entering a building site (work has finished for the day; there is no piece of equipment installed which is higher than foundation level; the person concerned is only going just inside the perimeter of the site). Nevertheless the rule 'no one is to enter without wearing a hard hat' may be considered one that is to be applied without exception, roughly because if any exceptions are allowed, the risks of someone sometime allowing themselves an exception which turns out to be disastrous are too great.[4] The person going just inside the perimeter may say that as a matter of principle he is going to wear a hard hat (whereas if he said that 'as a rule' he wears a hard hat, he would be suggesting that he would be likely to make an exception from time to time).

A further point is that, as the last chapter should have made clear, we can use the words 'rules', 'principles', or 'norms' — and indeed others, including 'standards' — for what can be internalised. But we are probably more likely to speak of principles or norms, rather than rules, when referring to something which often operates without being consciously verbalised at all.

The point of this excursus into the vagaries of the English language is partly to warn the reader not to be too concerned about thinking up counterexamples to my own use of the terms: there are always going to be counterexamples. A more important point is that education for shared public understanding needs to take account of ordinary usage. It would be too much to expect formal education to promote a completely consistent usage of the words we have been considering. It is not, I think, too much to expect formal education to direct people's attention to the distinction, which still seems to me the fundamental one, between broad considerations which are always relevant but which do not in most circumstances mandate specific forms of conduct, and prescriptions which are fairly specific in what they prescribe or prohibit. With this distinction in place one can also make a distinction within the latter category: between rules to which, when general principles require it, one may make an exception, and rules which, precisely because of the general principles, are to be treated as exceptionless.

ARE THERE ABSOLUTES AFTER ALL?

An interesting consequence of all this is that, if there are any norms which are (to be treated as) absolutes in the sense that no exceptions are ever to be made (cf. the discussion above in Chapter 8), they are either very broad principles or quite specific rules. At the broad end of the spectrum there are principles like 'consider people's interests'; this does not tell us that there cannot be occasions when, for other reasons, it is right to do something which goes against people's interests — so it does not, for instance, tell us that violent action is always wrong — but it does tell us that there are never any circumstances (what kinds of circumstance could they be?) in which one should give no consideration to people's interests at all. (This in turn does not mean that one must be actively at every moment thinking about other people's interests; it does mean that one should always be receptive to the possibility of other people's interests being affected: cf. Scheffler, 1992, p. 32.)

At a similar broad level of generality there are norms which refer to the motivational aspects of actions, not just their externally observable features. Thus one of Griffin's examples of a 'maximally reliable' moral norm is 'don't be cruel'.[5] This does not just mean 'don't cause pain', which would have no plausible claim to be an absolute norm (doctors and dentists could hardly be expected to adhere to this one). It means something like 'don't cause pain for your own satisfaction' (Griffin, 1996, pp. 79–80; McGinn, 1997, pp. 61 ff.). Apart from far-fetched philosophers' constructions, it is more difficult to think of exceptions to this ('sometimes you have to be cruel to be kind' does not mean 'sometimes in order to be kind you have to cause pain for your own pleasure').

At the other end of the spectrum there are likely to be some quite specific rules which have claims to be exceptionless. Consider the following: 'Never shake a baby'. It may not have occurred to you to include this in any list of moral rules.[6] It might seem more like one of Kant's imperatives of skill (*Groundwork*, 1948, p. 79), one variety of hypothetical imperative: 'if you want to look after a baby, never shake it', where the imperative is grounded in knowledge of the dangers in shaking a baby. So one might think that any well-intentioned person in charge of a baby will have the sense not to shake it; assuming either a minimal attitude of care for the baby, or respect for a principle of non-maleficence, or both, the person concerned will avoid the dangerous action.

But, as Kant is well aware, an imperative of skill can equally be turned to different ends: even the grisly: 'if you want to kill a baby, without it being too obvious, try shaking it'. Why not treat the rule itself, 'never shake a baby' as a moral imperative? Even though it is far from being at the kind of broad level of generality and abstraction from context of Kant's own categorical imperative, this could reasonably be taken to be a rule to which no exception is ever to be made. Of course, any philosopher (or any philosopher with a certain sort of training) will easily be able to think up a counter-example: if I do not shake this baby you are going to press the button which will set off the explosion which will trigger the earthquake under the maternity hospital, and so on. But as Hare long ago argued (1981, Chapter 8), the possibility of imagining counterexamples, and even the slight possibility that such a counterexample might one day become reality, is not a good basis for refraining from promulgating a rule as one to which no exception is to be made.

It may be asked what is the point of a rule such as 'never shake a baby', if broader norms such as respect for life and non-maleficence are in place. The point is that the more specific rule may be what is needed in a specific kind of situation. Someone who does have respect for life and who has no wish to do harm may nevertheless not realise that shaking a baby may be so bad; or if he or she has learned of the possible causal connection between shaking and possible injury or death for a baby, may nevertheless not call that connection to mind, under stress, at the appropriate moment. Whereas if that specific rule, 'never shake a baby', has been learned, it may prevent an action which the more general principle would not have prevented.

PRINCIPLES IN PUBLIC DISCOURSE

If that was one end of the spectrum of specificity of rules, at the other end, to come back to that, are the very broad principles such as non-maleficence and consideration of interests. These can have a different kind of function, in that they are publicly acknowledged as reference points. The idea, for instance, of respect for human life often functions in this sort of way. It does not resolve debates about abortion or capital punishment, military responses to terrorism, or how far the police should be armed, but it stands as a factor which serious debate cannot ignore.

A set of four very general principles — beneficence, non-maleficence, respect for autonomy and justice — have been influential in health-care ethics, especially through their advocacy and dissemination by Beauchamp and Childress.[7] In recent years there has been a tendency in that field to give more attention to an ethic of care, and to the virtues which it is desirable that practitioners in health-care should develop. The reasons for the (partial) shift away from a principle-based ethic towards a virtue- or care-based one are the reasons familiar in moral philosophy more generally: that practitioners need to make decisions in all the complexities of concrete situations, responding to the needs of persons, and that the broad principles may give answers which are too abstract, or conflicting or insufficiently determinate.

What is less often noted is that broad principles of the Beauchamp and Childress kind may have an important role in public-policy debate about health-care. The general public — which in a sense, in relation to health-care, includes politicians — are not in the front line of care for patients; they cannot, in the relevant sense, exercise care for patients — or display some of the virtues relevant to doing so — however important they think it that care should be exercised. For the general public, to say that nurses and doctors should be caring people is itself to talk at the level of general principles, which is the only level at which the general public can talk when considering health-care policy.[8] Perhaps some would argue, precisely for this reason, coupled with a distrust of argument at the level of general principles, that all health-care decisions should be left to the practitioners in the front line. But not only would that probably be quite impossible in practice, it would also go against the idea that a liberal democracy requires some sort of public oversight over the work of professionals. Whether that idea must be accepted can in turn be debated; and that debate too will invoke general principles. Discourse at the level of general principles is surely inescapable at public-policy levels.

It is no part of my argument to suggest that if there is public agreement on broad principles there will necessarily be agreement on the details of practice. Broad principles keep open great scope for disagreement, partly because it is rarely possible in any case to deduce specific and incontrovertible conclusions from the principles, and partly because principles on which there is agreement at a verbal level may still be open to very different interpretations.[9]

That principles such as 'respect for human life' are open to different interpretations is not, as I see it, an objection to appealing to such principles, especially if the possibilities of dialogue are taken seriously (cf. Haydon, 1999b). In moral discourse, people *may* discover that they share an understanding of what it is to respect human life; if so, they may go on from there in attempting to reach agreement on more particular matters. Or they may discover that they interpret 'respect for human life' in significantly different ways; but even that will have clarified what is at issue, and so will have constituted a progression in mutual understanding.

Even, then, where differences remain at a deep level (which may be true of some of the differences between certain more-or-less fundamentalist religious outlooks and certain more-or-less godless liberal outlooks), there is the possibility of an increase in mutual understanding. Far from public moral discourse being insubstantial or trivial, it is only public moral discourse that makes such an increase in understanding possible.

I suggest it is in this light that we should read the Statement of Values produced by the SCAA Forum (discussed in Chapter 3, and again below in Chapter 13). This Statement contains many prescriptions which are clearly open to interpretation, such as 'we should respect others, including children' and 'we should understand and carry out our responsibilities as citizens'. Some critics have seen such statements as merely platitudinous. But we should see them, I suggest, as having a function in interpersonal discourse in the sorts of way mentioned above. They are reference points which, at least at a verbal level, would be widely agreed on; within a school, as more widely, people may find that they agree on an interpretation of them and can go on from there; or they may, in the attempt to clarify the interpretation and application of such prescriptions, come to a better self-understanding and mutual understanding. Thus consideration of prescriptions such as these (taken seriously because there *is* widespread agreement on them at some level) will itself be a contribution to and enrichment of public moral discourse.

NOTES

1. See also my remarks on Warnock's position, p. 71 above.
2. Notice that nothing that I or, for instance, Peters have said in putting weight on rules has denied this.
3. The example can also be used to illustrate Hare's distinction between the general and the universal. 'Do no harm' is more general, 'don't hit anyone' more specific; but both are equally universal.
4. There are, of course, parallels here with discussions in the literature of act- and rule-utilitarianism. The example used is not morally neutral: indeed if there is a professional ethics of the construction industry this is surely part of it.

5. Here the languages of norms of conduct and the language of virtues seem to overlap, but there is still a difference. As I suggested in Chapter 8, Griffin's norm means 'don't act in a cruel way', not 'don't be a cruel person'.

6. It would not have occurred to me but for the 1997 case in which nanny Louise Woodward was acquitted of the murder of a baby in her care. It is important to make explicit that in the remarks I make below I am exercising the philosopher's prerogative of using imaginary examples. No opinion is implied (nor do I think I am in any position to have one) about the actual events preceding the Louise Woodward trial.

7. Beauchamp and Childress's text *Principles of Biomedical Ethics* has gone through numerous editions since its first publication in 1979. The four principles mentioned above have remained central in the text, but it has also — responsive to developments in moral philosophy — given progressively more space to virtues and caring.

8. Arguably, the need for a caring attitude and responsiveness to individual circumstances should be added to the four principles of Beauchamp and Childress — or alternatively it may already be covered by those four principles, sensitively interpreted.

9. This point is made in a discussion of the SCAA work by Smith and Standish in *Teaching Right and Wrong*, pp. 143–144. I am not sure how far Smith and Standish see this as an objection to thinking in terms of general principles at all.

Chapter 11 Moral Motivation

GEORGE (about McFee): Oh *no*, you don't understand. He wouldn't *kill* anyone. He's against it. He thinks it shouldn't be allowed. He would prefer it to be kept to a minimum. Otherwise — shambles. He's no more capable of killing someone than the Archbishop of Canterbury. (*Small pause.*) Not *as* capable. (*Jumpers*, p. 49)

MOTIVATION IN LAW AND MORALITY(n)

If people do not violate moral norms, does it matter *why* they do not violate them? Morality(n), like the law, expects people to act in certain ways and refrain from acting in certain others, but does not demand that they do so out of one kind of motivation rather than another. This is another of the ways in which, for public purposes, the language of norms may seem preferable to that of virtues. As Schneewind (1997, p. 180) has put it: 'The rules or principles can be known and applied by someone who has no desire or concern for acting on them'.

The points I made at the end of the last chapter may reinforce this view. Where rules or principles are functioning in a public discourse on policy issues, it is indeed possible for someone to know and apply the principles without any desire to act on them, since the people who apply the principles — in the sense of thinking what kind of action they require — and the people from whom the principles require some kind of action, may be different persons. However, I did not claim that this kind of role in public discourse is the only role for publicly-acknowledged principles; to the contrary, the norms of morality(n) have their primary importance to the extent that people do act in accordance with them.

There are still many possible motivations which can lie behind people's acting in accordance with the norms — if this means acting in ways which do not violate the norms. On different occasions I may be acting from unthinking habit, or from calculated self-interest, or from affection for another, or 'on the spur of the moment' for no articulated reasons, and on any of these occasions I might be acting in ways which do not in fact go against any of the norms. To that extent, one might say that it should not matter, from the point of view of morality(n), what my motivation is, provided my action is in fact in accordance with the norms.

However, morality(n) could not function if it were only a matter of chance whether people's actions are or are not in accordance with the norms. People can act in accordance with the norms without consciously acting *on* the norms.[1] It is not a matter of logical necessity that the more people consciously act *on* the norms, the more they will act in ways that are in fact in accordance with the norms (people might be so ineffective in doing what they are trying to do, that they would have acted in accordance with the norms more often if they had not been trying to). Nevertheless, it is a reasonable assumption that there will be many occasions when people's actions would not be in accordance with the norms were it not that they were consciously acting on the norms. This means that for morality(n) to function it must be possible for the recognition that something is required by the norms to be a motivation for action. It must after all be possible for people to have some sort of 'desire or concern' to act on moral norms.[2]

From this there are two implications for education. First, that in so far as the aim of moral education is not only that people should understand morality(n), but also that they should act in accordance with its requirements, educators will need to encourage this form of motivation (though not only this form). Second, that the public understanding of morality, in so far as it is an understanding of morality(n), will have to include understanding of the kind of motivation which morality(n) sometimes needs. (These are two different points, because it may be possible both for someone to be motivated in a certain way without understanding their own motivation, and for someone to understand a certain form of motivation — what it involves, how it is possible — without actually being motivated in that way themselves.)

So far we have not seen that a desire or concern to act on moral norms should be of any particular kind. (Part of the contrast between norm- and virtue-based accounts is that on norm-based accounts there is no one particular kind of motivation which morality(n) is exclusively concerned with, whereas a virtue-based account is focusing on some particular kind of motivation in the case of each virtue it distinguishes.) So far, the position of morality(n) is still parallel to that of the law. It matters to the functioning of the law that the existence of legal norms should sometimes enter into people's motivation — that people can have some sort of desire or concern to act according to the law — but there is more than one form this desire or concern can take. To mention the most obvious (which are not mutually exclusive), people may obey the law because they do not want the inconvenience and sanctions which may ensue on their breaking it, or because they respect the law and think that they ought not to break it.

One way in which morality(n) differs from the law is that the norms of morality(n) — in cases where they are not also legal norms — are not backed up by coercive sanctions. Some theorists would still say that morality(n) works through sanctions of a kind, though these might be sanctions only of more-or-less public disapproval. It is an important difference, though, that legal sanctions are designed to be hard to take for anyone with certain common human motivations (people do not like being locked up or forced to hand over large amounts of money), whereas it is possible for people to be indifferent or defiant towards the disapproval of others, which is not itself coercive. The desire or concern to avoid coercive sanctions, which are usually accompanied also by social disapproval, is not a sufficiently effective motivation to deter all action in violation of the law; it is not to be expected that avoidance of social disapproval alone would be a sufficient motivation to deter all action in violation of norms which are not backed up by coercive sanctions.

The other motivation for obeying the law which I distinguished above also has its analogue for morality: the motivation which is operating when someone refrains from doing what they want to do because they think they ought not to (or think it would be wrong), or does what they are reluctant to do because they believe it is the right thing to do (or that they ought to do it). As the writer of a book on moral education for the popular market puts it:

> The great battleground of morality is between obligation and desire. When somebody says 'I ought to do so and so' we understand that she doesn't really want to do it, or would prefer to do something else, but feels she should nonetheless (Houghton, 1998, p. 59).

In her first sentence, this writer is perhaps expressing a view of the matter which has been influenced by a certain kind of theory — though not only philosophy; we might cite much of mainstream religious traditions too. Arguably, this use of 'obligation' as a noun form of 'ought' is itself a philosopher's input. But certainly it is not a philosophical invention that people use the word 'ought' to express something which they themselves see as pulling against their own wishes or inclinations (though this does not preclude their acknowledging that they may in some sense want to do what they think they ought to do). And it is, I think, a fact of experience that people do sometimes act other than the way their wishes and inclination would lead, because they think they ought to. In other words, such thoughts, involving words like 'ought' and 'right' and 'wrong', can function as an element in people's motivation. And some approaches to moral education see the development of this form of motivation as central. The same writer, for instance, goes on to speak of the need for (self-)

discipline: 'doing what you do not want to do, and not doing what you would like to do' (*ibid.*).

When people use 'ought' with the sense that the 'ought' pulls against their inclination, it is not necessarily the case that they are consciously referring to a rule or principle. (I outlined in Chapter 9 a form of reasoning which could issue in an 'ought' without referring to norms.) But often it will be the case that there is a sense of some rule or general principle which should be followed and which applies in the particular case — and for some people acting on principles may be central to their experience of morality(n). There may also be the sense — since the ought pulls against inclination — that it takes an effort of will to act in accordance with the principle. Thus we have the notion that was seen as central to morality in the discussion document on *Spiritual and Moral Development* from the National Curriculum Council for England and Wales (NCC, 1993, republished as SCAA, 1995), which put at the head of its list of the qualities to be developed in moral education: 'The will to behave morally as a point of principle.'

VARIATION OF ETHICAL MOTIVATION

This is a way, then, in which motivation can function in morality(n). Is it, however, desirable that it function in such a way? There is a strong strand in recent moral philosophy and philosophical writing about moral education which plays down the value of such motivation and might like to exclude it altogether. Anscombe (1997, first published 1958) examined and found wanting the 'ought' which she saw as central to modern moral philosophy. Williams (1985) put a deconstruction of the notion of obligation at the centre of his critique of 'the morality system' in *Ethics and the Limits of Philosophy*. Taking up this theme of moral obligation John White (1990, p. 53) writes:

> Children are brought up to believe that ineluctable duties are laid on them to do or refrain from this or that. . . . They also learn, as part of this same scheme of thought, to feel guilt and remorse when they fail to live up to their obligations. They come to blame themselves and their shortcomings. And not only themselves. They are trained to see other people, too, through the same reductive spectacles, as abiders by, or deviants from, their moral duties.

White goes on to comment that 'our ethical life does not *have* to be as unlovely as this'. If we accept that an ethical life centred on and dominated by a sense of moral obligation is unlovely, we need to look for alternatives. And much recent moral philosophy has, of course, been exploring alternatives. There are the neo-Aristotelians, the Humeans, the proponents of an ethic of care. There is a variety of positions here, but they tend to converge on one or other, or both, of two points. They move away from such general (one could almost say 'all-purpose') motivations as a sense of obligation to more particular motivations, such as are incorporated into the various virtues (where each of honesty, courage, fidelity and so on has a motivation specific to it; cf. Jackson, 1978; McDowell, 1997). Also, they see moral behaviour as motivated by desire or affects in one way or another, so that rather than there having to be a 'battleground' of obligation and desire, the important question is the nature of the person's desires and affects. Thus an ethic of care finds the underlying motivation of the ethically responsible person in *caring*, which is surely an essentially affective matter. Again, when White suggests that for moral education we should substitute an education in altruism, he is speaking of something which has to be manifested in people's feelings. At a minimum, the altruistic person will sometimes be motivated by compassion, whereas we can imagine a rigid moralist, adhering to general principles, and capable of the will to follow them, never actually *feeling* compassion.[3]

In the face of so much counterargument, is there any point in trying to hang on to the notion of a sense of moral obligation as a motivation? In the next section I shall reinforce the point already made, that it is not sufficient to rely on other forms of motivation even if they do seem more attractive.

THE CASE FOR A SPECIFICALLY MORAL MOTIVATION

To a moral philosopher, the kind of motivation we are now talking about comes, so to speak, with the label 'Kantian' attached. This can be misleading, both because we do not have to accept all of Kant's ethics in order to recognise a role for a sense of moral obligation, and because it is possible to defend its role on other than Kantian grounds.

On the first point, it is in the first chapter of his *Groundwork*, where he is still analysing what he calls 'common rational knowledge of morality', that Kant first gives an account of the motive of moral duty, well before he introduces the notion of the categorical imperative, let alone the notoriously difficult conception of the noumenal and phenomenal standpoints. To Kant himself, then, the experience of this kind of motivation is recognisable prior to the rest of his own theory; in this sense, there need be nothing specifically Kantian about it. It is striking that when Mill writes in Chapter 3 of *Utilitarianism* about the sanction of morality — for which he uses the word 'conscience', and which he describes as an inner feeling — he seems, if one can put on his words the phenomenological interpretation which they seem to demand, to be talking about something which, in experience, would be very like the sense of reverence for the moral law which Kant talks about. The sense that one *ought* to act in a certain way, even though it is against one's immediate inclinations, is certainly present in Mill (and in many utilitarians, as Williams, 1985 p. 184, recognises).

It is also possible, with Mill, to defend the salience of a sense of moral obligation on consequentialist grounds, that is, by showing that things are likely to go better on the whole if people are capable of acting out of a sense of obligation. Kant himself points out that someone who is so absorbed in his own troubles that he feels no inclination to help others may nevertheless do so out of a sense of duty. The picture of someone who takes account of the interests of others only out of a sense of duty is not an attractive one. But our question here is this: is it desirable that this sort of motivation is available as one among the possible kinds of motivation that can move people to take account of the interests of others?

In earlier writing (*Teaching about Values*, p. 78; see also Haydon, 1999a) I have used the example of the Milgram experiments on obedience: many of the subjects in these experiments, believing that they were inflicting severe electric shocks on other people, went on doing so on the instructions of the experimenter. Notice that what these people thought they were doing could well be described as violence.[4] I suggested, not that people who defied the experimenter's instruction could not have had a variety of motivations for doing so, but that it is important that there is the possibility of people saying 'No. This is immoral, I will not do it.' (Some people, but not many, did respond in that sort of way.) It is possible that there are cases in which someone defies the experimenter, not out of benevolence or altruism, but simply because he or she thinks that what she is being asked to do is morally wrong. The mere possibility that this kind of motivation might operate in the service of morality(n) in cases where no other motivations would is, I suggest, enough to show that this kind of motivation is worth maintaining. In other words, it is important that there should be the possibility that a thought such as 'I ought not to do this', 'it would be wrong to do this', 'this is against the (moral) rules', can function for an individual as a reason, and sometimes a sufficient motivating reason, for doing the action.

LANGUAGE AND PSYCHOLOGY

If there is to be that possibility, it has to be a possibility within the public discourse of morality. It is not only that people must sometimes say to themselves, privately, things like 'I am not going to do this because it would be wrong'. For if such things were only ever said privately by people to themselves, new speakers could never learn to say such things. That is the importance of the language in which such thoughts are expressed being part of public discourse.

In earlier writings I have put some weight on the possibility that the very meaning of words like 'ought' in such contexts might be mysterious. I was perhaps unconsciously working — though I should have known better — with a picture theory of meaning by which there has to be something in the world for a word to correspond to if it is to have meaning. Then one would be puzzled by the meaning of 'ought', and related words, because there seems to be nothing in the world to which an 'ought' corresponds. On a more Wittgensteinian view of meaning it need be no surprise that the practice, in discourse, of using terms such as 'ought' and 'right' and 'wrong' can exist, and have effect, even though the participants in the practice may be quite unable to give an abstract account of the meaning of the words.

We do not, then, have to follow Anscombe's advice from 1958 that 'the concepts of obligation, and duty — *moral* obligation and *moral* duty, that is to say — and of what is *morally* right and wrong, and of the *moral* sense of "ought", ought to be jettisoned if this is psychologically possible; because they are survivals, or derivatives from survivals, from an earlier conception of ethics which no longer generally survives . . .' (Anscombe, 1997, p. 26).

Even if they are survivals from a publicly defunct conception of ethics — which is a conception of morality as law where the lawgiver is God — this does not mean that these terms cannot be put to service in the cause of a different conception, such as that of morality(n) understood in secular terms. Forms of discourse which are incorporated into social practices are quite capable of surviving changes in the interpretation of terminology (this has happened for many people with religious language).

Arguably all we need to say about the meaning of terms such as 'ought' is what Griffin (1996, p. 83) says: 'To say "You ought not to do it" is . . . to say that there is some norm or standard to which your not doing it would conform.' Within philosophy of education, Straughan (1982, Ch. 3; 1989, Ch. 1) has a more thoroughly worked-out account based on what is essentially the same idea.

An account of how the word 'ought' functions in relation to norms does not by itself constitute an account of motivation: for that it would need at least to be supplemented by an account of how it is that certain norms can be recognised as having authority over people's conduct (which will be the topic of the next chapter). But seeing 'ought' in Griffin's way may at least remove the sense (which non-philosophers may not share in any case) that there is something mysterious about the very meaning of 'ought'.

If the public discourse which uses terms such as 'ought' and 'wrong' can function without any articulated theory of the meaning of the terms, it can also function without any particular psychological account of what is going on when people's motivation involves the use of such terms (when people do something because they think they ought to, because the rules demand it, and so on). But four points are worth making in connection with psychological accounts:

1) Any plausible account is likely to include the idea that norms which have an existence in public discourse can be internalised. Such an account will not necessarily use the *word* 'internalised' but it will have to give an account of how norms which exist in public space before a particular individual exists at all can come to operate in some sense inside that individual. Mill, for one, offers such an account in Chapter 3 of *Utilitarianism*, before Freud came on the scene. I am not competent to say whether the most plausible account will turn out to be some kind of psychoanalytic one, but there are certainly a number of writers on morality and moral education, not themselves psychoanalysts, who have taken such accounts seriously, including Peters and, more recently, Scheffler (1992, Chapter 5), and Rustin in *Teaching Right and Wrong*.

2) It is not, so far as I can see, necessary for such an account to put great weight on guilt — which, as I have noted, is one of the things that bothers White and many others. If it were true that morality(n) could not function without people constantly being racked with guilt, this would suggest that morality(n) was defeating its own object of ameliorating the human condition. But first, while guilt may come into certain psychological accounts of moral motivation, the thought which moves the individual need not be 'I shall not do this because I shall feel guilty if I do (and feeling guilty will be an unpleasant experience which I would rather avoid)'. The conscious thought may contain no reference to guilt but may merely be 'I shall not do this because it would be wrong'. At the level of public discourse, it is a necessary condition of such motivation that the conceptual possibilities for it are available; whether the possibility of feeling guilt is or is not a necessary condition is a separate question.

Second, the negative features of guilt should not be exaggerated. Consider this example from Hare (written at a time when Czechoslovakia still existed, and doing philosophy there was a subversive activity):

I recently visited Prague to talk to some philosopher there. If, when I was crossing into Czechoslovakia, the officials had asked me the purpose of my visit, I should certainly have told them a lie, because if they had known they would most probably have expelled me. . . . And, just as certainly, I should have felt, not merely fear of being found out and getting into trouble, but a feeling of *guilt* at telling the lie (although I should have been in no doubt that I ought to tell it). (1981, p. 31)

If Hare had told the lie he would not have been *racked* with guilt; and his disposition to feel guilt in such circumstances (which he sees as a morally positive disposition) has not destroyed his quality of life (if it had I think we would have heard of this in his later writings). I do not think this is only because he is a philosopher. We should not think that any conception of morality which has a place for guilt is one that must be rejected by civilised benevolent people.

3) The same applies for conceptions which have a place for shame as a motivation, where shame differs from guilt in having more direct reference to the perception or opinion of others (cf. Taylor, 1985). In the last chapter I argued that a publicly shared understanding of morality will include a place for criticism, and for consideration, both individual and shared, of whether a criticised or potentially criticisable action can be justified. Shame seems to be the affective side of the disposition to consider whether one's actions can be or could be justified to others. It is not surprising that with increasing attention among moral philosophers to the social aspects of morality there have been recent acknowledgements of the role of shame.[5]

4) The public discourse which uses this idea of motivation presupposes that people *can* act in a particular way because they think that they ought to. That is not necessarily to say that it presupposes *freedom of the will*, with all the connotations that that term has had for some philosophers, but it is to say that the public discourse of morality will not too easily accept excuses of the form 'I couldn't help it, because. . . .' Of course, this public discourse can acknowledge that there are cases where people really could not have acted in a certain way, even if they did think they ought to: it may really be that some provocations, temptations or whatever, are too great. But if it were really thought that no one was ever able to choose to act in a certain way because they thought they ought to, there would be no role for such locutions in the discourse.

Since the thinking of individuals is never isolated from public discourse, the extent to which people think they can or cannot help what they are doing is itself in part a function of the nature of the public discourse. It is not unusual to hear on television talk shows[6] remarks such as 'I've been unfaithful to my partner ten times. I can't help it — it's my nature' (from someone who acknowledges in some sense that his or her unfaithfulness is a violation of shared norms). And given the apparently self-justifying nature of anger and the attacks it can lead to, as pointed out in Chapter 7, claims that violence was an inevitable response to provocation are part of a similar discourse. My point here is not that such an account of an individual's behaviour cannot be correct: conceivably it may be in certain cases. It is that if such thoughts become increasingly frequent within public discourse it will become increasingly likely that people do think they are unable to help what they are doing or should not be criticised for it, and so on. It is not just that people will avail themselves of whatever resources in public discourse serve their purposes. It is that the contents of our consciousness are formed at least in part by what is available in public discourse. If thoughts such as 'you could resist however great the temptation' are not available in public discourse, they may not be available to an individual; and it could be that very fact that makes the difference between the individual's being able, and being unable, to resist.

Recall the point cited in Chapter 7 from Larry May: that 'morality should not be diminished when the going gets tough'. We would not change May's meaning, but would bring it out, if we read 'morality should not be *seen to be* diminished when the going gets tough'. The point is about how morality must be publicly perceived, if it is to fulfil its function. It must not be seen as too easy to escape from in the face of pressures; though it is at the same time true that it will lose credibility if it is seen never to make allowances.[7]

SCHOOLING AND MORAL LANGUAGE

As educators, fortunately, we do not have to be passive in the face of changes in public discourse: to some degree we can influence it. (I am actually trying, in a small way, to influence it through this book.) The overarching educational conclusion from the argument of this chapter is that children have to be exposed to the terminology of moral evaluation, and that it matters what kind of terminology of moral evaluation they are exposed to. It is not part of my argument that they should *only* be exposed to a thin vocabulary of 'right' and 'wrong', 'ought' and 'ought not'. There is the whole rich vocabulary of 'thick' ethical concepts to which virtue theorists have drawn attention. But I do maintain that a certain sort of motivation would not be available to persons who had not learned to use terms such as 'right' and 'wrong' and 'ought' and 'ought not'.

Should one take it for granted that schooling will get people into the way of using such terms? I think one should not. This is not to deny that schools are, by and large, very moral places, as Nick Tate said in his January 1996 speech; but it is to express a degree of scepticism about how far one can assume in schools any systematic and consistent use of moral language. It is not unusual to come across teachers who would be reluctant to use the terms 'right' and 'wrong' out of fear that they would be thought, or conviction that they must not be, 'judgmental' or 'moralistic' (cf. the quotation from Midgley in the previous chapter).

If one cannot assume a consistent use of moral terminology among teachers then it also cannot be assumed among the general public who include the parents of children coming into the schools. Possibly in a more homogeneous (and perhaps literally God-fearing) society it might once have been possible to assume that whatever initiation into moral discourse was needed could be left to home upbringing. But in our present situation few assumptions can be made about the current understandings of morality and moral language other than that there is a fair degree of subjectivism, scepticism and sheer confusion around.

Schools, then, have a responsibility for the maintenance of a certain sort of public discourse. This means that the willingness or otherwise of teachers to use a certain sort of vocabulary is important. Perhaps some anecdotal evidence will be admissible here. At a meeting of the Values Education Council (VEC) in May 1998, where most of the participants were or had been teachers and most were professionally involved in moral education, I raised the question whether the terms 'right' and 'wrong' (in a moral sense) should be abandoned. The question was taken up as a focus for discussion in small groups. Though no group did reach agreement that the terms 'right' and 'wrong' should be abandoned, it is significant that the question was taken seriously.

One might wonder what terminology if any people may use, other than 'wrong', if they wish to convey that some conduct goes against accepted norms. One term which appears to be growing in popularity is 'unacceptable': often used, it seems, to mark the difference between what is (to be) tolerated and what is not (to be) tolerated. In some ways the term 'unacceptable' may seem to carry its meaning on its face more clearly than does 'wrong'; the reference to recognised norms, while still implicit, may be easily understood. Thus at the same VEC meeting an educationalist and teacher of long experience said that she would tell the pupil who was disrupting a lesson by banging on the desk that his behaviour was unacceptable, but not that it was wrong.[8] No doubt part of the point was a concern not to condemn, or appear to be condemning, the child as opposed to criticising the behaviour (a distinction which is vital if the kind of criticism I referred to in the last chapter is not to be counter-productive). But I think there was also the idea that to call such behaviour wrong would be to make too grand a claim, as if it purported to refer to a universal or absolute norm; banging on a desk, after all, is not wrong *per se*. The term 'unacceptable', understood as something like 'ruled out by the norms which the teacher has decided to apply in this classroom' makes a more modest claim.

Later in the same discussion participants were wondering what they would say about rape. I think there was a shared sense of the incongruity of using the term 'unacceptable' both for desk-banging and for rape. If 'unacceptable' becomes an everyday term of criticism, something stronger will be needed for other occasions. Perhaps (of the terms available within a relatively thin vocabulary) 'wrong' is the sort of word to do the job.[9]

My own argument, at any rate, is that morality(n) needs the availability of terms such as 'wrong' (though 'ought' and 'ought not' may be even more central); and not just their availability, but their being taken seriously. This certainly means that they should not be overused. They need to be used with reference to norms which are seen as important, not purely local or temporary, and subject to wide consensus.

It has not been the argument of this chapter that people are necessarily motivated to do what they think they ought to do. It is possible to see what one ought to do by reference to certain norms or standards, while not taking those norms seriously at all. And there may be nothing wrong with this — if the norms, say, are those of a particular game which one has no interest in playing. What we need to do now is consider what is involved in people taking certain norms, those of morality(n), to be authoritative.

NOTES

1. A parallel distinction is important both in Aristotle's ethics (cf. *Nicomachean Ethics* II.4) and Kant's (cf. *Groundwork*, e.g. Ch. 1, 397).
2. Nothing in my argument requires that all motivation has to be construable in terms of desires: cf. Scheffler, 1992, Chapter 5.
3. To some degree, a broadly Humean tendency is manifested in the recent turn in moral philosophy towards 'virtue ethics', though the writers within this tendency more often take their cue from Aristotle than from Hume (though see A. Baier, 1985). Advocates of virtue ethics will often see themselves as presenting an Aristotelian account in contrast to a Kantian one. The point needs to be mentioned here, because while I shall in what follows be suggesting that an aspect of the Kantian approach needs to be retained, I would not want to be read as defending Kant against Aristotle; it does not appear that there is necessarily a large contrast between Kant and Aristotle on this matter of motivation. An Aristotelian ethic does not suppose, as some modern accounts seem to, that people ideally would act

mainly out of fellow-feeling (in fact a distinctly altruistic motivation does not figure largely in Aristotle) and it does have to do with the basic structure of an agent's desires rather than with adventitious feeling. The National Curriculum Council document's 'will to act morally as a point of principle' may not be alien to Aristotle's ethics, even though the modern phrase could not be translated exactly into Aristotle's vocabulary. Certainly Aristotle believed that the possession of the virtues involved acting according to the right rule or principle (cf. Chapter 7 above), and he has the conception of doing what is noble for its own sake. One can imagine that if Aristotle and Kant could converse now, they might agree on a good deal, including some notion of 'how the upright gentleman behaves' (where the gender reference is deliberate).

4. They did not usually describe it to themselves in that way. Why not? No doubt in part because the experimental situation tended to present their action to them as being justified; hence it would not be described as violence if that description carried the connotation of unjustified infliction of pain and harm. And also because their action did not involve any sudden or forceful physical movements directly against another. They were pulling levers or pushing buttons — the sort of thing many of us do many times a day.

5. See, e.g., Williams, 1993; Tombs, 1995.

6. I do not often listen to them, and I have heard this sort of thing several times. For some remarks on the way American talk shows focus on the victim, thus diverting attention from the blameworthiness of the perpetrator, see Lamb, 1996, pp. 123–127.

7. cf. Scheffler's (1992) discussion of the stringency of morality.

8. Acknowledgements to Janet Edwards.

9. President Clinton, in his television statement on 17 August 1998 following his evidence to a Grand Jury on the Monica Lewinsky affair, admitted that his relationship with Lewinsky had been 'inappropriate — in fact, wrong'. This shows the usage of 'inappropriate' as another word which, like 'unacceptable', indicates that something is ruled out by certain norms — in this case the norms pertaining to public office. It also shows Clinton's awareness that 'wrong' is a stronger term of condemnation of the behaviour. Later he moved to a term which is presumably even stronger in American public discourse, though it would not be part of a secular morality(n): 'I have sinned'.

Chapter 12 Moral Authority

BONES: Well, if that's the case, I don't see any difference whether he thinks he's obeying the Ten Commandments or the rules of tennis.
GEORGE: The difference is, the rules of tennis can be changed.
(*Jumpers*, p. 49)

MELANIE PHILLIPS AND THE NAZIS

Many observers are worried by what they see as the questioning of moral authority in the modern world. A not untypical example occurred in Melanie Phillips's (1996) polemic on educational standards, *All Must Have Prizes*. It is particularly pertinent here because she was commenting on something I had written in 1993. Her somewhat selective quotation from my article is as follows:

> It still must be said forcefully that accepting uncritically what someone tells you because they are seen to be in authority is not a good thing. . . . Doing what is right cannot be a matter of doing what one is told. Schools must produce people who are able to think for themselves what is right. . . . It will not take an exceptionally clever pupil, or an exceptionally bolshie one, to ask 'How do we know this is right or that is wrong?' Any pupil who is being taught to think ought to be asking such questions. And the same pupil ought to see that 'Because I say so' is not an acceptable answer. Nor is 'Because these are the values of your society.' When exposed to a little more teaching of history, perhaps, this pupil will see that by such an argument the values of slave states and Nazi states would have to be endorsed.

Phillips's comment is:

> But this reasoning was specious and dangerous. Of course pupils should be taught to think for themselves and should understand the reasoning behind the moral rules they are taught. But the answer to the pupil's question was surely: 'Because these are the values of our common humanity and are the basis of human flourishing.' Not to answer it in that way leaves it up to the pupil to decide that sometimes the end may justify the means, for example; or that stealing may be permissible if you are poor; or that lying to Parliament is justified to protect the sale of arms. Far from preventing us against succumbing to totalitarian regimes, it provides the means to endorse them. Quite contrary to Haydon's own example, it might legitimise Nazism because it would say in effect that the Nazi view of the world was merely what the Nazi thought was right and was therefore as valid as the pupil's own view. If there is

no absolute right, it follows that there can be no absolute wrong, just as if there is no absolute truth there can be no lies. If rightness is simply what is right-for-me, then who is to say that Nazism was an absolute wrong? But of course it was just that, because it offended the common moral code of humanity. Haydon's attitude, however, opened the way for his pupils to say that racial prejudice was no less right than tolerance; or that it was permissible to kill people because they were genetically imperfect. Moral relativism leads directly to despotism and tyranny. It was no accident that Nietzsche, in whose long shadow our relativist society was formed, represented a significant milestone on the road to the Final Solution. (pp. 221–222)

In his contribution to *Teaching Right and Wrong*, Paul Standish comments on Phillips's attribution to me of moral relativism on the basis of the passage quoted:

> Now this is a bit odd given that Haydon's point of view derives very much from the tradition of liberal education (with the questioning Socrates in the background) which in other respects Phillips seems eager to embrace. Is this the relativism that must be so roundly condemned? . . . Haydon's purpose is hardly to endorse the idea that we cannot know what is right and wrong. It is to favour reason-giving over blind acceptance of authority. (p. 49)

Standish is exactly right about my purpose in the 1993 article. One could leave the matter there, except that Phillips's reaction is an example of the current state of the public understanding of morality, and anyone concerned with the improvement of that understanding needs to give some regard to writings which may typify current confusions, and which may themselves have some influence on the views of a wider public.

These are some of the things Phillips is doing in her comments.

1) She is accepting that reasons can be given for something being right or wrong. I have no problem with this.
2) She is offering her own account of the fundamental kind of reason for something being right or wrong. In her view the fundamental reasons are of a broadly naturalist or neo-Aristotelian kind. These reasons are broadly in line with what I have said here about the function of morality(n).
3) She is suggesting that pupils should be given the correct reason for the norms they are expected to follow. Perhaps what matters here is the interpretation of 'give'. If a teacher simply tells pupils a reason this may have little or no effect on their thinking. A reason which they come to through their own thinking may be one they take more seriously. In fact I do not think the relevant teaching need be or should be either purely didactic or purely a matter of 'discovery learning' on the pupil's part. In the passage immediately following that quoted by Phillips (but ignored by

her) I referred to the rich resources within moral philosophy for answering the pupils' questions about how we know what is right and wrong. Such resources can be used both to structure discussion and to give content to it; answers which emerge from philosophical discussion are neither impositions by the teacher nor the pupils' unguided thoughts.[1]

4) Phillips displays — as I think, do many commentators on moral education — a scepticism about the abilities of ordinary people to 'see reason' in moral matters. Her concession — as it seems — that 'pupils should be taught to think for themselves' is immediately followed by the assertion that they should understand 'the reasoning' (not apparently their own reasoning) behind the moral rules they are taught, and then that they should be given the correct reason. As Standish also sees, one encounters — not only in Phillips — a curious brand of anti-intellectualism or anti-rationalism when the topic is one of right and wrong. People who are concerned about educational standards will usually believe that there are appropriate ways of thinking in particular areas of the curriculum, so that when pupils are thinking about a problem in, say, maths or physics, it does not follow, just from the fact that they are doing their own thinking, that there is no limit to what they can reasonably come up with. Yet where questions of right and wrong are concerned, these same people seem to believe that if pupils think for themselves they might come up with anything at all — at which point we begin to get invocations of Nietzsche, relativism, and various other bogies, including Nazism. This actually suggests that these critics themselves subscribe to a kind of irrationalism about morality, believing that morality does not rest on any rational basis, and therefore that there is no such thing as a right way of thinking about moral matters. If they believed there to be a rational basis for morality, why would they be so worried that other people, doing their own thinking, would come to the kind of answers which they (the critics) think are wrong? If they believe there are right answers in morality, why should they be so sceptical about ordinary people's capacity to see what these answers are?

5) Phillips does not separate the question of how we know what is right and wrong from the question of whether other people have the authority to tell us what to do. But it has to be said that I also did not make that distinction in the article from which she quotes. Certainly I was expressing a scepticism as to whether the authority of society should be accepted. Since in my present argument I am giving a large role to the social

recognition of norms, it may look as if I am contradicting myself. Here then may be the crux, both of what is at issue between Phillips and myself, and of whether my present argument hangs together.

KINDS OF AUTHORITY

In this book I have not been satisfied with accounts of morality which could do away with the notion of authority altogether. I have argued that we cannot do without an imperative or prescriptive conception of morality in which there are norms telling people what to do. For many Aristotelians and neo-Aristotelians morality or ethics, being intimately connected with the good life, has an attractive rather than imperative force.[2] If the attraction of a moral life were sufficient, or could be made sufficient, we would not need to worry about the authority of morality — and we should, therefore, not need to stress this aspect of the morality/law analogy.

Though I have not tried to undermine such 'attractive' accounts, there are at least two reasons for paying attention to imperative accounts. One is the argument of the last chapter, that morality(n) cannot dispense with a certain kind of motivation: where people act in a certain way because they think they ought to. The other is that popular conceptions of morality at present probably do see it largely in imperative terms. While it is not inconceivable that public education about morality might involve an attempt to subvert such understandings, there is much to be said for working from where people are in their present conceptions, or at least taking these seriously rather than dismissing them. The thought, widespread in public conceptions, that young people should be taught certain norms which will be taken to have authority over their actions, will not just dissolve in the face of positive accounts of virtues or of caring.

To put it differently, if norms are important, it is important that they are in some way taken as carrying authority, since norms which left it a purely voluntary matter whether people followed them or not could not do the job of morality(n). One might wonder at this point whether it is essential that all those who see themselves as subject to the authority of the norms of morality(n) must have the same conception of that authority. The SCAA Forum acknowledged in the Preamble to its Statement of Values that agreement on the values is compatible with disagreement on their sources. One might read this as applying something like Rawls's (1993) notion of overlapping consensus to the authority of moral norms: people can have different ideas about the nature of that authority, so long as they all think the norms have some kind of authority.

It seems likely, though, that a shared morality in which there is no shared sense of the authority of that morality would risk coming apart. Different sources of authority would be unlikely to coincide completely in the norms they underpin; acknowledgement of different sources of authority by different people might tend to pull attention away from the consensus on norms that are shared towards those that are not. It is a fact, certainly, that different sources of moral authority will be acknowledged in a plural society; the point is to see whether, compatibly with this, there can be acknowledgement of one shared source of authority attaching to morality(n). (There does not, after all, seem to be any inconsistency in acknowledging more than one source of authority — say, the law of the land and God — for the norms against murder.)[3]

Is there a candidate as a source of authority which can be acknowledged by all in a plural society? I take it that the authority cannot in a plural society be divine; also that a Kantian universalist understanding in which the authority of moral norms is the authority of Reason is too problematic — even among philosophers — for it to provide a source of authority which can be publicly acknowledged. What of the idea that the authority of morality over the individual is the authority of Society?

In the literature of philosophy of education a distinction between two kinds or senses of authority has often been made (e.g. Peters, 1959, 1966; K. Baier, 1973). There is the authority of the expert who has knowledge which others (lay persons in relation to that authority) do not have, and the authority, often conferred on particular persons under publicly recognised norms, to tell certain others what to do. Thus the teacher may be (relative to her pupils) an authority on a certain area of curriculum content, and she may have the authority to tell her students what to learn and in various ways how to behave. The first claim may be used as a premise in an argument to support a claim to the second kind of authority, but they are two different claims.

In terms of this distinction, what kind of authority, on moral matters, could society have in relation to the individual? It will not be the authority of knowledge of what is right and wrong. If we were to say that society 'knows' what is right and wrong, we would presumably have to unpack this in terms of a social consensus being the criterion of right and wrong. There is one kind of case, conceivable rather than actual, where consensus can be taken as the criterion of what is right. This is the kind of case envisaged hypothetically in Habermas's (e.g. 1990) communicative ethics, where all those affected by a given norm are able to discuss and raise objections to that norm, under conditions of unconstrained communication (as defined by Habermas's ideal speech situation). If all those who would be affected by a given norm would — because of conditions of full information and so on — see any objection which there might be to that norm from their point of view, and none of them in fact do see any objection, then *ex hypothese* we can say that there *is* no objection to that norm: then the consensus is the criterion of its being justified.[4]

This possibility affords an answer to some of the worries which people often have about the idea of a morality based in consensus. It will often be objected that consensus does not make something right, and examples like that of Nazi Germany will be cited: if consensus makes something right, then Nazi policy was right because there was a consensus on it in Germany in the 1930s. The reply is that this was not a consensus in the relevant sense: namely a consensus of all those who would be affected by the norms in question. There were whole sectors of the society, very much affected by the norms in question, which were not part of the consensus.

The conditions written into Habermas's test for the justification of norms are empirically unlikely to be realised as regards norms applying to a whole society (let alone even more widely). It is not possible for all those who will be affected by a given social norm to participate directly in discussion on it (even if we confine our attention to *humans* who will be affected by it);[5] and for those who are involved in discussion, it is unlikely that the discussion will be free of all bias and pressure such that, in Habermas's terms, the only force is the force of the better argument.

In ordinary conditions, the fact that there is a broad consensus across a society on certain norms does not establish — or should not be taken to establish — that these norms are right or beyond criticism.[6] My alternative formulations here are intended to take account of the possibilities of a range of realist or non-realist interpretations, so that it will not be necessary here to go into metaethics. If a realist account is wanted by which certain norms are correct, I am saying both that being norms on which there is a social consensus is not what it is for norms to be correct, and that a social consensus on norms is not infallibly correlated with their being correct. If we take a non-realist route, then of course social consensus is not a criterion of actually-held norms being the 'real' ones, because there is nothing which is a criterion of actually-held norms being the 'real' ones; but this need not worry us if we can recognise the possibility of actual norms being criticised and changed in ways which will be seen as improvement. The reason for objecting to taking consensus as authoritative in the sense of establishing correctness will now be that to take it this way would be to insulate the norms against criticism.

Thinking in terms of morality(n) it is clearly important that the possibility of criticism and change be retained, both because the actual norms recognised by a society at a given time may not be the ones that best serve the purposes of morality(n), and because even if they are the ones that best serve it at a given time, circumstances may change. I shall say more about criticism and change in the next two chapters.

So, society is not the measure of right and wrong. We now need to consider the possibility that society nevertheless has authority in the second of the senses distinguished, namely the authority to tell people how to behave. We could unpack this in terms of the publicly recognised norms of a society being authoritative for the conduct of individuals — at least provisionally. By saying 'at least provisionally' we can recognise that the norms are subject to criticism and improvement, and still hold that — unless and until they are changed — people ought to abide by them.

THE ANALOGY WITH LAW AGAIN

It will perhaps be clear that we have returned to the analogy between morality(n) and law. The sort of authority we are now talking about is the kind of authority that can be attributed to the law. In broadly liberal-democratic societies, people do not generally think that there is some model of ideal law to which the actual law either does or does not correspond (or if they do think in this way, arguably this shows a certain deficiency in citizenship education); people can think that the law has authority over their conduct — that they ought by and large to obey the law — while acknowledging that it is subject to criticism and change.

It is worth pursuing the analogy again, to see something further of the conditions on which law can have acknowledged authority, and whether these conditions do or can apply to the moral norms of society.

The law can appear to the people who are subject to it to be an alien force: something imposed from the outside. Morality can appear this way also. To people who are in any case in a position of a certain subordination to others — which to some degree applies to all school pupils — it may appear that the norms which others expect them to adhere to are nothing but disguised ways of saying 'we don't want you to do this', or even 'don't do this, or else!'

And when it appears that there are no particular sanctions which follow violation of these norms — unlike legal ones — morality may appear to be not so much an alien force as an alien presence which lacks any force. This is just the sort of condition which can contribute to a widespread scepticism about morality, to lip service at best, or to an alienated 'so what?' attitude towards moral norms. And this is the sort of way in which morality comes to have a bad name (Hare, 1992;

cf. Midgley, 1991, and the passage from Standish in *Teaching Right and Wrong*, p. 50, quoted in Chapter 2 above).

The democratic tradition in politics over several centuries has, with varying success, worked against the sense of law as an alien power. In a democratic system it is possible — though in the absence of an effective education for citizenship it will often not happen — for people to see themselves as subject, not to alien demands, but to a system which they themselves are part of. This is, I suggest, the sort of conception which moral education also needs to be aiming at, where people see themselves as on the inside of morality. If I am right that a language of norms allows more readily than a language of virtues for the public articulation of shared standards, there is a further reason here for giving priority to a language of norms. As Annette Baier (1997, p. 273) puts it, 'significant power is possessed by those shaping our conception of the virtues and expecting us to display them, approving when we do, disapproving and perhaps shunning us when we do not'. Baier thinks this power is less coercive than the power exercised by those setting up an ethics of norms one is obliged to follow. But it seems to me it could be the other way round: if the formulation and promulgation of norms is a public, transparent process, there will be less danger of manipulation in it than in the attempt to bring people up as certain sorts of people. (cf. *Teaching about Values*, pp. 124–6, and my references to Patricia White in Chapter 5 above).[7]

What is involved in seeing oneself as on the inside? One point is that one can see reason for the norms of morality (as one can see point in the law). This does not in itself mean that one will endorse those norms, but is perhaps a precondition of that. This suggests that education needs to educate people about morality. Far from representing it as something mysterious (or ignoring it as too problematic) education needs to focus attention — not only through philosophy, since a variety of empirical disciplines will have a role here too — on the nature of morality(n).

A second point, already made in Chapter 5, is that people are able to agree to norms, not just in the sense of agreeing that there is reason for them, but in the stronger sense of agreeing to adhere to them (I suggested in Chapter 5 that this is more practicable where morality is expressed in terms of norms than where it is expressed in terms of virtues). There is a partial model in the way that people, joining a particular club or association, will often not just agree that they see the point of its rules, but agree to abide by its rules. For the law, an analogous position is possible though not often realised: one could imagine that people, perhaps on reaching the age of majority, undertake as citizens to adhere to the law (the closest to this that happens in practice may be when adult immigrants are granted citizenship of their new state). For morality, we can hardly imagine anything like a ceremony; but we can see it as a possible attitude that people can have towards the norms of their society, that they have undertaken to live by those norms — though not, as we shall see, in an uncritical spirit.

A third point, which can also use the analogy of joining a club, is that one may take the norms the more seriously to the extent that one sees oneself as belonging to and valuing the community whose norms they are. This is one reason why one of the most important tasks for education where morality is concerned is to try to overcome the alienation that many people may feel from their community (one of the respects in which it is important for liberals to learn from communitarianism). I do not have in mind here only the sort of notional sense of membership in a community which could go with, for instance, acknowledging oneself as a member of Kant's kingdom of ends (though for some people this might work: cf. Haydon, 1999a). I mean that a society which wants people to take morality seriously has to tackle in all sorts of ways — which will often be more directly describable as political and economic — the danger of people feeling left out of their society.

This, coupled with the previous point, constitutes an acknow-ledgement of what the reader may feel has got left behind in this discussion of the public aspects of morality, namely the affective aspect. A person can *care* about norms and care about adhering to them, if they are the norms of a community which he or she is part of and values. And then both the consciousness of the fact that these are shared values (where the fact that a society has shared values may itself be valued), and the consciousness of having played some part in the forming of a shared sense of values, can be positive factors in motivating persons to take such values more seriously, in the sense of seeing them as having authority over their own conduct.

A fourth point is that people can see themselves as sharing with others a responsibility for the norms of morality(n) to the extent that they can participate in criticism and change of those norms. Again the analogy is clear with the way in which democracy hopes that people will see themselves as part of the system because they are able to criticise and make changes within the system.

If moral education can work with this sort of analogy, it will in effect be saying to young people: 'This is the prevailing morality of your society, on which people by and large do agree, even though they may have come to this consensus from different starting-points. Other people are not, on the whole, stupid, and the experience of society over generations is not irrelevant, though at the same time your study of history will show you that some moral ideas which hardly anyone would now accept were in their time surprisingly resilient, and would not have changed if they had not been criticised. So, given that you have the possibility of criticising the prevailing morality, and given that it can change as a result of criticism, it is reasonable for society to expect you, for the moment, to go along with it. Your criticism will have more weight to the extent that it is based on an understanding of the reasons behind the prevailing morality, on your own experience of life and on your reflective understanding of your experience and that of others. These kinds of understanding and experience are ones which we hope your education will help you to develop.'

It is important to this position that it is possible not only for the prevailing morality to be criticised, but also for it to change as a result of that criticism. This introduces a disanalogy between morality(n) and law. The democratic conception of the law holds that people are at liberty to campaign to get the law changed, but should abide by it (unless in exceptional circumstances) until it is changed. In the case of law there is a definite procedure of legislation. This makes it possible to say that a given law is in force at a given time — even until a precise time on a precise date — and that thereafter it is not in force. This in turn makes it possible to say to people 'you should go along with this law while it is in force, but if you, in conjunction with others, succeed in getting it changed, then once it is changed you need take no further notice of it'. If there were such a thing as moral legislation, we could transfer this model to morality. But there is no moral legislation as such. Does this make the whole process by which morality is criticised and changed too fluid for the democratic analogy to be applied?

We should not exaggerate the difference. Though laws can cease to apply or come into force at a given time, there is often lying behind such changes a more gradual process. Laws can come into disrepute, can cease to be enforced, can come to be ignored, before they are actually repealed. Legislation may be the 'outward and visible sign' of a change in popular thinking which has been going on for some time. Morality does not get changed by acts of legislation; nevertheless it does get changed. The sexual morality of Britain, for instance, is changing.[8] (It remains open to people to say, from a universalist perspective, that sexual morality has not changed; it is just that people are behaving less morally. But a greater tendency for people to do, without thinking it wrong, what once was thought wrong, and a greater tendency, not just to tolerate conduct that once was condemned, but to think of it as not wrong at all, are precisely the kinds of change we are interested in.) The important point here is that the morality of a society gets changed through processes which are intelligible and which it is possible for persons to participate in. That there is less deference to the views of certain social elites, and a wider dissemination of ideas and arguments, than there used to be, makes it easier to defend the idea that the prevailing morality has a provisional authority. For the processes by which morality changes are, increasingly, ones which are visible to all and available to all. The more we can see the influences on the changes as being ones to which everyone has access, the more we have an analogy between the processes by which law is changed (in principle, in a democratic society) and the processes by which morality changes. And the more we can say that people, as they become full members of the society, will have the opportunity to participate in such processes, the more we can say that, in the meantime, they should see the prevailing morality as having authority over them.

NOTES

1. The original 1993 article was in the *Times Educational Supplement*, 19 March 1993 (Phillips has the wrong reference). I have argued further for the importance of philosophy in moral education in Haydon, 1993a, and briefly in *Teaching about Values*, pp. 151–152.
2. For this distinction see Larmore (1996) and Korsgaard (1996), cited by Callan (1998).
3. The Preamble to the SCAA Forum Statement of Values also says that 'the only authority claimed for these values . . . is the authority of consensus'. If the consensus itself is seen as a source of authority people will have a reason (a publicly sanctioned one) for going along with the consensus even when they also acknowledge a different source of authority which pulls in a different direction. This can admittedly put individuals, and possibly whole communities, in a difficult position; but this is a difficulty which already exists. It may be clarified, but is not created, by conceiving of morality(n) and its authority in the way suggested here.
4. It is doubtful whether this argument can apply to any norms which are not concerned with, and seen by those affected to be concerned with, the protection or promotion of interests (cf. *Teaching about Values*, p. 144). Some norms — including some which are seen by their adherents as deriving from divine authority — are not seen by their adherents as being about human interests at all. One response to this would be that it should not be a problem where morality(n) is in question; but see Chapter 14 below. Another response would be to argue with Khin Zaw (1996) that wherever there is a conflict of moral beliefs, the beliefs can be treated as moral interests. If she is right, it may be possible to bring even beliefs which are not about human interests in the normal sense into a Habermas-like schema.
5. I consider how norms may relate to non-human animals in Chapter 14.
6. Critics of the SCAA Forum who say that empirical findings cannot establish the correctness of norms are right; cf. *Teaching Right and Wrong*, p. 142. Whether such claims were actually made on behalf of the Forum is a different question.
7. If one is worried about power relations within society, one may have some reason to be suspicious of the adage that morality is 'caught not taught'. At least the power relationship is more evident in teaching.
8. Some recent empirical evidence is presented in *Young People, Politics and Citizenship: A Disengaged Generation?* (Citizenship Foundation, 1998), which is the report on a Colloquium held in December 1997. Unfortunately, this publication will not help to promote public understanding of morality(n), since changes in attitudes towards premarital sex are the *only* matters reported on under the heading 'Moral matters'.

Chapter 13 Consensus, Criticism and Change

DOTTY: It's not the voting that's democracy, it's the counting. (*Jumpers*, p. 35)

THE NEED FOR AN INSTITUTIONAL BASIS

I have sketched an understanding of morality(n) as having a provisional authority in being subject both to consensus and to criticism and change in a broadly democratic way. But I have also admitted that we lack the formal processes of criticism and change which exist for the law. The reader could reasonably demand that I say at least something more than I have said so far about ways in which the processes of consensus, criticism and change I have in mind could be given some sort of institutional basis. Without that, the kind of understanding of morality that I have been speaking of is likely to remain no more than an understanding which some members of society — perhaps some of those who are both somewhat reflective and somewhat pragmatic — are likely to have. And then it will not be a shared public understanding at all.

It should come as no surprise that I consider formal education — that is, schooling — could be the main channel through which a shared public understanding of morality can be institutionalised. No other social institution has as much opportunity, across generations, of reaching parts of society which other institutions cannot reach. This is indeed one respect in which critics of schooling such as Illich were right when they held that school has become the Church of our modern society; I am, if you like, trying to pick up one positive aspect of that analogy. At the same time there are important differences between the way that the Church[1] might once have promoted a shared understanding of morality and the way that one can now envisage schooling doing so.

The most obvious difference is that the Church works with a broader interpretation of morality which refers to a quite different source of authority from that I have envisaged here. This difference in 'curriculum', though, could be exaggerated. In one direction, there has always been at least some overlap in content between the morality preached by the Church and morality(n); the Church has in fact served a social function of promoting the content of morality(n) whether or not it has seen its role in that way. In the other direction, it is no part of my argument that the only ethical or indeed spiritual concern of schools should be with morality(n). Schools should, as a Church does, have an eye to the broader ethical or spiritual development of their pupils; here the difference is, as I brought out in Chapter 3, that secular schools cannot work to a single model of spiritual or indeed ethical development, given the scope for individual variation and choice.

Having stressed that what I am talking about here is not the whole of a school's concern with 'spiritual, moral, social and cultural development', or with Personal and Social Education, or even with moral education, I return to the responsibility of schools in maintaining morality(n). In this respect the most important differences between schools and Churches is, so to speak, in teaching method rather than curriculum. Churches have often been somewhat static and dogmatic in their teachings. I do not intend that as a criticism; perhaps static and dogmatic, in certain respects, is just what Churches should be. That point at least is arguable. But I do maintain that static and dogmatic is just what schools should not be in *their* moral teachings. Why not? For several reasons which I have already anticipated, so that I need only list them briefly here.

1) There would be a risk that certain norms would be set in stone when they ought to be open to criticism and revision.
2) By seeking merely to promulgate a set of norms already decided on, schools would make it less likely that individuals would see these norms as having authority over them, for reasons I have set out in the previous chapter. In particular, any centralised procedure, through which some government body sought to promulgate norms through the schools, would be likely to reinforce the appearance of morality as an alien imposition.
3) To put the same point in a social/political mode, the promulgation of a predetermined set of norms would be undemocratic. A small body of people would be laying something down for the rest of their contemporaries in society (this is akin to White's (1998) complaint about sectionalism). Further, what was laid down would be expected to have force not only for the present generation but for the next generation and even (to the extent that the norms were set in stone) for further generations beyond. This is what I dubbed in *Teaching about Values* (p. 123) 'generational imperialism' (see also Haydon, 1993).

At the same time, if a shared public understanding is the aim, some public co-ordination across a school system seems to be essential. It will not be sufficient to encourage schools to do something about moral education, while merely assuming that what is promoted will be the same in every school.

To remain in the spirit of the kind of authority which a publicly shared morality(n) can have, any public body trying to promote a shared understanding will have to work at least partly through consensus. While I have already indicated in the previous chapter my agreement with the commonly expressed philosophical view that empirical consensus does not establish that certain values are correct (a point made by Smith and Standish in *Teaching Right and Wrong*, Chapter 11, and also implicit in the preamble to the SCAA Forum Statement), this does not mean that a choice has to be made for consensus *rather than* philosophical argument; the point is to find a way in which these two can be complementary rather than mutually opposed. To suppose that they have to be mutually opposed is, I think, to repeat the sort of mistake that I suspected Melanie Phillips of making: having too little faith in people's ability to 'see reason'. We do not have to subscribe to the division of labour by which the only people who can explain or understand the rationale for certain norms are philosophers. Indeed once stated this seems an unlikely division, as if philosophers were a special class of person.

Philosophers are people who have had a certain sort of education; which people go in for that sort of education is often a rather accidental matter. The role of both education and philosophy in relation to consensus is to make it more likely that the consensus on which it will be possible to move forward is a rational and informed consensus (where 'rational' is not meant to imply that there is only one possible consensus that would be rational).

It is likely, then, that the way forward would not be *entirely* unlike the process by which the SCAA Forum produced its Statement. It may be worth briefly reviewing that process. There were 150 members in the Forum, divided into ten groups, each made up of people sharing certain common interests; the groups did not meet in a plenary session until a draft of the Statement of Values had already been produced (and was in the public realm). Thus, as White (1998, p. 17) correctly surmises, 'once the Forum began to meet there must have been some way of managing its deliberations so as to eventuate in the neat, four-category list of values. . . . What part did SCAA officials and consultants play in this? How far did they regiment what must have been pretty diverse and diffuse data into more manageable categories unconsciously reflecting their own value-preferences?'

Certainly the initial getting together of a draft was not the work of the groups collectively; after the first meeting of each group, the group came back for its second meeting to consider a draft, which was further revised before the next meeting, and so on. One SCAA official[2] attended virtually all of the meetings and, as I understand it, was largely responsible for the drafts which were written, circulated, criticised and revised during the first round of three meetings for each group. The set of four categories — self, relationships, society and environment — was settled during this period though not from the beginning; I recall that at one stage 'family' and 'community' were candidate categories. Presumably the categories were intended to reflect the concerns which were actually coming out of the groups.[3] I have no answer to the 'how far' questions: that is, both 'how far did the writer of the drafts regiment?' and 'how far was it according to her own value-preferences?'

Apart from the initial remit (repeated in the Preamble to the Statement; and see Chapter 3 above), the Forum members were not given any advance instructions about what they were looking for. It is not, then, surprising if the resulting list turned out to be something of a mixed bag, given a degree of structure by the items being put into the four categories, and by their all being expressed as norms. Though, for the reasons I gave in Chapter 3, I think they are best read as an attempt at drawing up an outline of the norms of morality(n), a different list might well have resulted if the Forum members had seen their task explicitly in those terms.

It is not, I think, a problem if the items in the list turn out to differ amongst themselves in their level of specificity or generality. I have argued in Chapter 10 that there is a place among public norms both for specific rules and for very broad principles. For the most part the items in the Forum list, even if some are more general than others, need to be treated as principles, which leave a good deal of discretion rather than mandating or prescribing particular actions. I have already commented at the end of Chapter 10 on the way such principles might function as reference points in public discourse.

What is perhaps more problematic is that some of the items in the Statement do not seem to be of the kind appropriate to morality(n). (This of course, is perfectly possible; as I pointed out in Chapter 3 the mere fact that there is a consensus on certain values does not make them moral values.) In particular, one might instance from the first category:

- develop an understanding of our own characters, strengths and weaknesses;
- clarify the meaning and purpose in our lives and decide, on the basis of this, how we believe that our lives should be lived; and
- strive, throughout life, for knowledge, wisdom and understanding.

While it would certainly be possible to make out an argument that if people took these norms seriously the purposes of morality(n) would thereby be furthered, they do not in themselves seem to be norms that fit comfortably within morality(n), since, consistently with my argument about motivation in Chapter 11, morality(n) can be satisfied (so to speak) even if people lack much self-knowledge and wisdom or sense of meaning in their lives.

Probably, while treating the whole statement as an attempt to draw up a content for morality(n), we should also reckon that several of the items in the first category are there because many members of the Forum had their eye on broader educational goals, and in some cases particularly on the idea of spiritual development.

While the SCAA initiative could well, then, be read as a step towards the promotion through schools of a shared public understanding of morality, it is (from that point of view) a shaky step. A new and more focused attempt to promote such an understanding could start by seeking to find, not simply a consensus on values which happen to be shared, but a consensus on norms which people could see as serving the functions of morality(n). It might on practical grounds be convenient to combine this exercise with a broader remit concerning personal and social education more generally, but there would be advantages in making the concern with morality(n) an explicit aspect of any wider remit. The norms thus arrived at could form a basis for work done in schools,[4] but that work would also need to incorporate a clear sense both of the idea of morality(n) — that is, not only of its content at particular time — and of the ways in which norms could be both justified and criticised. Over time, these forms of justification and criticism could themselves become part of a public consensus.

CRITICISM OF NORMS

Law can often be criticised by reference to moral norms which are publicly acknowledged. But it is not clear that any equivalent account can be given of criticism of prevailing moral norms. For (tautologously) there will not be any publicly recognised moral norms to appeal to outside those which are publicly recognised at a given time. So outside of the set of publicly recognised norms there will be no other authoritative reference point for criticism; but if that is so, it seems to leave the publicly recognised norms having not merely a provisional authority but an absolute one (if they have any at all).

If my account leads into this impasse it is a serious problem. But the logical neatness of the argument just made conceals the fact that in the concrete situation there is a degree of flexibility which does in fact allow for criticism. The situation is one not unfamiliar to modern philosophy — it is the idea that criticism and improvement of beliefs does not have to have foundations to refer to. In that sense, there can be no appeal outside of shared understandings, though understandings can gradually change. But the field of actual and potential shared understandings is broad enough that there are constantly different possibilities of criticising some parts by reference to other parts; there does not have to be a firm unchanging foundation at the bottom of it all (or above it all) for reasoned criticism and change to happen.[5]

There are several ways in which this is so.

1) The publicly recognised norms of one society are not — especially in the modern world — isolated from those of others. Criticism of the norms of one society will sometimes involve comparison with those of another.

2) The publicly recognised norms of a society will not necessarily form a consistent set, nor (as I have pointed out in Chapter 10) will they all be at the same level. It will often be possible for criticism of certain norms to appeal to other norms which are also publicly recognised: for instance, criticism of a relatively specific rule may sometimes be criticised by reference to a broader principle. (This is not unlike the way in which legal argument can go on within a structure in which both temporary and local statute law, and also broader principles, are recognised.)

3) There can be appeal to how inclusive a perceived consensus actually is — a point which will be relevant again in the next chapter.

4) There can be appeal to the underlying point of morality(n): that is, arguments may be made that currently recognised norms do not in fact tend to check undesirable motivations, or do this at unnecessary cost, or do not facilitate co-operation, and so on. (In line with my remarks above I do not see this as an attempt to find foundations by getting outside the sphere of public discourse to something incontrovertible, perhaps in evolutionary psychology; the appeal will still be to public understandings.) It is plausible that as a general understanding of morality(n), in something like the terms in which I have described it here, becomes more widespread, criticism of this kind would become more common.

In Chapter 8 I distinguished four sorts of relationship (actually points in a spectrum) in which norms might stand to the underlying purpose of morality(n). What happens to the authority of norms when these differences in terms of underlying rationale come to be explicitly addressed (as they inevitably would be in an education which seeks to promote both understanding of morality(n) and a reflective disposition towards it)? For my categories (1) and (4) at opposite ends of the spectrum there should be no special problems. The kind of fundamental rules to which White refers in *Teaching Right and Wrong* (such as the prohibitions on killing and grievous bodily harm) should be able to retain as much authority as they have ever had; there is no reason, here and now, to suppose they will ever cease to be part of morality(n).[6] The taboos which have no underlying rationale should lose any vestige of authority.

The case for the categories between is more difficult. Category (3) was of norms which give a particular shape to human life, though it can be recognised that there is no underlying argument for one shape rather than another. It is difficult to see how far norms in this category can survive critical reflection, a point related to that Williams (1985, Chapter 9) makes about the loss of ethical knowledge. I shall not attempt here to assess how far there is or is not significant loss; we may in any case have to accept that human societies are becoming, to stick to the metaphor, more shapeless than they used to be.

Category (2) perhaps raises the greatest problems. These are cases where there are (or it is widely believed that there are) good reasons of a consequentialist kind for having certain norms, but where there are many cases (not just rare exceptions) in which there seems no harm in someone going against the norms, and even many where it is (still on consequentialist grounds) better for individuals in particular circumstances if they do not adhere to the norms. Suppose, to take up again the example I used in Chapter 8, that things will go better overall if people in society in general adhere to traditional norms of monogamy, where these are taken to include a prohibition on premarital sex (whether we could reliably know this is a further question). What then would be the advice to be given to a person wondering whether there is any reason not to enter into what might be a short-term cohabiting relationship? Apparently this: Do not, because things will go better overall if people in society in general adhere to traditional norms of monogamy. This seems unlikely to be a very convincing reason to the individual. (Notice the difference between this and instances in category (1), albeit the difference may be one of degree; it is important that in the case of killing and injuring we can give other kinds of reason than just 'things will go better overall if people in society in general adhere to norms of not killing and injuring'.)

Norms of category (2) are, then, likely gradually to lose their authority. But there may well be reasons, again of a consequentialist kind, for wanting them not to lose their authority too quickly. Society takes time to adjust. In the meantime there are different people trying to work to different norms; and in an area like this the possibilities of special pleading by individuals in their own interests — or to satisfy their own inclinations — are particularly strong (cf. Chapter 9, p. 81 above). The best situation we can realistically hope for is probably the one already envisaged, in which society's norms are taken to have a provisional authority, but are not, as a body, expected to remain static.

In Chapter 2 I referred to Cupitt's view that morality can for the most part be left to look after itself. I have shown, I think, that the evolution and renegotiation of the rules which Cupitt has in mind cannot be an automatic process: it is one that takes knowledge, intelligence, and discussion, and hence it is very much a process in which education, including formal education, has an important role.

THE ROLE OF TEACHERS

What, then, is the role of teachers in the processes of consensus-building, criticism and change? We can ask two questions here. What would the role of teachers be if there were a public body charged with the promotion, through schooling, of a shared public understanding of morality? And what is the role of teachers when in fact, as now, there is no such body with that responsibility? Though these are two different questions, the answers will to a large degree coincide. A public body with the responsibility to promote through schools a shared understanding of morality would have to make certain demands on teachers in terms of their own knowledge and understanding, and their approaches to teaching in the area of morality. But, bureaucratic details aside, these are the demands which, individually or collectively as a profession, teachers might reasonably make on themselves even in the absence of some public co-ordinating body. I shall, then, give just one set of answers to both questions.

If my argument so far is accepted, it should be clear that the role of teachers will not be confined to transmitting some set of norms which is taken as fixed. This is for at least three reasons. One is that, even in relation to the norms which may be subject to a consensus at any given time, teachers' role is not to transmit them didactically.[7] A second, the positive converse of the first, is that teachers need to develop in their students the understanding and capacity necessary to reflect on current norms, so as to endorse them with understanding, and where appropriate criticise them. Teachers themselves, then, will need to have an understanding of the nature of morality(n) and of ways in which its norms can be justified and criticised.

A third, taking up a point made above, is that the role of teachers in promoting a shared public understanding of morality(n), onerous though that may be, is not the whole of their role in moral education. The reason for this is that the promotion of a shared understanding of morality(n) will not by itself remove — and is not intended to remove — the existing diversity across society in understandings of morality or ethics in the broader sense. Even supposing a shared understanding of morality(n) is achieved, that does not mean that the differences that remain can be ignored. To the contrary, in a plural and democratic society it is important that people should have knowledge not only of what they share but also of their differences. If I do not spend time on that point here it is because it is already widely acknowledged. I have myself argued for it, on grounds both of what is necessary for tolerance and of what is necessary for the functioning of democracy, in Haydon (1995) and in *Teaching about Values* (see especially pp. 140–142, 154–155).

Even from the little that has been said here, a good deal could be drawn out about the knowledge and understanding that teachers need to have to fulfil their role in public moral education: knowledge, for instance, about existing norms, both those widely shared and those which are shared only within certain groups, and the capacities to facilitate in pupils the kind of discussion of values which will help to promote both individuals' understanding of their own values and their understanding and tolerance of other people's.[8] Above all, teachers need to be able to use, and to be confident in using, both a language of norms and languages of virtues.

Reflection on the demands that a systematic approach to moral education would make on teachers can only heighten the realisation that teachers now standardly get very little preparation for this aspect of their role. I have argued in other places (Haydon, 1996; *Teaching about Values*, Chapter 13) that the teaching profession as a whole could give more attention than it does — in any explicit and systematic way — to its own values. This might be done, as in many other professions, through the formulation and promulgation of a code of ethics, though there may be other ways also. Within any profession, there are arguments for a shared sense of ethics which to some degree parallel the arguments for a shared sense of morality among the general public. One difference will be that whereas a shared morality(n) will probably not, in a liberal society, include an articulation of some collective overall goals, the shared ethic of a profession usually will include some such articulation of goals, such as health in the case of the health-care professions.

For teaching, a statement of shared goals is likely to be multifaceted. But it should, I would argue, include an acknowledgement of the role teachers have in the public aspect of moral education. As John Tomlinson, one of the authors of a draft Code of Ethical Principles for the Teaching Profession,[9] has put it: 'Teachers . . . discharge public responsibility for the socialisation and value-world of the next generation. They must be expected to encourage personal and social responsibility in their learners, and accept it for themselves.' (Tomlinson, 1995, p. 185).

What I have tried to do above all in this book — and it is significant that one can try to do this even in advance of tying down any detailed content for morality — is to indicate that it is possible to have a conception of morality which people could converge on, without particular metaphysical commitments, without hypocrisy, without authoritarianism. For any individual teachers who may on their own initiative come to read my arguments, I hope I will have helped them to feel that they can know what they are doing in this area. The question remains of how much can be achieved through teachers working on their own initiative; any individual's influence is limited, especially when a shared understanding is the aim. So there is a temptation to think that some sort of public agency (perhaps the Public Understanding of Morality Authority, which would, of course, be generally known as the PUMA) would be essential to co-ordinate the relevant work and tell teachers what to do. This carries its own dangers. Any appearance that a quango is trying to impose its own conception of morality on teachers risks being antithetical to the spirit of a shared public understanding of morality.

There may yet be room for a middle way: a understanding of morality(n), which teachers could feel comfortable with, initially shared across the teaching profession itself, which that profession, through education and without imposition, could try to spread more widely through the general public. This could not be achieved without channels of communication and policy-making existing for the profession as a whole. There would have to be a professional body working in such a way that teachers really could feel themselves to be part of a single profession sharing certain commitments and understandings; it would also have to be able to listen to and respond to the general public. This is a public role which one could imagine a General Teaching Council performing. Unfortunately, this would not be the kind of General Teaching Council which it appears, at the time of writing, we are actually going to get.

NOTES

1. To avoid complications in what is not a central part of my argument, I shall speak here in a way applicable to an established Church like the Church of England; what I say could generally be adapted to other varieties of organised religion and other religions.
2. Barbara Wintersgill. (The Oxford philosopher Marianne Talbot came on the scene as a consultant somewhat later.)
3. Notice that these four categories are quite distinct from the spiritual, moral, social, cultural categorisation used by OFSTED (see Chapter 3 above). I suspect the discrepancy was not by design; certainly it led to complications in the development of the guidance for schools; cf. Haydon 1998, pp. 10 ff., p. 19.

4. In addition to the question of how a consensus is to be established, there is the question of how it is to find its way into practice in schools. White (1998) states that whereas the later QCA investigation into the aims of education was due to eventuate in a report for the Secretary of State for Education, the SCAA Forum exercise fed its outcomes direct into policy changes in schools. This does not fit my understanding of the events. SCAA sent a report of the work of the Forum to the Secretary of State shortly after the General Election of May 1997; the report was accepted by the Secretary of State. Only after that did SCAA produce pilot materials on SMSC development to be tried out in schools; the pilot exercise, in a total of 100 schools, began in Autumn 1997 and is due to run for about two years. As yet, then, no outcomes have been fed directly into policy changes at school level.

5. If the reader versed in the literature expects at this point a reference to Neurath's boat I am happy to oblige, pointing out that the same analogy is used in the context of the law by Dworkin, 1986, p. 111.

6. White includes the norm against stealing (see the quotation in Chapter 2 above). Despite Biblical precedent, this does not seem to me to be in the same category, since it is conceivable that the conventions establishing a sense of property could change so much as to render this norm inapplicable.

7. See *Teaching about Values*, Chapter 11 for problems with the idea of teachers as transmitters.

8. See Haydon, 1999b.

9. Published by the Universities' Council for the Education of Teachers (UCET).

Chapter 14 The Content of Morality(n)

DOTTY: . . . all our absolutes, the thou-shalts and the thou-shalt-nots
that seemed to be the very condition of our existence, how did *they* look
to two moonmen with a single neck to save between them? Like the local
customs of another place. When that thought drips through to the
bottom, people won't just carry on. There is going to be such . . .
breakage, such gnashing of unclean meats, such coveting of neighbours'
oxen and knowing of neighbours' wives, such dishonourings of mothers
and fathers, and bowings and scrapings to images graven and incarnate,
such killing of goldfish and maybe more . . . (*Jumpers*, p. 75)

BEYOND THE MINIMUM

If the reader expects, under this chapter's title, a list of norms which
are to constitute the content of a publicly shared morality(n), then he
or she will have missed the point of much of my argument in the last
several chapters. Such a content is not something to be laid down by
a philosopher: it is to be arrived at through consensus and criticism in
the light of a shared understanding of morality(n).

The reader might, however, feel short-changed with nothing but
that. I shall then, without stipulating the details of content, say more
about the kinds of question that need to be addressed in the attempt
to articulate relevant norms, and in doing this I shall pay some special
attention to the theme of violence which has been my dominant
example throughout. It will emerge that both in general, and in
relation to violence particularly, there is a question of how minimal
or expansive the shared norms are to be.

As part of a broader ethical outlook, someone might reasonably be
concerned that a morality(n) resulting from a consensual process would
be rather limited and inward-looking. People sharing an understanding
of morality(n) might think (i) that while they and their fellow-members
are bound by the terms of this morality(n), it has no prescriptive force
for anyone else. People might also think (ii) that the agreed norms tell
them how to behave towards the fellow members of their own society,
but do not tell them how to behave towards anyone else (let alone
towards animals or the environment). And people might think (iii) that
morality(n) predominantly requires them to hold off from interference
with others, but does not make much demand on them to bring positive
benefit to others.

These three possibilities give us three questions worth exploring here.

(i)   To what range of moral agents do the norms of morality(n) apply, that is, who is subject to those norms?

(ii) To what range of beneficiaries do the norms apply, that is, who or what needs to be taken into account in applying the norms?

(iii) Are the norms going to be minimal and predominantly negative, or far more extensive and positive, in what they require?

The kind of position I have sketched, at its worst, is one I would be far from wanting to endorse (I am, of course, occupying a particular evaluative stance in saying 'at its worst'). There is (relating to the first question) a variety of relativism which says (for example) 'English people should behave in this sort of way but we can't say anything about how other people should behave'. Then (relating to the second question) there can be an ethnocentric or otherwise group-centred morality in which people think they should behave well towards their fellow group members but do not think it matters how they behave towards anyone (or anything) else. And (relating to the third question) there can be a minimal morality in which people think that provided they respect other people's basic (negative) rights, it does not matter whether they do any positive good in the world.

I shall not attempt the empirical assessment which would be necessary to tell us how far such positions are widespread at the moment. The three positions put together may well form a picture the reader finds recognisable. But at the same time there are counter-weights to those positions. Many people do think that basic moral norms apply to everyone, that they themselves should not just take fellow members of their group into account, and that they should positively help others. This mixed picture is the one that educators have to start from. My present question is whether the broad approach I am suggesting, working through criticism and consensus, will inevitably tend towards an inward-looking and minimal sense of morality.

A BRITISH MORALITY?

There is, if not a tradition, then at least a recent practice of certain educational initiatives being taken at national level,[1] including the SCAA Forum. If the approach I am suggesting were to be encouraged and facilitated through the education system, this would be likely to give it a national focus. If there were an attempt, as British educational policy, to promote a public consensus on the nature and content of morality, it would be a consensus across the British public that such a policy would be aiming at. Does this mean that the consensus would be on 'British morality'? There are at least two aspects of my argument that might lead us to expect this.

One is the point first made in Chapter 8, that many moral norms are not the only possible response to certain features of the human condition: they are norms that give a particular shape to what Standish (in *Teaching Right and Wrong*) calls our moral geography, where other shapes would also be possible. There is, then, room for a degree of relativity in morality, and we should expect this to be reflected in the public understanding which is already present or which is arrived at in different parts of the world. For instance, there appear to be strong norms of filial piety in many parts of East Asia, and in terms of the purposes of morality(n) such norms make good sense as a response to human vulnerability with advancing age. A shared sense of morality(n) in Western societies will equally need to respond to that (and arguably to find rather better ways of responding to it than are widespread now). But ideas of filial piety are not the only possible response, and with such traditions not now in place in Western societies it is to be expected that Western understandings of the requirements of morality(n) in this respect will not be identical with East Asian ones. That is why, though the notion of morality(n) does not itself contain any culture-relativity, it was possible to say in Chapter 8, pursuing the analogy with positive law, that any set of moral norms will be the norms of a society.

A second element in the preceding discussion that could point toward a rather inward-looking understanding of morality is the conception of moral authority that I have adumbrated. This is in line with the claim made in the Preamble of the SCAA Forum Statement, that the only authority claimed for the norms listed is 'the authority of consensus'. In the context, this can only mean 'consensus across our society'. Pragmatically, one can see how teachers and others involved in education may more confidently work with the understanding of the morality they are subscribing to as being that of their own society; they will seem to be making more modest claims if they are saying 'This is our society's morality' rather than 'This is (universal) morality *per se*'.

The more modest claim also fits with the point made first in Chapter 5, and taken up again in the discussion of moral authority, that people can agree on norms, not only in the sense that they agree that certain norms would be a good idea, but in the stronger sense that they agree to act according to the norms (p. 48 above). There is something here of a social contract understanding of morality: for mutual benefit, the members of a society agree with each other that they will regulate their behaviour towards each other in certain ways. And indeed, given the importance of a shared sense of membership of a community to which I referred in the last chapter, I do think this is an important element in the shared moral understanding of a society.

At the same time, there is a temptation to claim more than local validity for the norms that may be agreed across a society. Smith and Standish in *Teaching Right and Wrong* seem to have interpreted the SCAA Forum as claiming that a consensus found empirically in Britain somehow establishes universal validity. Of course, an empirical finding across one society does not establish this; on the other hand, an appeal to the underlying point of morality(n) will give a backing to norms which is not merely local.

One needs, I think, both a recognition of local consensus and a recognition that the norms on which there is consensus do not apply only to members of the group within which the consensus is arrived at. (It would be a fine thing if English football fans undertook not to fight each other; but not so fine if this goes with the idea that there is nothing wrong with fighting fans of foreign clubs in the streets of French or German cities.) Fortunately, there is no incompatibility here. There is no incoherence in the idea that an agreement with others of one's own group to observe certain norms in relation to each other can coexist with a recognition that those same norms apply to members of the group in relation to others outside the group. To take up Mary Warnock's example from Chapter 8, it is not, so far as I can see, absurd that there might be an agreed rule within a school that there is to be bullying or theft within the school, coexisting with the recognition that there is to be no bullying of or theft from anyone outside the school either. Indeed this could also be part of what members of the school have agreed with each other. So also across a whole society, a shared public acknowledgement that theft is wrong will certainly be understood as implying that members of the society should not steal from each other, but will at the same time be a shared acknowledgement that stealing from anyone is wrong. (One implication of this is that if shame is to figure at all in people's motivation for observing the norms, shame before one's fellow group members may be felt not only for transgressing the norms against fellow group members, but for transgressing those same norms also against others.)

It will be part of the responsibility of educators to see that the developing understanding of morality on the part of their students does not become too inward-looking. They may do this in part by referring to the underlying point of morality(n). Since morality(n) is a response to elements of the human condition which are in no way limited by national boundaries, there is no inherent reason why its most important norms should not be universal ones (universal at least across human beings, rather than across rational beings as in Kant). Educators wishing to resist inwardness should very much be helped by the evident fact that cultures and countries are not in impermeable compartments. Cultures coexist in a classroom and, with increasing travel and through the media, people who are not fellow-citizens are frequently encountered. Promoting within one society a shared sense of a morality which is not confined to that society ought to be easier now than at any time before.

ONLY HUMAN?

How far will the requirements of morality(n) be understood as applying to actions of which the major effects are not on human beings? There are several approaches which seem to be compatible with an underlying appreciation of the importance of morality(n). On some issues, where damage to the environment makes the world a worse place to live in, even from the point of view solely of human interests, the norms prohibiting that damage can be straightforwardly part of morality(n). Where that is not the case, some would see norms against harming animals or the environment as extensions to morality(n) — that is, part of an extended morality(n) — and ones which are from a logical point of view gratuitous, even though explicable. This is Mackie's (1977, pp. 194–195) approach in relation to animals.

Another possibility, which may more clearly apply to the environment than to animals, is to see the concerns for the non-human as not part of morality(n) at all, but as part of morality or ethics in a broader sense. On this view, taking action for the sake of the environment might be part of some people's conception of a good life but would not be a part of a shared morality(n). Griffin (1996, p. 127) takes this view.

Others see norms against harming animals as rationally required extensions from an initial appreciation of the way in which morality(n) serves human interests; given that morality(n) requires norms against the causing of suffering, it is simply irrational not to recognise that these norms apply to suffering as such, whether human or animal. (We could add that where moral norms are articulated in terms of violence, there will be no good reason to define violence in such a way that only human beings can be its victims.) This is Peter Singer's approach, and my approach in *Teaching about Values* (see p. 108, n. 4). Something different, however, needs to be said about the environment, which cannot in the same literal sense suffer. Where violence against animals can be violence in the same literal sense as violence against human beings, violence against the environment will be violence in a metaphorical or extended sense.

Yet another approach in applying norms to animals and the environment is to extend one's sense of the community of which one sees oneself to be a member. We are all — humans and non-humans — animals sharing the biosphere; for that matter, we are all — animals, plants, even mountains — part of the same common world (cf. *Teaching about Values*, p. 96 n. 15; Clark, 1977, 1993).

For my argument here, there is no need to decide for one or other of these approaches. They all exist, and not only among philosophers. They exist already within that public whose understanding of morality I am talking about. In any attempt, then, to arrive at a more widely and explicitly shared understanding of morality, these points of view would be represented. To speak only of Britain, it is unlikely that a shared sense of morality would not include norms on the treatment of animals and the environment. Certainly this held good of the SCAA Forum Statement, which includes a section on the environment in which animals are mentioned. The item relating to animals — that we should 'understand our responsibilities for other species' — probably represents fairly well the present state of agreement. It does not attempt to say what these responsibilities are; but it does, importantly, rule out the idea that we do not have any responsibilities towards animals. That is enough to enable even this apparently rather vacuous prescription to function as a reference point in the way I suggested in Chapter 10.

A MINIMAL MORALITY?

The question of how minimal or otherwise a shared morality(n) may be cuts across the question about animals and the environment. There can, for instance, be a minimal conception of responsibilities towards animals — that we should not be deliberately cruel towards an animal — or far more extensive conceptions. But it would apply also even within a morality in which no responsibilities were recognised towards anything non-human. The spectrum extends from the most minimal morality of a recognition of certain basic and negative rights[2] to the most extensive utilitarian conception — not actually held by most utilitarians — that everyone ought at all times, and at the expense of any projects of their own, to be doing all they can to promote human happiness. Various conceptions of virtue ethics will fall somewhere between the extremes, if they can be placed on the same spectrum at all (it will depend partly on what weight is given to the virtue of benevolence and how that is interpreted). An ethics of care is likely to demand that those who are able to 'put themselves out' for at least some others, but nevertheless may fall towards the minimal end of the spectrum because caring is in the first instance a response towards the perceived needs of particular others who are immediately present.[3] Within philosophy of education, the issue of where our conception of morality should be placed on this spectrum has been extensively discussed by White (1982).

It may seem that a consensus approach to the content of morality(n) will tend towards a conception of responsibilities which will do as much as, but no more than, is necessary to satisfy the interests of those who are party to the consensus. This is by no means necessarily so, since those who are party to the consensus need not be motivated only by self-interest. But suppose it is so. Then the content of the consensus depends very much on how inclusive is the process by which the consensus is arrived at. People in comfortable circumstances might agree on norms which would require them to do little more than refrain from interfering with each other. A consensus which includes the homeless, people with disabilities, people with chronic illness, and so on, would be unlikely to be so minimal.[4]

Again, there are heavy implications for education. By its nature, compulsory formal schooling takes in a wide cross-section of any population. Apart from a minority whose parents choose to educate them at home, formal schooling takes in everyone at a certain stage in their life. So if there could be a consensus to which everyone in all the schools in a society had agreed, there could hardly be any way in which any more inclusive consensus could be arrived at. It should be possible in schools, if anywhere, to see that people do not grow up with a conception of morality which overlooks the needs of those who are less well-placed than themselves. If, as a society, we do end up with a shared public understanding of morality which is minimal and inward-looking, it will be at least in part because teachers have not taken up some of the opportunities which schooling makes possible.

NORMS ABOUT VIOLENCE

Any publicly shared set of norms would be incomplete — as would this book, in the light of my initial concerns — without some attention to violence. Indeed it might be a criticism of the SCAA Forum list that it says almost nothing explicitly about violence. The closest it gets is the item under 'Relationships' which reads 'resolve disputes peacefully'.[5] Of course, violence might be taken to be ruled out by other items, such as 'respect others, including children'. But given that some adults will argue that they are respecting children in using corporal punishment on them, this stops well short of an explicit prohibition on violence. Perhaps the SCAA Forum list is an instance of the phenomenon I noted in Chapter 2, of taking the wrongness of violence — and even of killing — for granted.

Rather than the wrongness of violence being taken for granted, and thus not articulated, an articulation of norms is surely needed. But beyond this point, of course, matters are not simple. In his discussion in *Teaching Right and Wrong*, for instance, White does not speak of a rule against violence as such: he sees the basic moral rules as ruling out 'injury' or, later, 'grievous bodily harm'. Violence, even violence which is unambiguously physical, does not always cause injury, and injury is not always grievous. The ruling out of violence as such would not be so uncontroversially part of the framework of basic rules to which White refers.

Publicly acknowledged norms, however, have to draw lines, and the lines have to be recognisable and applicable in practice. A line between some acceptable level of hurt and some unacceptable level of injury as a result of physical violence is going to be too easily blurred. Any physical violence, even if not intended to have serious results, runs the risk of doing so. And any physical violence at least raises a presumption that those on the receiving end are not being respected. There is good reason, then, for erring on the side of caution and drawing the line against physical violence as such.

It is difficult, however, to rule out physical violence without ruling out more than that. Some schools have rules saying 'We keep our hands, feet and objects to ourselves' (cited by Skillen, 1997, p. 376, but by no means unique to his children's school). This may indeed, as Skillen suggests (*ibid.*, p. 381) 'suppress . . . the very impulses of friendship'; but it is presumably an attempt to set up the sort of norm which will at least ensure an absence of physical violence until more subtle nuances can be appreciated. The initial improvement in subtlety needed here would be the realisation that, as we have seen in Chapter 7 and Chapter 10, norms can refer to motivation and not only to the outwardly observable aspects of action.

If some sort of ruling out of interpersonal physical violence is taken here as basic and minimal, then again there is a question of how far a shared understanding is to go beyond the minimal. There are several ways in which the scope of norms against violence can be understood more broadly. One question is whether the same norms apply in institutionalised contexts, the police and military, for instance, as in 'private' interpersonal contexts. This is a question which in educational contexts provides ample scope for the kind of thinking about justification and criticism to which I referred in the last chapter.

Probably more problematic, because it will seem to many to call into question the meaning of the word 'violence', are questions about what sort of actions and states of affairs, other than deliberate use of physical force by persons against persons with intent to hurt or harm, are to be brought under norms against violence. As I pointed out in

Chapter 1, it is possible to give reasons for using the term 'violence' in a broader way. But whereas the question may have seemed at that point to be one about the meaning of a word, it is perhaps clearer now that the primary question is about the norms which are to constitute the content of a publicly shared morality(n). How a particular word is to be used, while far from unimportant, is — or can reasonably be treated as — a question about how our norms can best be articulated.

Norms that refer to the outwardly observable aspect of actions and norms that refer to motivation categorise conduct in different ways. The notion of violence cuts across both categorisations, which is one reason why it is so problematic. 'Keep your hands and feet to yourself', as Skillen notices, puts blows intended to hurt in the same category (probably unintentionally) as friendly pats on the back or hugs. 'Don't be cruel' puts blows intended to hurt in the same category as words intended to hurt. If 'don't be cruel' means something like 'don't cause pain for your own satisfaction' (cf. Chapter 10 above), this can apply to the causing of emotional as well as of physical pain. If the cruel infliction of physical pain counts as violence, then so can the cruel infliction of emotional pain, which may or may not accompany physical pain. Thus it is possible to count some verbal attacks as violence, in a way fully compatible with what I said in Chapter 7 about the link between anger and violence:

> This kind of verbal violence frequently goes with anger and shouting, often directed at someone not in a position to answer back. The aim is to hurt the other person emotionally, to cause them mental pain and anguish. This can substitute for, or supplement, the causing of physical pain by bodily means. It can, indeed, be worse in its effects than passing physical violence. (McGinn, 1992, p. 41)

What is important here, morally speaking, is that people should not do this sort of thing — in other words, a norm against behaving in a certain kind of way. Whether or not we do call this way of behaving violent is surely not a question of great interest in its own right — other than a specialist lexicographical question — independently of the moral questions. One could argue the question of terminology both ways. On the one hand, if 'violence' is restricted to the physical variety, then 'don't be violent' sets up a clear line which people know they are not to transgress. Maybe in certain circumstances it is justifiable or excusable to get angry and to express the anger — and it may not be easy to stay on one side of the line between expressing justified criticism and being angry — but at least you know you must stop short of hitting the person. But by the same token, if you think that the most important thing is that you should not attack physically, you may feel justified in any amount of verbal attack, and go too far in that way. If we put great weight on a norm ruling out physical attack, we also have to accept a responsibility to moderate the forms of verbal assault we use.

Though the norms in such cases refer to the agent's motivation, they do also refer to harm done. Notice, for instance, that McGinn in the passage above does not simply equate the motivations behind certain verbal and physical attacks: he also points out that the effects of the one can be worse than that of the other. More generally, as I have pointed out before (in e.g. Chapters 1 and 6 above), thinking in terms of norms for conduct does tend to direct our attention towards the consequences of actions. If we object to action which will cause injury, and object to this not because of the motivation of the agent, but because of the injury itself, then we have reason for objecting, not only to deliberate cruelty, but also, say, to the state of affairs which allows people to be killed and maimed in road accidents. If we count among physical harms, not only such things as being hit, stabbed or shot but also, say, dying of cold and hunger, then we have reason to object to the state of affairs which allows old people in affluent countries to die of cold in the winter, and many thousands in less affluent parts of the world to die of hunger. Since these are harms which could be avoided or at the very least mitigated through deliberate human actions, it is not extending the meaning of the term unintelligibly to speak in such cases of violence by some people against others.

In that kind of case the extension of meaning putatively goes through because the causing of physical harm — or responsibility for avoidable physical harm — is still there. But the notion of psychological violence already shows that the element of physical harm is not essential to the notion of violence. So the way is opened for a notion such as that of systemic violence, already referred to, which can refer to any 'institutional practice or procedure that adversely impacts on individuals or groups by burdening them psychologically, mentally, culturally, spiritually, economically or physically' (Epp and Watkinson, 1996, p.i), or the rather similar notion of structural violence which was probably first used by the peace researcher Galtung (1969).

At this point it should be clear that we have arrived at a notion rather close to that of injustice or oppression. My own feeling about this (which I do not take to have any argumentative or evidential value) is that at some point in the gradual extension of the meaning of 'violence' we have come too far from its central meaning. But the extensions are not arbitrary. It is worth remembering that, given the vulnerable physical nature of human beings, many forms of injustice and oppression do have physical effects in the end: the poor are more likely to get ill and do not (statistically speaking) live so long. This is one of the main planks of Honderich's (1980) comparison between violence and injustice, though he himself keeps to a fairly restricted use of the term 'violence'. And there are strong arguments from moral philosophers (e.g. Glover, 1977) for thinking that ordinary moral thinking puts too much weight on the distinction between acts and omissions.[6]

When I started writing this book, I thought I was going to argue for a public morality of clearly articulated norms, where something simple like 'don't be violent' would be among the norms. I also thought I was going to argue for sticking to a narrow definition of violence. And I wanted to argue that there is something specially horrible about violence (thus defined) even within the whole field of ways in which people can treat each other badly and ways in which things can go badly wrong. I have not, at least not here, found the arguments for the last point. As for the narrow definition, as a philosopher by profession, I could defend that in terms of clarity in public discourse and the avoidance of confusion. But we should also recognise that sticking to a restricted meaning makes it easy for us to believe that we, individually, cannot be responsible for anything like, or as bad as, violence. To insist on a narrow definition is, then, to take a position which we, that is, I and probably most of my readers, can comfortably live with. But having read Frankfurt (1988) and Charles Taylor (1977) on second-order or strong evaluation, we should not be comfortable with something so comfortable to live with. I prefer, then, to leave the question of how violence is to be defined as a question to be worked out within the public sphere, as we try to articulate the norms by which we wish to and are prepared to live.

Earlier in this chapter I gave reasons for thinking that, even taking a consensual approach towards the content of morality, we are not bound to find that our morality becomes or remains minimal. There are sufficient voices already in the public sphere, including but by no means confined to the voices of philosophers, to make it likely — provided education plays its role — that shared conceptions of morality will be more expansive than this. I suspect that something similar will happen with our understanding of the category of violence. Already in the public sphere there are sufficient arguments, difficult enough to ignore, in favour of expanding our understanding of violence, for it to be likely that the boundaries around a narrow understanding will not prove impregnable. This is something on which neither philosophers nor educationalists can legislate, though we can add our voices to the public discourse. To some degree we are observers, but we can remain ready to help people to think clearly and not to be misled by their language.

Will it then be an irrevocable loss of clarity if the term 'violence' comes to incorporate categories which our ancestors would not have recognised as violence? It will not, provided a degree of self-consciousness and reflectiveness about language can be retained. Will there be an irrevocable loss of moral clear-sightedness? Not necessarily. Indeed it may be the other way round: we may be helped to see clearly wrongs that we might have overlooked before.

Of the things I set out thinking I would do, I have argued for a public morality of articulated norms, even if they cannot unproblematically take such forms as 'don't be violent'. But while I have thought at times that I would be arguing for a language of rules and principles and against a language of virtues — consciously going against the recent tendency in the literature — it now seems all the more clear that both are indispensable, and that both need careful educational attention: neither can be taken for granted.

NOTES

1. For strong historical and political reasons, educational policies initiated by the British government have usually been for England and Wales, with different provision for Scotland. For the public understanding of morality this might make particularly good sense, since there have been numerous initiatives on values education in Scotland in recent years, and there was once a strong Scottish tradition of public engagement in moral discourse (see MacIntyre, 1987). Here, though, simply for convenience, I shall refer to a putative national policy as British.

2. In my doctoral thesis I have argued that such a conception is too minimal to be viable as a basis for moral education.

3. Cf. *Teaching about Values* p. 80. Also, compare Peter Singer's (1972, 1979) arguments on the obligation to relieve famine with Noddings (1984). (For a Kantian perspective on the same issue, cf. O'Neill, 1986).

4. I made a similar point in Chapter 12 when discussing whether consensus can ground the authority of norms. In various ways the same point is present, of course, in Habermas, Rawls and Kant.

5. At one point in the drafting this read 'try to resolve disputes peacefully'. (Indeed at one point virtually every item in the list began with 'try' or 'strive'.) In line with points made in Chapter 10 above, there is nothing wrong in itself with norms being articulated as broad principles which allow discretion in their interpretation. In this instance, however, my own expressed view was that the item left far too much room for discretion as to what would count as sufficient trying ('Please Miss, I did try to reason with him before I hit him'). One might think that what is to be ruled out is, not merely resorting to violence before trying anything else, but resorting to violence at all as a way of winning (rather than resolving) disputes.

6. Coady (1986) is a useful discussion of the arguments over the meaning of 'violence'. Coady defends a fairly conservative position.

Chapter 15   The Moral Development of Society

CROUCH (about McFee): 'Henry', he said to me, 'Henry, I am giving philosophical respectability to a new pragmatism in public life . . .' (*Jumpers*, p. 80)

As I stressed in Chapter 13, I have by no means addressed all aspects of moral education in this book, let alone all aspects of personal and social education or of a school's concern for spiritual, moral, social and cultural development. Even within the notion of 'moral development' there is much about which I have said little. In Chapter 3 I sketched a rather crude notion of moral development by which it could be said that someone has developed morally to the extent that he or she has come to share the values which are central to a given society. That way of conceiving of moral development leaves out a great deal: it says nothing about individual attitudes and feelings towards others or about the degree of responsibility the individual takes for his or her own behaviour. Nor does it tell us what balance is to be struck in the overall educational task between putting across received norms, trying to develop virtues, and encouraging the capacity for and disposition towards autonomous thought. I do not, therefore, put it forward as a conception of moral development *tout court*. Nevertheless, it does point to an aspect of moral development in which society has a legitimate interest, but which education has not in recent years done much systematically to address. It is my contention that this is an important aspect of moral development for education to take into account, not least because it can at the same time be seen as an aspect of education for citizenship.

When people speak of moral development, it is nearly always the moral development *of individuals* which they have in mind. Contrast this with talk of moral decline. That notion is more likely to be predicated of society as a whole. Indeed the thought that our society is in some sort of moral decline is quite a common one. Smith and Standish, for instance, refer to the Bulger and Lawrence murders as 'symptomatic of a more general moral destitution in our society' (*Teaching Right and Wrong*, p. vii). The thought here is not simply that people, individually, are behaving in a less moral way than people used to (indeed Smith and Standish quite rightly show that we could argue the other way). It is the thought of something lacking 'in the moral as well as the social fabric of society' (p. viii).

The popular view of violence from which we started seems to buy into this notion of moral decline, and couples with it the kind of limited notion of moral development to which I have just referred. And it offers the latter as a solution to the former. Individuals have to behave better (as judged by widely agreed norms), and have to be brought to behave better through moral education. So the moral development of individuals seems to be regarded as the cure for the moral decline of society. There is at least an asymmetry here that invites examination.

Interestingly, though it is often forgotten, the formative 1988 educational legislation which led directly to the National Curriculum in England and Wales, and indirectly to the present school inspection system, required schools to have a curriculum which would promote 'the spiritual, moral, cultural, mental and physical development of pupils at the school *and of society*' [emphasis added]. On the face of it, a contribution from schools to the moral development *of society*, not only of individuals, could be just what is needed to counteract a moral decline of society — if, that is, we can make sense of the idea of the moral development of society.

INTERPRETATIONS OF THE DEVELOPMENT OF SOCIETY

I shall try here to bring out what we might understand by the moral development of society, by taking up again the contrast I made in Chapter 3 between spiritual and moral development, but now transposing each of these onto a social plane. I argued there that there is more likely to be social agreement on what constitutes moral development than on what constitutes spiritual development *of individuals*. It does not directly follow that we can make better sense of the idea of moral than of spiritual development of *society*, since it is not yet clear how we are to make sense of the idea of any kind of development *of society*.

I suggest that we can interpret the idea of the development of society in two ways, reductionist and non-reductionist. In a reductionist sense, the development of society is nothing over and above the development of individual members of the society. Consider one of the other categories in the 1988 Act: physical development. If we can make sense at all of the physical development *of society*, it is probably only in the reductionist sense, in which that development is nothing over and above the physical development of (all, or most, or many) individual members of the society. Similarly in a reductionist way it would be possible to speak of the economic development of society and mean *nothing but* the fact that (all, or most, or many) individuals were becoming better off.

But such thoroughly reductionist interpretations do not look plausible for most categories of development. Economists speaking of economic development are not in fact using the notion in a reductionist way. They will have in mind many processes — trade, banking and so on — which are inherently *social* processes. And with the rather notional idea of the physical development of society we can contrast the idea that a society is becoming healthier. This certainly includes the idea that individual members of the society are likely to be healthier than individual members of the same society at some previous time, but it is doubtful whether it can be reduced purely to that. For instance, a society which has introduced clean air legislation, in which smoking in public places comes to be frowned on and in which provision is made for safe cycling and walking to school and work might be judged to have become a healthier society. This assessment might be made even without detailed knowledge of trends in individual health, because part of what constitutes a change to a healthier society would be a change in public attitudes and policy.

In Haydon (1994), discussing secularisation, I followed Hirst in describing this process as involving 'a decay in the use of religious concepts and beliefs'. It is individuals who have or do not have beliefs and who use or do not use concepts. But suppose that very many individuals suffer a loss of faith but keep this to themselves, while continuing in all their interactions with others to express the same beliefs as before and use the same concepts. Publicly, little would have changed, so there would not in fact have been a secularisation of society. Now suppose the opposite: that individuals carry on privately, in their own thinking, having a religious faith and using religious concepts, but that these beliefs only get expressed in private to like-minded others and that religious concepts fall out of use in public discourse. This *would* be a case of the secularisation of society. In other words, secularisation is a change in a society — and at least in an evaluatively neutral sense a development in society[1] — which cannot be reduced to changes in the thinking of a multiplicity of individuals. It is, above all, a change in public discourse.

THE IDEAS OF THE SPIRITUAL AND MORAL DEVELOPMENT OF SOCIETY

How does the reductionist/non-reductionist distinction apply to the ideas of the moral and spiritual development of society? The limited notion of moral development to which I referred above would fit easily with a reductionist interpretation of the moral development of society. A society will be developing morally just to the extent that the individuals within it tend to behave better (from the standpoint of publicly agreed norms). Many of those who call for moral education to counteract violence and other perceived ills in society, and thus to reverse the perceived moral decline, may recognise nothing but this reductionist idea of the moral improvement of society (and it is an interpretation which is comparable with the little that has been said about the moral development of society in official documents). But it is a crude account, and there is room for a less reductionist one.

A reductionist interpretation is also available for the spiritual development of society: a society will be developing spiritually to the extent that individuals within it are developing spiritually. But in this case, since we would have no observable criteria and no shared standpoint as to what constitutes improvement, we would not in fact — in a plural society — be able to apply such a notion of the spiritual development of society. A reductionist interpretation in this case would amount to no interpretation at all. But it is also not clear — in a plural society — whether any non-reductionist account is available. To see whether a non-reductionist account is possible, both for spiritual and for moral development of society, we need to look to the nature of public discourse.

Bringing together the points made so far, I can suggest that the moral development of society will be a matter of changes for the better in the moral aspects of the public discourse of a society, and similarly for spiritual development of a society. This is still to use the minimal evaluatively positive notion; but how do we know what to count as a change for the better within public discourse? Here it will be helpful to introduce a somewhat richer interpretation of development, not because such an interpretation is necessarily required by all uses of the word, but because it brings out a relevant continuity between the kinds of case we are interested in here. Often when we use the notion of development in an evaluatively positive way, we have in mind that the development of something involves the attainment or maintenance of some sort of unity or coherence in it.

The development of an argument, for instance, results in a position which hangs together rather than falling apart. Similarly for a person, we would see the attainment of integrity and a sense of identity as development, but going to pieces mentally is not the sort of thing we mean by personal development. Moral development of the individual is in most accounts (if they go beyond reference to observable behaviour) a development which results in some sort of coherent set of values and a consistent way of exercising them. Whether we follow Kohlberg, or an Aristotelian virtue ethic, or a feminist ethic centred on caring, we will consider that the morally developed person has 'got it together' to a greater extent than the less developed. In discussions of spiritual development there is often the idea of a person attaining some sort of coherent sense of his or her place in the world — which is contrasted with the kind of floundering in which people have no idea of who or what they are, and perhaps change their ideas from one day to the next. Of course, a lot of floundering may take place along the road of spiritual development, but it is not the kind of thing that would be seen as a desirable end-point.

If this is the way we are using the notion of development, then the moral or spiritual development of society would also be a development towards some sort of coherence or unity — and that would have to be, not just within individual members of the society, but across the society.

For spiritual development, at the level of the whole society we would be looking for an analogue of a person's having a coherent sense of his or her place in a wider scheme of things. It is also important, and in line with a number of accounts in the literature, that in the individual case we would expect that this sense of 'place' — which we could also call a sense of 'meaning' — would be both cognitive and affective, and that the two elements would be integrated. Thus while it is a possible condition that someone has an intellectual sense of their place in the universe but feels alienated from it, we would expect spiritual development to be towards a more integrated outlook in which reason and feeling do not come apart.

If this kind of account is right there are two reasons why it is difficult, in a plural society, to use the notion of the spiritual development of society. First, in such a society there will not be a shared understanding, even on a verbal level, of the human condition and of the place of persons within some wider scheme of things.[2] Second, if affective experience is indispensable to spiritual development, then the relevant shared understanding across a society would have to be not just cognitive but also affective. Is such a thing possible?

In certain conditions, it probably is. We can talk of people sharing an experience, in a sense that involves mutual recognition and empathy: the sense, roughly, in which two people who know each other well, sitting in the same room listening to a piece of music, may be sharing the experience of that music, whereas two strangers, in different rooms, listening to the same piece of music on the radio, are not sharing the experience of it.[3] Extending that sort of case, we could probably make sense of the idea that a community of worshippers could develop spiritually not just as individuals but as a group. But such development would depend crucially on both shared background assumptions and shared experience — just the elements which are missing across the life of a whole society in modern conditions.[4]

THE MORAL DEVELOPMENT OF SOCIETY

I suggest, then (though I have not tried to argue the point in detail), that we have to reach a negative conclusion about the possibility of the spiritual development of a modern plural society. But it does not follow that the conclusion about moral development will be negative. To the contrary, there are at least two complementary reasons for distinguishing the cases. First, the role of the affective is not so central in the case of moral development. I do not mean to deny that affective development is an important aspect of moral development in the individual; but at the level of public discourse the more cognitive, linguistically expressed aspect of morality can, so to speak, take on a life of its own. What there is convergence on at that level is not dependent on each individual party to the public discourse having the same feelings, or any particular feeling. Second, there are in fact several possibilities for convergence at the level of public discourse where morality is concerned. Reviewing these here will also serve as a summary of some of the points for which I have argued in this book.

1) Though it may sound paradoxical to start with this, there can come to be greater mutual understanding of differences in values and in conceptions of morality. As I pointed out towards the end of Chapter 13, one of the educational tasks in relation to values (a task to which I have given more attention in other places) is to promote understanding of the diversity found within modern societies. In such societies there are likely in the foreseeable future to be different conceptions of morality coexisting (secular and religious understandings, for instance), not to mention different values across the whole broader field of values. The existence of such differences is not, of course, a case of convergence; but there could be convergence towards a shared understanding of the differences which exist. Within an understanding of the human condition in both its biological and cultural respects it is understandable that there will be differences in beliefs and values. A society in which, through education, such an understanding is promoted will in one sense be a better educated society, and is likely to be a more tolerant society, than one in which people find the values of others unintelligible.

2) Even while different values and different understandings of morality in the broader sense coexist, it should be possible for people to share an understanding of morality(n). (This especially brings out the difference between the spiritual and moral cases: while in a plural society there will not be convergence on the meaning of 'life, the universe, and everything', there could be convergence on the meaning of morality(n).) It may be that already many people do think of morality in something like this way, but such an understanding coexists with a variety of other beliefs and attitudes about

morality. I am suggesting that educators, while not denying and certainly not attempting to suppress other understandings, can quite consciously seek to promote a shared understanding of the nature and importance of morality(n).

3) If society is to converge on a shared understanding of morality(n), then it needs a common language in which to articulate that understanding. Actually it is not strictly true that there must be one common language: there could be a plurality of, perhaps overlapping, languages, provided that each is understood by all. And I have in fact suggested that there is a role in public discourse for both a language of rules and principles and a language of virtues. I have also suggested that we are at present some way off having a shared language of virtues, and that a language of rules and principles has a certain priority in the articulation of morality(n).

4) For morality(n) to fulfil its function, it is not sufficient for people to recognise the concept and have a common language in which to articulate their understanding: it is also necessary that there be at least a degree of convergence on the content of morality(n) (the loosely Wittgensteinian point referred to in Chapter 2).

All these forms of convergence, then, can be seen as constitutive of the moral development of society: that a society comes to share an understanding of its differences, to share an understanding of the idea of morality(n), to have a common language for the articulation of morality(n), and to agree — at least to some extent — on the content of morality(n). I shall pause at this point to consider briefly whether we have any reason to think the fourth kind of convergence is likely.

Many people would suggest that modern societies have been changing in exactly the opposite direction, away from agreement on any moral norms. Yet there are some areas in which, plausibly, certain substantive moral positions are much more widely held now than used to be the case: the moral wrongness, for instance, of discrimination on grounds of race. The appearance of great diversity may in part be the result of our failing to make the distinction between morality(n) and other fields of values.

It might be objected that convergence of this kind is in what people say, not necessarily in their private opinions or their actions. But this is part of the point: there has in certain matters been convergence in public moral discourse, on what can acceptably be said and on what must be taken into account. And in all sorts of social and political ways, that itself is morally important. It is morally important, for instance, that there be a public recognition of equality across ethnicity and gender, even if that recognition is not shared privately, or on an affective level, by all members of the society (cf. P. White. 1996, p. 73)[5]. And it is morally important that there be a public recognition that certain sorts of behaviour are not to be tolerated; this is part of the way in which the shared understanding of norms about violence has to be worked out. It is rather in this spirit that the Gulbenkian Commission (1995, pp. 80 ff.) proposes the working out and adoption of a public commitment to non-violence.

So this convergence at the level of public discourse on certain values is one aspect of the moral development of a society. It is important too that people become aware of their convergence: it is not just that as a matter of fact individuals become less inclined to say certain things and more inclined to say others, but that people are mutually aware of this fact, and take it into account in their own speech and action. We could say that this is a development in the moral self-awareness of a society.

The forms of convergence I have picked out so far have not included the idea that people will behave better, even according to norms which are publicly agreed. I have not stressed this point so far because I wanted to distinguish my understanding of the moral development of society from the purely reductionist notion which would have it that this moral development consists simply in people behaving better. But having seen that there are various possibilities of convergence at the level of public discourse that can be constitutive of the moral development of society, it is not unreasonable to ask whether these kinds of convergence, up to and including agreement on norms of conduct, would do anything to make it likely that people would actually conform to the norms on which they agree. Of course, convergence in public discourse cannot guarantee anything about what people will do; nor can any other aspect of moral education, though we can reasonably expect that a mixture of approaches, provided they are not incompatible with each other, will have more effect than any single approach.

That said, there are grounds for thinking that convergence in public discourse will make a difference to individuals that, at least for many individuals, will go beyond lip-service. Moral ideas and moral language, and thoughts expressed in such language, will make a difference to people's conduct to the extent that people take these ideas seriously. People are more likely to take these ideas and this language seriously if they can see themselves as involved in morality, rather than perceiving morality as an alien imposition on them. My stress on understanding and — where appropriate — convergence at the public level, and hence my concern for education towards this public understanding, is motivated by the concern that we should be able to continue to take morality seriously.

NOTES

1. In the evaluatively neutral sense a change can be described as (a) development whether it is considered to be for better or for worse (there may be certain other conditions of a factual rather than evaluative nature which a process of change has to meet if it is to be appropriately described as development, but these are not my concern here). In an evaluatively positive sense of development, secularisation will only be counted as development by someone who sees it as a change for the better; to the opposite point of view it will be a matter of decline rather than development. Indeed secularisation might to such a viewpoint be a candidate case of the spiritual decline of society.

2. I am not suggesting that such a shared understanding is an impossibility in all places and at all times; it may have been present in the past in certain societies with a strongly held and shared religious faith.

3. Cf. Taylor, 1989a, p. 169.

4. It may be true that many people shared in the experience of grief after the death of Diana, Princess of Wales. More would be needed before we could say (as was suggested by some commentators) that this experience contributed towards the spiritual development of the nation. We would need some idea of how widely the grief was in fact shared; media reporting may have been misleading in neglecting the numbers who remained relatively indifferent. We would also need to know more of the character of what was experienced: given the scope for different interpretations of the significance of the life and death of Diana, was it the same experience that was shared by so many? In any case, one shared experience would not constitute a development of society unless it had lasting effects which were not reducible to the effects on the individuals concerned.

5. Iris Murdoch, whose main preoccupation was not with morality(n), makes a similar point: 'Lip service is not to be despised. The triumph of good causes partly depends on people, at some point, becoming ashamed of saying certain things.' (1993, p. 358).

Bibliography

Anscombe, E. (1997), Modern moral philosophy, in: Crisp, R. and Slote, M. (1997), *Virtue Ethics*. (Oxford: Oxford University Press). (first published in *Philosophy* 1958).

Aristotle (1954), *Nicomachean Ethics* (trans. Ross). (Oxford: Oxford University Press).

Baier, A. (1985), *Postures of the Mind*. (London: Methuen).

Baier, A. (1997), What do women want in a moral theory? in: Crisp, R. and Slote, M. (1997), *Virtue Ethics*. (Oxford: Oxford University Press).

Baier, K. (1973), Moral autonomy as an aim of moral education, in: Langford, G. and O'Connor, D. J. (eds), *New Essays in the Philosophy of Education*. (London: Routledge).

Bauman, Z. (1993), *Postmodern Ethics*. (Oxford: Blackwell).

Beauchamp, T. and Childress, J. (1989), *Principles of Biomedical Ethics*. (Oxford: Oxford University Press).

Benhabib, S. (1992), *Situating the Self*. (Oxford: Polity Press).

Blum, L. (1994), *Moral Perception and Particularity*. (Cambridge: Cambridge University Press).

Bourdieu, P. and Passeron, J.-C. (1970), *Reproduction in Education, Society and Culture*. (London: Sage).

Callan, E. (1998), Liberal virtue and moral enfeeblement. Paper presented at Institute of Education, London, May 1998.

Campbell, T. (1983), *The Left and Rights*. (London: Routledge).

Citizenship Foundation (1998), *Young People, Politics and Citizenship: a Disengaged Generation?* (London: Citizenship Foundation).

Clark, S. R. L. (1977), *The Moral Status of Animals*. (Oxford: Oxford University Press).

Clark S. R. L. (1993), *How to Think about the Earth*. (London: Mowbray).

Coady, C. A. J. (1986), The idea of violence, *Journal of Applied Philosophy*, 3.1.

Cooper, N. (1981), *The Diversity of Moral Thinking*. (Oxford: Oxford University Press).

Cooper, D. E. (1998), Educational philosophies and cultures of philosophy, in: Haydon (1998), *Fifty Years of Philosophy of Education: Progress and Prospects*. (London: Institute of Education).

Crisp, R. (1996), *How Should one Live? Essays on the Virtues*. (Oxford: Oxford University Press).

Crisp, R. and Slote, M. (1997), *Virtue Ethics*. (Oxford: Oxford University Press).

Cupitt, D. (1995), *Solar Ethics*. (London: SCM Press).

Dancy, J. (1992), Caring about justice, *Philosophy* 67.

Dancy, J. (1993), *Moral Reasons*. (Oxford: Blackwell).

Dent, N. (1984), *The Moral Psychology of the Virtues*. (Cambridge: Cambridge University Press).

Driver, J. (1996), The virtues and human nature, in: Crisp R. (1996), *How Should one Live? Essays on the Virtues*. (Oxford: Oxford University Press).

Dworkin, R. (1977), *Taking Rights Seriously*. (London: Duckworth).

Dworkin, R. (1986), *Law's Empire*. (London: Fontana).

Epp, J. and Watkinson, A. (eds) (1996), *Systemic Violence: How schools hurt children*. (London:Falmer).

Frankfurt, H. (1988), *The Importance of What we Care about*. (Cambridge: Cambridge University Press).

Foot, P. (1978), *Virtues and Vices*. (Oxford: Blackwell).

Galtung, J. (1969), Violence, peace and peace research, *The Journal of Peace Research* 6.

Garver, N. (1981), "What violence is", in: Bierman, A. K. and Gould, J. (eds) *Philosophy for a New Generation*. (New York, Macmillan).

Gibbard, A. (1990), *Wise Choices, Apt Feelings*. (Cambridge, MA: Harvard University Press).

Glover, J. (1977), *Causing Death and Saving Lives*. (Harmondsworth: Penguin).

Griffin, J. (1996), *Value Judgment: Improving our Ethical Beliefs*. (Oxford: Oxford University Press).

Grimshaw, J. (1986), *Feminist Philosophers: Women's Perspectives on Philosophical Traditions*. (Brighton: Wheatsheaf).

Gulbenkian Commission (1995), *Children and Violence*. (London: Calouste Gulbenkian Foundation).

Habermas, J. (1979), *Communication and the Evolution of Society*. (London: Heinemann).

Habermas, J. (1990), *Moral Consciousness and Communicative Action*. (Cambridge: Polity Press).

Hampshire, S. (1983), *Morality and Conflict*. (Oxford: Blackwell).

Hare, R. (1981), *Moral Thinking*. (Oxford: Oxford University Press).

Hare, R. (1992), How did morality get a bad name? in: Hare, R. (1992), *Essays on Religion and Education*. (Oxford: Oxford University Press).

Harré, R. (ed.) (1986), *The Social Construction of Emotions*. (Oxford: Blackwell).

Harris, J. (1980), *Violence and Responsibility*. (London: Routledge).

Hart, H. (1961), *The Concept of Law*. (Oxford: Oxford University Press).

Haydon, G. (1978), On being responsible, *Philosophical Quarterly*, 28.1.

Haydon, G. (ed.) (1987a), *Education for a Pluralist Society: Philosophical Perspectives on the Swann Report*. (London: Institute of Education).

Haydon, G. (ed.) (1987b), *Education and Values: The Richard Peters Lectures*. (London: Institute of Education).

Haydon, G. (1993a), *Education and the Crisis in Values: Should we be Philosophical about it?* (London: Institute of Education).

Haydon, G. (1993b), Values education in a democratic society, *Studies in Philosophy and Education*, 12.1.

Haydon, G. (1994), Conceptions of the secular in society, polity and schools, *Journal of Philosophy of Education*, 28.1.

Haydon, G. (1995), Thick or thin? The cognitive content of education in a plural democracy, *Journal of Moral Education*, 24.1.

Haydon, G. (1996), Values in the education of teachers: the importance of recognising diversity, in: Selmes, C. and Robb, W. (eds), *Values in Teacher Education*, Vol. 1. National Association for Values in Education and Training.

Haydon, G. (1997), *Teaching about Values: a New Approach*. (London: Cassell).

Haydon, G. (1998a), Between the common and the differentiated: reflections on the work of the School Curriculum and Assessment Authority on values education, *The Curriculum Journal*, 9.1.

Haydon, G. (ed.) (1998b), *Fifty Years of Philosophy of Education: Progress and Prospects*. (London: Institute of Education).

Haydon, G. (1999a), Behaving morally as a point of principle: a proper aim of moral education? in: McLaughlin, T. and Halstead, M. (eds), *Education in Morality*. (London: Routledge) (forthcoming).

Haydon, G. (1999b), Discussion of values and the value of discussion, in: Leicester, M., Sohan, C. and Sohan, M. (eds), *Values, Diversity and Education*. (Brighton: Falmer) (forthcoming).

Haydon, G. (1999c), Understanding the diversity of diversity, in: Leicester, M., Sohan, C. and Sohan, M. (eds) *Values, Diversity and Education*. (Brighton: Falmer) (forthcoming).

Haydon, G. (1999d), What scope is there for teaching moral reasoning? in: Gardner, R. (ed.) *Values Education*. (London: Kogan Page) (forthcoming).

Honderich, T. (1980), *Violence for Equality*. (Harmondsworth: Penguin).

Houghton, Brenda (1998), *The Good Child: How to Instil a Sense of Right and Wrong in your Child*. (London: Hodder Headline).

Hursthouse, R. (1995), Applying virtue ethics, in: Hursthouse, R., Lawrence, G. and Quinn, W. (eds), *Virtues and Reasons: Phillippa Foot and Moral Theory*. (Oxford: Oxford University Press).

Hursthouse, R. (1996), Normative virtue ethics, in: Crisp, R. (1996), *How Should one Live? Essays on the Virtues*. (Oxford: Oxford University Press).

Hursthouse, R. (1997), Virtue theory and abortion, in: Crisp, R. and Slote, M. (1997), *Virtue Ethics*. (Oxford: Oxford University Press).

Innes, M. (1964), *Operation Pax*. (Harmondsworth: Penguin).

Jackson, J. (1978), Virtues with reason, *Philosophy* 53.

Kant, J. (1948), *Groundwork of the Metaphysics of Morals*, translated in Paton, H. (1948). *The Moral Law*. (London: Hutchinson).

Khin Zaw, S. (1996), Locke and multiculturalism: toleration, relativism and reason, in: Fullinwider, R. (ed.), *Public Education in a Multicultural Society: Policy, Theory, Critique*. (Cambridge: Cambridge University Press).

Korsgaard, C. (1996), *The Sources of Normativity*. (Cambridge: Cambridge University Press).

Kymlicka, W. (1995), *Multicultural Citizenship*. (Oxford: Oxford University Press).

Lamb, S. (1996), *The Trouble with Blame*. (Cambridge, MA: Harvard University Press).

Larmore, C. (1996), *The Morals of Modernity*. (Cambridge: Cambridge University Press).

Leseho, J. and Howard-Rose, D. (1994), *Anger in the Classroom*. (Calgary: Detselig Enterprises).

Louden, R. (1997), On some vices of virtue ethics, in: Crisp, R. and Slote, M. (1997), *Virtue Ethics*. (Oxford: Oxford University Press).

Lukes, S. (1985), *Marxism and Morality*. (Oxford: Oxford University Press).

McDowell, J. (1997), Virtue and Reason, in: Crisp, R. and Slote, M. (1997), *Virtue Ethics*. (Oxford: Oxford University Press).

McGinn, C. (1992), *Moral Literacy, or How to do the Right Thing*. (London: Duckworth).

McGinn, C. (1997), *Ethics, Evil and Fiction*. (Oxford: Oxford University Press).

MacIntyre, A. (1981), *After Virtue: A Study in Moral Theory* (London: Duckworth).

MacIntyre, A. (1987), The Idea of an Educated Public, in: Haydon, G. (ed.) (1987), *Education and Values: The Richard Peters Lectures* (London: Intitute of Education).

MacIntyre, A. (1988), *Whose Justice? Which Rationality?* (London: Duckworth).

Mackie, J. (1977), *Ethics: Inventing Right and Wrong*. (Harmondsworth: Penguin).

Marcuse, H. (1969), Repressive tolerance, in: Wolff, R., Moore, B. and Marcuse, H. (eds), *A Critique of Pure Tolerance*. (London: Jonathan Cape).

May, L. (1998), *Masculinity and Morality*. (Ithaca and London: Cornell University Press).

Midgley, M. (1986), *Wickedness*. (London: Routledge).

Midgley, M. (1991), *Can't We Make Moral Judgements?* (Bristol: Bristol Press).

Murdoch, I. (1993), *Metaphysics as a Guide to Morals*. (Harmondsworth: Penguin).

National Curriculum Council (1993), *Spiritual and Moral Development: a Discussion Paper*. (York: National Curriculum Council).

Noddings, N. (1984), *Caring: A Feminine Approach to Ethics and Moral Education*. (Berkeley: University of California Press).

Nussbaum, M. (1993), Non-relative virtues: an Aristotelian approach, in: Nussbaum, M. and Sen, A. (eds), *The Quality of Life*. (Oxford: Oxford University Press).

O'Neill, O. (1986), *Faces of Hunger*. (London: Allen & Unwin).

Peters, R. (1959), *Authority, Responsibility and Education*. (London: Unwin).

Peters, R. (1966), *Ethics and Education*. (London: Allen & Unwin).

Peters, R. (1981), *Moral Development and Moral Education*. (London: Unwin).

Phillips, D. Z. and Mounce, H. O. (1969), *Moral Practices*. (London: Routledge).

Phillips, M. (1996), *All Must Have Prizes*. (London: Little, Brown).

Pincoffs, E. (1983), Quandary ethics, in: Hauerwas, S. and MacIntyre, A. (eds), *Revisions: Changing Perspectives in Moral Philosophy*. (Notre Dame: University of Notre Dame Press).

Rawls, J. (1967), Two concepts of rules, in: Foot, P. (1967), *Theories of Ethics*. (Oxford: Oxford University Press).

Rawls, J. (1972), *The Theory of Justice*. (Oxford: Oxford University Press).

Rawls, J. (1993), *Political Liberalism*. (New York: Columbia University Press).

Ross, W. (1930), *The Right and the Good*. (Oxford: Oxford University Press).

Ross, W. (1939), *The Foundations of Ethics*. (Oxford: Oxford University Press).

Sabini, J. and Silver, M. (1982), *Moralities of Everyday Life*. (Oxford: Oxford University Press).

SCAA (1995), *Spiritual and Moral Development: a Discussion Paper*. (London: School Curriculum and Assessment Authority).

Scheffler, S. (1992), *Human Morality*. (Oxford: Oxford University Press).

Schneewind, J. (1983), Moral knowledge and moral principles, in: Hauerwas, S. and MacIntyre A. (eds), *Revisions: Changing Perspectives in Moral Philosophy*. (Notre Dame: University of Notre Dame Press).

Schneewind, J. (1997), The misfortunes of virtue, in: Crisp, R. and Slote, M. (1997), *Virtue Ethics*. (Oxford: Oxford University Press).

Schostak, J. F. (1986), *Schooling the Violent Imagination*. (London: Routledge).

Searle, J. (1967), How to derive 'ought' from 'is', in: Foot, P. (1967), *Theories of Ethics*. (Oxford: Oxford University Press).

Shklar, J. (1986), *Legalism: Law, Morals and Political Trials*. (Cambridge, MA: Harvard University Press) (first published 1964).

Singer, P. (1972), Famine, affluence and morality, *Philosophy and Public Affairs*, 1.

Singer, P. (1979), *Practical Ethics*. (Cambridge: Cambridge University Press).

Skillen, T. (1997), Can virtue be taught—especially these days? *Journal of Philosophy of Education*. 31.3.

Slote, M. (1992), *From Morality to Virtue*. (Oxford: Oxford University Press).

Slote, M. (1996), Virtue ethics, utilitarianism and symmetry, in: Crisp, R. (1996), *How Should one Live? Essays on the Virtues*. (Oxford: Oxford University Press).

Smith, R. and Standish, P. (1997), *Teaching Right and Wrong: Moral Education in the Balance*. (Stoke on Trent: Trentham).

Statman, Daniel (ed.) (1997), *Virtue Ethics: A Critical Reader*. (Edinburgh: Edinburgh University Press).

Steutel, J. (1997), The virtue approach to moral education: some conceptual clarifications, *Journal of Philosophy of Education*, 31.3.

Stoppard, T. (1972), *Jumpers*. (London: Faber).

Straughan, R. (1982), *I Ought to But—A Philosophical Approach to the Problem of Weakness of Will in Education*. (Windsor: NFER-Nelson).

Straughan, R. (1989), *Beliefs, Behaviour and Education*. (London: Cassell).

Strawson, P. (1974), Social morality and individual ideal, in: *Freedom and Resentment*. (London: Methuen).

Tattum, D. P. and Lane, D. A. (eds) (1988), *Bullying in Schools*. (Stoke-on-Trent: Trentham).

Taylor, C. (1977), What is human agency?: in: Mischel T. (ed.), *The Self: Psychological and Philosophical Issues*. (Oxford: Blackwell).

Taylor, C. (1989a), Cross-purposes: the liberal–communitarian debate, in: Rosenblum, N. (ed.), *Liberalism and the Moral Life*. (Cambridge, MA: Harvard University Press).

Taylor, C. (1989b), *Sources of the Self*. (Cambridge: Cambridge University Press).

Taylor, C. (1995), A most peculiar institution, in: Altham, J. and Harrison, R. (eds) (1995), *World, Mind and Ethics: essays on the ethical philosophy of Bernard Williams*. (Cambridge: Cambridge University Press).

Taylor, G. (1985), *Pride, Shame and Guilt: Emotions of Self-Assessment*. (Oxford: Oxford University Press).

Tombs, D. (1995), 'Shame' as a neglected value in schooling, *Journal of Philosophy of Education*, 29.1.

Tomlinson, J. (1995), Professional development and control: a General Teaching Council, in: Bines, H. and Welton, J. (1995), *Managing Partnership in Teacher Training and Development*. (London: Routledge).

von Furer-Haimendorf, C. (1967), *Morals and Merit: A Study of Values and Social Controls in South Asian Societies*. (London: Weidenfeld & Nicolson).

Warnock, G. (1971), *The Object of Morality*. (London: Methuen).

Warnock, M. (1977), *Schools of Thought*. (London: Faber).

White, J. (1982), *The Aims of Education Restated*. (London: Routledge).

White, J. (1990), *Education and the Good Life*. (London: Kogan Page).

White, J. (1998), New aims for a new national curriculum, in: Aldrich, R. and White, J. (1998) *The National Curriculum Beyond 2000: the QCA and the aims of education*. (London: Institute of Education).

White, P. (1996), *Civic Virtues and Public Schooling*. (New York and London: Teachers College Press).

Williams, B. (1985), *Ethics and the Limits of Philosophy*. (London: Fontana).

Williams, B. (1987), The primacy of dispositions, in: G. Haydon (ed.) (1987b), *Education and Values: The Richard Peters Lectures*. (London: Institute of Education).

Williams, B. (1993), *Shame and Necessity*. (Berkeley: University of California Press).

Williams, B. (1995), Moral luck: a postscript, in: *Making Sense of Humanity*. (Cambridge: Cambridge University Press).

Wilson, J. (1990), *A New Introduction to Moral Education*. (London: Cassell).

Wolff, R. P. (1969), On violence, *Journal of Philosophy* 66.

Wolfgang, M. (1977), Freedom and violence, in: McPartland, J. & McDill, E. (eds) *Violence in Schools: Perspectives, Programs and Positions*. Lexington, Mass: Lexington Books.

Young, I. M. (1990), *Justice and the Politics of Difference*. (Princeton: Princeton University Press).

Index